How Nations Remember

How Nations Remember

A Narrative Approach

JAMES V. WERTSCH

OXFORD
UNIVERSITY PRESS

OXFORD
UNIVERSITY PRESS

Oxford University Press is a department of the University of Oxford. It furthers
the University's objective of excellence in research, scholarship, and education
by publishing worldwide. Oxford is a registered trade mark of Oxford University
Press in the UK and certain other countries.

Published in the United States of America by Oxford University Press
198 Madison Avenue, New York, NY 10016, United States of America.

Library of Congress Cataloging-in-Publication Data
Names: Wertsch, James V., author.
Title: How nations remember : a narrative approach / James V. Wertsch.
Description: New York, NY : Oxford University Press, [2021] |
Includes bibliographical references and index.
Identifiers: LCCN 2020044249 (print) | LCCN 2020044250 (ebook) |
ISBN 9780197551462 (hardback) | ISBN 9780197551486 (epub)
Subjects: LCSH: Nationalism—Psychological aspects. | Collective memory. |
International relations.
Classification: LCC JC311 .W453 2021 (print) | LCC JC311 (ebook) |
DDC 909—dc23
LC record available at https://lccn.loc.gov/2020044249
LC ebook record available at https://lccn.loc.gov/2020044250

DOI: 10.1093/oso/9780197551462.001.0001

1 3 5 7 9 8 6 4 2

Printed by Integrated Books International, United States of America

To Zadie Morgan Roberts Wertsch

Contents

Preface   ix

1. Different Memories, Different Worlds   1

2. A Conceptual Tool Kit   31

3. National Narratives   87

4. Selectivity and Emplotment in National Memory   115

5. Narrative Dialogism in National Memory   161

6. Managing National Memory   199

Acknowledgments   233
References   241
Index   255

Preface

Anyone who has ever been in a family knows that individuals can disagree over the past. Who hasn't heard something like, "But Dad, it just didn't happen that way!"? Disagreements over the past also occur between entire groups, including large groups like nations, and these can encourage dangerous tension and conflict. This begs questions such as: How do members of a group end up with such striking agreement among themselves about the past? What happens when one group believes something about the past that another rejects out of hand? What if no amount of evidence produced by one group can dislodge the other group's belief about the past? And what happens when one group uses memory to encourage violence against another?

These questions take on special significance with the resurgence of nationalism around the world. After decades of assuming that globalization would continue its inexorable rise, nationalist and populist movements have sprung up in places ranging from Russia and Hungary to India and China. Of course, the United States qualifies as well with its recent calls for "America first," decoupling, and the like. The reasons for these developments are puzzling, as are their consequences, but one thing that is clear is that they can impede forms of cooperation needed to deal with major global issues. As I write this, for example, the world is in the midst of the COVID-19 pandemic, and scientific inquiry that would normally and productively flow across borders has been stymied by disputes between American and Chinese leaders.

An even more unsettling case is climate change, where global cooperation is needed both for research and policy implementation.

But here again, cooperation has been hampered as nationalist leaders insist on furthering local interests. Young people from around the world "get it" with regard to climate change and fully understand that carbon emissions have no regard for national boundaries. Many of them even see this as a debate between generations, rather than nations, but even in such cases where it is obvious that "we are all in this together," nationalism has retained its power to pull people back into local communities and pit them against one another.

Scholars have long struggled to understand the hold that group identity can have over us. At an abstract level, discussions sometimes turn to a primordial tribalism that stems from our evolutionary origins, but if we wish to understand concrete cases, it is clear that shared memories about particular pasts must be taken into account. Memory plays a particularly important role in such cases because in contrast to attitudes and values, where we recognize group differences and can agree to disagree, memory is assumed to be about *truth*, which is a recipe for trouble when different groups have different accounts of the past.

The groups at issue may be religious, ethnic, generational, or familial, but my specific focus is on nations. National memory is distinguished from other forms of collective memory by the fact that it is backed up by the modern state. Just as it has been proposed that language can be defined as a dialect with an army, national memory can be thought of as an account of the past with a state to back it up. The power of the state manifests itself in formal education, the media, and other institutions, which can be quite effective in inculcating beliefs in citizens, who then can be mobilized to pursue grand causes—both beneficent and deleterious.

To illustrate, consider the Soviet campaign mounted in schools and the media during the Cold War about the dangers of American imperialism. These dangers were presented as part of a story about the past that seemed to lead inevitably to a state of implacable conflict between the USSR and the United States. While this was going on in the Soviet Union, schools and the media in the United States were busy claiming that the USSR was out to destroy the American way of life and urged American citizens to be prepared to go to any lengths to make sure this did not happen. Both sides knew of their brief period of friendship during World War II, but the story of their relationship then descended into obdurate hostility, which on more than one occasion led to the brink of nuclear war.

This was the context in which I came of age in the 1950s and 1960s. For Americans, it was a time permeated by fear of the Soviet Union. We learned the song "Duck and Cover" and practiced doing just that by hiding under our school desks in case of a Soviet nuclear attack. In my small Midwestern town, volunteers built an observation tower for the national "Operation Sky Watch" program and staffed it day and night to watch for Soviet bombers. And on my family's farm, we knew that the storm cellar built to protect us from tornadoes could also shelter us in case of a Soviet nuclear attack. All this might sound bizarre, indeed paranoid, from today's perspective, but it was part of a cultural landscape at the time, a landscape in which it seemed to many in the United States that Russians woke up every day trying to think of new ways to bury America.

To be sure, this was not a monolithic perspective for the entire country, and doubts and questions did occasionally manage to surface through the haze of hostility. When I was in fourth grade, for example, the Soviet Union launched Sputnik 1, which I could see streaking across the night sky in Illinois, and my parents and I had to admire the people who were able to do this. And in fifth grade I saw photos of Russian families in *National Geographic* and mused, "That kid looks like he could have come from the farm down the road," which made me wonder if he was really so different from me after all.

But such episodes were the exception rather than the rule, and what remains astonishing is the extent to which Americans agreed about dangers they saw. Their views were part and parcel of a story about Russian perfidy in Eastern Europe, where nations like Poland,

Estonia, and Hungary had valiantly resisted Soviet aggression but ended up being subjected to the brutality of an occupying power. This sad state of affairs was presented as predestined by events in the past, as baked into a story about evil Russian intentions from the outset. For an American to question this amounted to a form of heresy and invited censure. During those same years, official Soviet memory had it that the Poles, Estonians, and Hungarians were boundlessly grateful for being included in the Soviet bloc. It was the outcome of a struggle to be free of American imperialist aggression. And for Soviet citizens to question this could lead to much more trouble than mere censure.

In this ongoing struggle, each side relied heavily on national memory as a tool, if not a cudgel, something that became very clear to me in the 1970s when I first had a chance to live in Moscow. It was then that I discovered how different Soviet history textbooks were and how distant my ideas about the past were from those of my Russian friends. At a rational level, I could understand why Russians had such a different view of history. Their nation, after all, had a completely different historical experience than mine, and learning about its rich and often tragic past was eye-opening. But it also became obvious that our differences were not just about fact and rational argument. They ran much deeper and reflected conflicting worldviews grounded in incompatible national memories.

Indications of this came from episodes in which my Russian friends and I ended up at complete loggerheads when discussing historical events. On more than one occasion I found myself looking at a friend and thinking, "You can't possibly believe what you just said about that episode from history, can you?" But the problem was that my Russian friends was looking at me and thinking exactly the same thing. And as I met more and more Russians, I realized this gulf existed not just between us as individuals but between our two national communities. It was as if entire communities lived in different worlds when it came to the past. This could sometimes make it tempting to say that my Russian friend (never I, of course!)

was brainwashed or a victim of false consciousness, but that only served to bring the conversation to a testy and abrupt end. These discussions could end up being as puzzling as they were difficult, and it sometimes seemed that along with every insight I discovered a new point of confusion, leading to a deeper appreciation for Winston Churchill's quip that Russia is "a riddle wrapped in a mystery inside an enigma."

My time to Moscow during the 1970s and 1980s provided me with much more than exposure to another national memory, however. It also introduced me to an intellectual tradition that would help address some of my confusion. This is a tradition that had been developed over decades in the 20th century by figures such as L.S. Vygotsky, A.R. Luria, and M.M. Bakhtin. Their account of how social discourse is internalized to form mental life provided a powerful alternative to the individualistic approaches to psychology I had previously encountered in the United States, and it provided a means for understanding how social, psychological, political, and cultural forces are all wrapped up together in national memory.

A starting point in this conceptual approach is the notion that language is a cultural tool that shapes, even co-authors, what we say and think. For me, this led to the recognition of the central role that narratives play in national memory. When engaging with others across national boundaries, we are engaging with other stories provided by national communities. These take the form of not only stories about particular events but also the narrative habits that flow from them. It is sometimes possible to detect how these habits constrain the thinking of others, but they are much more difficult to see in ourselves. We are likely to naïvely believe that we are simply reporting what really happened, and the power of our unconscious narrative habits may come to light only when we are confronted by those equipped with a different national memory.

My incessant concern with Soviet national memory may stem from having heard the "Duck and Cover" song too many times or from seeing the 1959 film *On the Beach* about the world after a nuclear war. Such experiences bring home the fact that different views of the world might be capable of encouraging people to be willing to annihilate entire nations. Even in that context, however, we usually do not lose all sight of the fact that we may have more in common with people from other nations than implacable animosity. Indeed, it sometimes dawned on us that our concerns were the mirror images of those of others. This was made apparent to me years after my childhood when I discovered that during the very years I was learning what to take into the storm cellar to survive a Soviet nuclear attack, my future friends in Moscow were practicing how to go down to the safety of their subway system shielded by massive blast doors to survive an American nuclear attack.

The concerns in this volume, however, have more to do with the present than the past. The forms of nationalism we are witnessing today may not be the same as earlier ones, but they could end up being even more destructive, and a key to understanding them will be the national memories that they rely on for support. This will require delving into the cognitive dimensions of national memory but also its emotional appeal as part of identity projects. The combination can bring out the best but also the worst in all of us. Remembering injury and humiliation from a national past is an ideal way to encourage anger in the present, suggesting that we need not only to understand national memory but also to find ways to manage it. These issues have been of ongoing concern for my generation, with its unhappy experiences with nationalism. But going forward, the real issue is how nationalism will be understood and managed by generations of the future. Will they be able to keep destructive predilections under control in order to deal with issues like climate change?

It is naïve to believe nations and national identity will disappear anytime soon, and in fact, there are good reasons why they should not. After all, local collective identities are the source of much good in our world and can be the bedrock on which the beneficial outcomes of cultural diversity can be built. Instead of trying to eradicate or transcend national identities, the ideal world might be one in which they are celebrated as a source of the strength and resilience that diversity brings. But the all-too-familiar path of national identity to devolve into aggressive nationalism or xenophobia is one that we have to find better ways to avoid.

My conversations with young students from around the world suggest that many of them are aware of these dangers and may be able to maintain a healthy balance between commitment to their national community and working with people from other national groups. Continued success on this score will depend on appreciating and managing differences in national memory, and that is one reason I explore the topics included in the chapters that follow. Addressing these issues does not require jettisoning the national memory of one's own group nor does it mean there are no truths about the past. Instead, it requires an appreciation of the powerful forces we are up against when it comes to national memory and a level of cognitive humility about the truths we hold dear.

My own generation has done some things well, but we have also managed to do many things badly, including demonstrate a surprising inability to move beyond the constraints of parochial nationalism. I wish I could review the research on the topic and report that we have a clear recipe for moving beyond this failing. Instead, I think the best we can do is provide some reflections on the forces at work that we still do not control. In 2020 my wife Mary and I became grandparents for the first time with the birth of Zadie, and this does a great deal to focus one's mind on the hope that the generations to come will find better ways to meet these challenges.

1

Different Memories, Different Worlds

1.1. Introduction

In the 1970s I lived for several periods in Moscow as a research scholar in psychology and linguistics. During my time there I spent countless hours discussing everything under the sun with Russian colleagues, several of whom became lifelong friends. One of these was Vitya, a young man from Ukraine who was studying neuropsychology and also working as an English-language translator. It was in this latter capacity that I met him in December 1975 as he was serving as a guide and interpreter for the American psychologist Jerome Bruner, who was visiting Moscow State University.

Vitya had never visited America and had no hopes of ever doing so in those Cold War years, but like many Soviet citizens he was fascinated with my country. His insatiable curiosity led him to soak up all he could about the United States. In the face of heavy-handed Soviet censorship, he worked hard to understand America and had developed sophisticated views on its politics, history, and culture. Indeed, he was in awe of all things American, and this sometimes bordered on the naïve. On more than one occasion I cautioned him that things in my homeland were hardly perfect, but this did little to dampen his admiration.

Private conversations with Vitya and others like him in those Cold War years stood in sharp contrast to the ideologically tinged exchanges of public discourse, and like other citizens, Vitya maintained a clear distinction between the two spheres. In private he had little use for the official teachings of Marxism-Leninism and dismissed out of hand the daily diatribes in the Soviet media on

How Nations Remember. James V. Wertsch, Oxford University Press (2021). © Oxford University Press.
DOI: 10.1093/oso/9780197551462.003.0001

imperialist aggression and "Pentagon—Wall Street cliques." To be sure, he was proud of Russian accomplishments in music, literature, and science, but the bottom line for Vitya was that most things were better in America.

Given Vitya's deep knowledge and admiration of America, it sometimes surprised us when we encountered sharp differences where we had assumed we would be in agreement. Despite our close friendship and the knowledge we had about each other's society, these episodes reminded us that in some ways our mental worlds remained distinctly separate. One such episode arose in a conversation I had with Vitya in the spring of 1976 at a friend's apartment, where he ("V") and I ("JW") had the following exchange[1]:

v: Jim, one thing I still don't get is why the U.S. dropped atomic bombs on Japan in 1945.

JW: Well, we knew that the bombs would shock Japan into surrender, shorten the war, and reduce the number of people who would die.

v: (With a pause and look of incredulity) But you don't really believe that, do you? Everyone knows that the Japanese understood they were defeated, and when Stalin launched an attack against their forces [in 1945 in Manchuria], it became completely clear to them that they would surrender. Come on, Jim, Truman dropped the bomb to intimidate Stalin and stop any further Soviet advance in Europe.

JW: But that's not what happened, Vitya! Truman dropped the bombs to force Japan to surrender. Soviet propaganda may say something different, but Truman wanted to end the war, and the way he did it saved the lives of maybe a million U.S. troops. I've spoken with veterans who were on their way to invade Japan, guys who were scared to death, and they told me they broke down crying for joy when Truman dropped

---

[1] Based on fieldnotes written shortly after the encounter.

the bomb because it ended the war with Japan and saved
their lives.

v: But no one really believes that an invasion of the main island was
needed! The Japanese were ready to surrender. Maybe Truman
didn't say it, but he obviously believed that the real reason to
use atomic weapons was to scare Stalin and the Soviet people.
It's naïve to think otherwise.

Prior to this discussion, I had never encountered the account of
Truman's decision that Vitya espoused and had never questioned
the truth of my own. Indeed, I had no idea that an alternative existed.
Like most Americans, it was a matter of faith for me that the United
States used atomic weapons to try to force Japan's surrender—and
that it worked. But Vitya was equally certain about what he said,
and the result was that he and I found ourselves in a "mnemonic
standoff" (Wertsch, 2008b). We both were convinced that our version of the event in 1945 was true, and neither of us seemed capable
of budging from this in the face of counter-evidence or argument.

Such impasses provide telling insight into hidden national
differences and the conflicts they can spawn, and for me, they raise
three questions explored in the following chapters. First, how is it
that there can be such strong disagreement between entire national
communities about the past? My conversation with Vitya involved
only a single Russian, but over the years I learned that nearly all
Russians line up with him and most Americans take the perspective
I had on the events of 1945. It is as if a largely invisible but impene-
trable wall separates the two national communities in general, and
the event in 1945 is just one illustration of how stark this divide
can be.

Second, why were Vitya and I so certain that our account
of the events in 1945 were *true*? Differences between national
communities can involve opinion or ideology, but when it comes
to accounts of the past, we assume they are about truth, and the result is that we are surprised when someone questions our version.

Whereas we can agree to disagree over opinions or values, debates over national memory typically don't leave this option open. Instead, we find ourselves blurting out things like my "But that's not what happened, Vitya!" or "That's just not true!" And all too often, this is followed by accusations that others—never ourselves—are ignorant or brainwashed, which serve to signal that the conversation has reached an unproductive and unpleasant impasse.

A third question raised by my mnemonic standoff with Vitya concerns the tenacity with which we held our views. Something deeper than differences over a particular event seemed to be at stake. As our discussion unfolded, it became clear that more general worldviews were at work that made our accounts impervious to evidence and counterargument. If I introduced a fact that contradicted Vitya's account, he quickly dismissed it or gave it another interpretation consistent with a broader view he had, and I did the same with his attempts to challenge my version. This suggests that both of us were committed to some sort of larger perspective than an account of a particular event, and this is what made us unwilling or unable to consider alternative accounts.

These questions guide my analysis of the illustrations I take up in this chapter, but before turning to them I should comment on a couple of issues reflected in the title of this volume. One has to do with the focus on the memory of nations as opposed to other sorts of communities, and the second concerns the centrality of narrative in my analysis.

1.2. Why *National* Memory?

My observations about the encounter I had with Vitya would appear to be relevant to the memory of many types of communities, not just nations. After all, towns, religious communities, universities, and even families engage in memory projects, and they have been the focus of much of the scholarship on collective memory since

Maurice Halbwachs (1980) introduced the notion nearly a century ago. I don't wish to discount the importance of memory in these other communities, and many of the claims I develop are relevant to understanding them.

But national memory is special. This is so first of all because of the role that nation-states play in today's geopolitical scene. They have resources, especially in the form of economic and military power, far beyond those of other collectives, and this makes the memory projects they pursue in textbooks, state holidays, and museums much more consequential. Demands that nation-states make on citizens' loyalty can outweigh those of just about any other community, making it seem to be only natural, for example, that citizens are willing to go to war on behalf of a nation, but not for other collectives. It should be noted that scholars such as Daniel Levy and Natan Sznaider (2002) and Chiara de Cesari and Ann Rigney (2016) have called into question assumptions of "methodological nationalism," which "posits the nation as 'the natural social and political form of the modern world'" (de Cesari and Rigney, 2016, p.1). Studies such as theirs have documented transnational memory projects that hold out some hope for moving beyond the tired and dangerous ways of nationalism. Nonetheless, however unfortunate it may be for today's world, the sort of "cosmopolitan memory" that they envision is still engaged in an uphill battle with national memory.

In making these points, it is worth remembering that nations are relatively recent inventions, emerging only over the past two centuries. In a discussion of the "new nationalism," for example, Andreas Wimmer (2019) notes that "in 1900, roughly 35% of the globe's surface was governed by nation-states," a figure that had jumped to 70% by 1950 (p.28). The youthfulness of the national project is especially evident in the United States, where Jill Lepore (2019) notes that Americans began thinking of themselves as belonging to "a nation, with a destiny" only in the 1840s, when "European nations were swept up in what has been called 'the age of nationalities'" (p.12). Nations went on to dominate the geopolitical scene for most of the 20th century—all too often with destructive consequences.

For a brief period after the Cold War ended, some observers thought that globalization had left the nation-state behind as a geopolitical player. In place of competing nations, Francis Fukuyama (1992) announced the "end of history," an era in which globalizing neoliberal economic forces replaced the parochial concerns of national communities. And Thomas Friedman (2005) marveled at how the internet, trade, and travel were making old national borders irrelevant, leading him to conclude "the world is flat." These confident assessments suddenly came into question in the 2010s, however, with the outbreak of populist nationalism around the globe. Instead of an atavistic force that had disappeared with the 20th century, the new nationalism has "come back with a vengeance" (Rose, 2019, p.9).

In trying to understand nationalism—new or otherwise—one of the few generalizations that seems to hold is that there are so few generalizations to be had. It often seems that there are as many kinds of nationalism as there are nations. This makes the search for common themes challenging at best. But memory is one theme that can serve as a basis for generalization across cases. This is a claim whose genealogy extends back to Ernst Renan's 1882 article "What Is a Nation?" In this famous essay, Renan systematically discounted race, territory, language, or religion as the foundation for a general definition of a nation, proposing instead two basic elements: "spirit" and a "rich legacy of memories."

What Renan called spirit has similarities with the ideas of Benedict Anderson (1991) about "imagined communities" in which media and other forces make it possible for people who have never met face to face to feel a sense of belonging and commitment. When Renan reflected on such forces, he wrote of "a daily plebiscite," a general set of practices carried out in the media and other sites that reproduce the spirit of a nation. The idea of "banal nationalism" put forth by Michael Billig (1995) explores such practices, which range from the raising of flags at post offices and other government offices to media coverage of sports and the weather as if they exist only within one's own national borders.

The other crucial ingredient of nations for Renan was their rich legacy of memories, and his observations on this score are as relevant today as they were in 1882. In this vein, Jill Lepore notes that the key to understanding "why modern historical writing arose in the nation-state" requires an appreciation of the need for a national community to imagine its past (2019, p.10). For her, this was part of a criticism of American colleagues for shying away from the study of the nation due to their concern with the dangers of nationalism. They seem to have concluded that "If nationalism was a pathology, . . . the writing of national histories was one of its symptoms, just another form of mythmaking" (p.18). But her point amounts to a call to action for her fellow professional historians, a plea to recognize that they are destined to "forever fight over the meaning of [the nation's] history" (p.19).

Implicit in Lepore's call to action is the notion that if objective, empirically based historical scholarship does not address a nation's past, "memory activists" such as those described by Carol Gluck (2007) will be all too ready to fill the vacuum. They sometimes play a beneficial role by taking on issues from the past that are not included in official histories, but in other cases their work is less beneficial and indeed can become downright dangerous. In the case of India, for example, the renowned historian Romila Thapar (2019) has accused Hindu nationalists of "peddling myth as history" in ways that threaten the Muslim minority and the secular state of India. These threats, which have sometimes been directed at her personally, are such that she was led to quip in an interview that "history is to nationalism what the poppy is to the opium addict" (2018b). These are issues I explore in discussions of the difference between history and memory, but for now the point is that discussions of the past take on special importance for nations as opposed to other sorts of communities.

1.3. Why a Narrative Approach?

By using "A Narrative Approach" as the subtitle of this volume, I signal the importance I attach to narratives as basic means for making sense of human action, memory, and identity. This is an old claim in philosophy dating to Aristotle (e.g., MacIntyre, 1984), but it has taken on new life in the social sciences over the past few decades. Jerome Bruner (1915–2016) was a leading figure in this as he placed narrative squarely at the center of his cultural psychology (Bruner, 1990, 2002). Other psychologists have built narrative into their approach in other ways. For example, Dan McAdams (1993, 2013) has conducted extensive research into the issue of "the stories we live by" and how they shape individual identity and life choices, and Rauf Garagozov (2019, 2020) has provided fascinating insights into the "narrative reconciliation" that may be required to address bitter disputes such as the one between Azerbaijanis and Armenians in Nagorno Karabakh.

More surprising, perhaps, is a recent development in economics, where Robert Shiller (2017, 2019) has outlined a proposal for a "narrative economics." Shiller takes as a starting point that "The human brain has always been highly tuned toward narratives, whether factual or not, to justify ongoing actions . . . Stories motivate and connect activities to deeply felt values and needs" (2017, p.2). He then goes on to formulate narrative economics as "the study of the viral spread of popular narratives that affect economic behavior, can improve our ability to anticipate and prepare for economic events. It can also help us structure economic institutions and policy" (2019, p.3).

The basic building block for this new field is the "economic narrative," which is "a contagious story that has the potential to change how people make economic decisions, such as the decision to hire a worker or to wait for better times" (Shiller, 2019, p.3). In his view, narratives are "an important new element to the usual list of economic factors driving the economy: contagious popular stories the spread through word of mouth, the news media, and social media" (Shiller, 2019, p.3). As an example, he notes the bitcoin story about how "investors have become rich simply by being aware of new things on the cutting edge" (2019, p.10).

It is encouraging to be in the company of Shiller and others in the social sciences when foregrounding narrative as a foundational construct, and their scholarship suggests that the social sciences may be in for a broader "narrative turn." But this can mean several different things. My motivation for focusing on narratives may be similar to Shiller's at a general level, for example, but the way I harness notions of narrative differs from his in crucial respects. For starters, my interest in narrative stems from a concern with national memory and identity, whereas his is with economic explanation and causality. Furthermore, his focus is what might be called an "external" analysis that takes the presence of narratives as a starting point and allows for large-scale quantitative studies, whereas mine is on an internal analysis that relies on textual analysis and ethnographic methods that produce qualitative analyses of particular cases.

In what follows, I shall be particularly concerned with how the internal structure and logic of narratives shape discourse and mental life. In addition, my analysis focuses on narratives as *cultural tools* (Wertsch, 1998) provided by cultural, historical, and institutional contexts. Also, much of what I explore concerns schematic underlying codes of narratives and the habits they spawn. In the end, however, these are points of complementarity rather than contradiction with Shiller and others, and a comprehensive account of the narrative turn in the social sciences would need to address how all the pieces fit into a larger whole.

A related question about a narrative approach to national memory is whether stories or narratives[2] are the *only* cultural tools that can mediate memory. The short answer is no, and my focus on narrative should not be taken to rule out other candidates. Astrid Erll (2011) has raised this issue in a discussion of the role of photography and film. Noting the challenges raised by Walter Benjamin when he wrote that "history decays into images, not into stories" (from Erll, p.134), she reviews the role of media other than stories. In the end, however, her overarching analysis of visual media leads her to observe, "Taken by itself, a photographic image does not tell a story . . . [Instead] What photography needs in order to function as a medium of memory is narrative contextualization" (pp.134–135). Like her, though, I do not take this to mean that narrative is necessarily involved in all forms of national memory.

There is much more to say about how various media play a role in our understanding of the past, but for my purposes the point is that narratives do play a central role in how nations remember. The implication of this claim, of course, depends on what one means by narrative, which is an issue I take up in the following chapters, but one point is worth making from the outset. My concern with narratives as tools entails a focus on their use in active processes of speaking and thinking. This contrasts with accounts of narratives as semiotic forms removed from a context of use, and among other things raises issues that Paul Connerton (1989) discusses in connection with "habit memory" in *How Societies Remember*.

My debt to Connerton is obvious from the title of the present volume alone. It extends to the fact that he emphasizes the need to consider the place of "habitual memory" that is "sedimented in the body" (p.72) as part of the analysis of how groups remember. Connerton's conceptual framework for discussing habit memory differs in several respects from what I shall lay out, but the general motivation for our two approaches is similar. Namely, we are both

---

[2] I use the terms "narrative" and "story" interchangeably.

concerned with the need for collective memory studies to transcend boundaries between the individual and society and between semiotic text and embodied practice. In my case this involves focusing on practices built around symbolic mediation in the form of narrative tools and the mental habits that ensue.

1.4. Disciplinary Collaboration in the Study of National Memory

The approach to national memory outlined in the following pages reflects a couple of choices about analytic strategy that distinguishes my claims from those of many others. First, national memory is viewed from the perspective of mental functioning, thereby inviting findings from psychology and cognitive science into a discussion that is often dominated by history, sociology, and political science. And second, special emphasis is given to narrative tools that serve as "symbolic mediation" for national memory, specifically in the mental functioning of members of a national community. Instead of narrowing the analytic lens, these two assumptions actually expand the range of research traditions that can be brought into the picture. In particular, they call for input from semiotics, cognitive science, sociology, anthropology, psychology, and narrative and literary studies.

The resulting approach that I present considers not only how narrative tools shape mental habits of individuals but also how they reflect historical, cultural, and political forces of a national community. These are concerns that have long been part of discussions in several disciplines, but often in relative isolation. In the human sciences generally, narratives have long been part of the basic data to be studied, and their analysis can be traced back to scholarship in folklore and philology such as that of Johann Gottfried Herder (1744–1803) and Alexander von Humboldt (1767–1835). And in the early years of cultural anthropology Franz Boas noted the importance of examining "the general structure of the narrative, the style of composition, of motives, their character and sequence" (1917, p.7). In recent years, linguistic anthropologists such as Patience Epps, Anthony Webster, and Anthony Woodbury (2017) have noted that this has been part of the "continuing centrality of texts" (p.41) that characterizes this area of study.

What I have to say in the following chapters can be viewed as continuing this tradition. My goal is not to lay out a complete account of what might be termed "narrative anthropology." Instead, it is limited to developing basic tenets for what would be required to provide insight into issues of national memory. Thus, I focus on stories whose source and content concern a particular kind of collective—the nation—rather than individuals or other groups. This distinguishes what I cover from the efforts of figures in narrative psychology such as Theodore Sarbin (1986), János László (2008), Michael Bamberg (2012), and Dan McAdams (1993, 2013), who tend to focus on narratives as they relate to personal identity.

Another issue that sets my analysis apart from what other accounts of narrative anthropology might consider is the focus on stories as symbolic mediation (Wertsch, 1998). This emphasis reflects the influence of ideas from European and Russian traditions. Specifically, it is an emphasis on how narratives "mediate" (Wertsch, 1985a, 1998) human social and mental functioning, with the result that a crucial part of mental life is the stories we receive and tell. My concern is on nonfictional, as opposed to fictional narratives, although this is a distinction that sometimes can be hard to maintain in national memory, and my focus is on texts (Lotman, 1976) that are bounded by a beginning and end point and have internal organization governed by a narrative "logic" (Brooks, 1984). These are issues I take up in more detail in chapter 2.

Finally, my approach differs from many other narrative analyses because of my concern with generalized narrative "templates" and habits. This involves introducing an additional level of analysis along with that concerned with the concrete narratives that are often the focus of the ethnography of speaking and related fields. This discussion of narrative templates and habits takes me into topics having to do with schemata[3] and other issues discussed in psychological anthropology (D'Andrade, 1995). Indeed, it owes so much to psychology and cognitive science that a more cumbersome subtitle for my project might be "a psychological anthropological approach to narrative."

1.5. Mnemonic Standoffs: Illustrations and Lessons

In order to pursue the three basic questions I have outlined above, I turn to a few illustrations of national memory. Two of these involve Russian national memory, and one concerns a Chinese account of the past, but in all cases, American national memory serves as a foil or counterpoint. The inclusion of counterpoints reflects the fact that national memory is often flushed out into the open only when confronted with an alternative. To be sure, it is possible to learn something about national memory simply by asking members of a group about their views of the past, analyzing history textbooks, and so forth, and these are methods that I myself employ in what follows, but the full significance of such evidence often becomes apparent only when we examine how one account of the past stands in opposition to others.

Using counterpoints brings up the fact that narrative tools often operate under the radar of conscious reflection, leaving us with the impression that we have a direct, unmediated picture of reality. As Alexander Luria (1976a) put it, language (including narratives) can be "transparent" in that we believe we are looking directly at reality. Or in Bruner's words, "Common sense stoutly holds that the story form is a transparent window on reality, not a cookie cutter

---

[3] Following the usage of others, this is the plural of "schema."

imposing a shape on it" (2002, pp.6–7), and it is only when we "suspect we have the wrong story" and ask "how a narrative may structure (or distort) our view of how things really are" (p.9) that the cookie cutter comes into view. As a result, one of the best places to find national memory in action is in such confrontations between members of different national communities (Wertsch, 2018). They provide the best opportunity we may have to recognize that stories organize information by grasping it together into plots and to overcome the impression that our accounts of the past simply reflect "what really happened."

1.5.1. American and Russian National Memory of World War II

In 2016, I gave a lecture on national memory to a class of undergraduate students at Washington University in St. Louis. Some of them had foreign-born parents, but all of the students had been educated in U.S. schools. I began by asking them to write down a list of the five most important events of World War II. After giving them a few minutes to do this, I asked for a volunteer to name an item on his or her list and then called for a show of hands of how many others in the class had included it. I repeated this procedure until we came up with a set of the core events that appeared on a majority of their original lists. The four items named that received a majority of the votes were:

Pearl Harbor (the Japanese attack on Pearl Harbor, December 7, 1941)
D-Day (the Allied invasion of Normandy, June 6, 1944)
Hiroshima and Nagasaki (the American use of atomic bombs, August 1945)
The Holocaust (an event that extends over the longer time of 1933 to 1945)

A few students nominated other events such as the German invasion of Poland in 1939 and the Battle of Stalingrad in 1942–43, but none of these received more than a handful of votes. On the basis of these results, we took these four items to represent the group's consensus on what needs to be included as core events in an account of World War II.

After the 25 students had settled on these events, I showed them a slide that I had prepared before class. I told them that it was my prediction of what they would say, a prediction that I made before ever having met them. When they saw the slide, some of them chuckled because it included the exact same four events they had just come up with. This is a sort of parlor trick that I have used countless times with university students as well as with middle-aged adults in community groups in the United States. The exercise always involves a new set of participants who had no contact with the other groups, but it turns out that I can unerringly predict what they will say as a group about the most important events of World War II.

As a next step in such presentations to U.S. audiences, I show them how deeply American their account is. I do this by contrasting it with the minimal set of events in Russian accounts of World War II. Some of the items Russians include are familiar to Americans, but others are completely unknown. The list I present in such settings comes from Russian students' responses in the same task, but it also reflects Russian textbooks, essays by Russian students, family discussions and popular culture, and Russian media.[4] This list consists of:

German invasion of the Soviet Union (June 22, 1941)
Battle of Moscow (winter 1941–42)
Battle of Stalingrad (winter 1942–43)

---

[4] In later chapters I will discuss an expanded list based on a survey research study, but the list I use here is the standard one I use in presentations to students and other audiences.

Battle of Kursk (summer 1943)

Opening the Second Front (June 6, 1944)

Battle of Berlin (spring 1945)

These events are largely unfamiliar to American audiences, so I usually provide a running commentary as I present them. I note, for example, that the German invasion on June 22, 1941, marks the beginning of what is known in Russia as the "Great Patriotic War" (Velikaya Otechestvennaya Voyna). For Russians, the Great Patriotic War is the most important and brutal part of World War II, beginning nearly two years after the German invasion of Poland in September 1939 and after almost two years of the "Phony War" that had been waged between Germany and European countries, including France, Great Britain, Belgium, Norway, Denmark, and the Netherlands.

I then tell American audiences that the Battle of Moscow derives its importance from the fact that it was the first time that the German army was clearly stopped in its attack on any European nation. In contrast to what had happened elsewhere, after overrunning huge parts of the Soviet Union in the summer and fall of 1941, the onslaught slowed and then halted at the outskirts of Moscow. This battle took place during the winter months of 1941–42 and saw the German army come within 15 kilometers of the center of the city of Moscow, a point beyond which it never advanced.

The Battle of Stalingrad is an event that American audiences often have heard about, sometimes thanks to the 2001 American popular movie *Enemy at the Gates*. But in my presentations, I found that it never rises to the point of being included by a majority of American students or older adults. For Russians, however, the Battle of Stalingrad is undeniably a pivotal event in World War II. It is also widely accepted by historians (e.g., Beevor, 2012)—non-Russian as well as Russian—as the decisive turning point in the war because it was the first time that the German army experienced crushing defeat.

It is very rare to find anyone in an American audience who has heard of the Battle of Kursk, but it was such a decisive battle that some historians (e.g., Clark, 2011)—non-Russian as well as Russian—take it to rival the Battle of Stalingrad as the most important turning point in World War II. It took place 450 kilometers southwest of Moscow in the summer of 1943 and was the largest set piece battle in history, involving 6,000 tanks, 4,000 aircraft, and 2 million troops. The success of the Red Army in this case stemmed from its superiority in numbers, but it also showcased a brilliantly executed strategy of encirclement that countered a German effort to trap Soviet forces. It proved to be a major turning point that saw the Soviet army seize the strategic initiative that it maintained to the end of the war. It is an event that is very well known by Russians, and its inclusion is considered by them to be indispensable for any serious account of World War II.

The opening of the Second Front in June 1944 is what Americans typically know as D-Day, a term that has no direct translation in Russian. For Russians the Second Front means a second*ary* front in the sense that it was a relatively small, second-tier event in the war. Russians clearly view the landings in 1944 as significant and welcome, but they also often make the point that these landings had been expected and would have been much more helpful if they had occurred in 1942 or 1943.

I have found that American audiences are also unlikely to know about the Battle of Berlin, which took place in the spring of 1945. It was another massive clash that resulted in a combined total of 1.3 million German and Soviet casualties and was the final push that ended with Hitler's suicide and German surrender in early May. The leaders of the Allied forces approaching Berlin from the west did not launch a corresponding attack because they recognized Russia's right to take this final prize of the war.

The most striking fact about the two accounts I have just outlined is their nearly complete lack of overlap. It is almost as if the American and Russian groups were coming from different worlds.

Further evidence of the gulf that separates them can be seen in the absence of the attack on Pearl Harbor on the Russian list and the absence of the Battle of Kursk in nearly every American's vocabulary. When asked about this, Americans often assert that Russians probably do not have access to information about Pearl Harbor or other such events. In fact, even during the Cold War students and adults in Russia were well informed about the specifics of the attack on Pearl Harbor and could recount details that even students in the United States were unlikely to know. And in the post-Soviet era, with ready access to the information through the internet and international travel, such an explanation is even less plausible.

After hearing all this, American students often say that the Russian and American accounts simply reflect a difference in what people learn in school. This, however, just begs the question of what the different worldviews are that would support such distinct patterns of history instruction. Furthermore, it is not an explanation accepted by all Americans, especially those born in the decades immediately following World War II. These older Americans are likely to insist that no adequate or legitimate account of World War II could be compiled without mentioning Pearl Harbor or Hiroshima, neither of which appears on the Russian list of main events. Conversely, Russians usually scoff at the list of events provided by Americans, viewing it as uninformed at best. For them the question is how any account of World War II could not mention the Battle of Kursk, let alone the Battle of Stalingrad. In both cases, they are also likely to say that the other version of World War II is incomplete and misleading, if not simply false.

How can the national memory of these two groups be so isolated from one another? The procedure I used to elicit answers from the various audiences yields lists rather than fully formed stories, but narratives are the key to understanding the differences in national memory. This is reflected in the events selected for inclusion, which represent high points of well-known narrative accounts of World War II. It is also indicated in Russian observations about the American list of most important events and vice versa. The concerns of members of both national groups virtually never are about the accuracy of dates, places, or actors. Instead, they are about whether or not an item deserves to be on the list of most important events in any adequate account of the war. This suggests that the underlying difference is over what the "real" or "right" story is, and this is also often taken to be a matter of truth—namely, "narrative truth" as discussed in chapter 2. If it were just a matter of opinion based on group perspective, we might be able to accept others' accounts of the past, agree to disagree, and move on. Instead, the mnemonic standoff reflected in the lack of overlap between the two lists seems intractable based on assumptions by the two communities that their account is the real truth.

1.5.2. National Memory for the Bombing of the Chinese Embassy in Belgrade

In 2014, I was teaching a seminar for Chinese and American students at Fudan University in Shanghai. In one of the sessions I asked the group what they knew of a 1999 event in which a U.S. Air Force plane dropped bombs on the Chinese embassy in Belgrade, killing three Chinese journalists. Suddenly a line of demarcation sprang up in the classroom. The students, who had bonded over working together on a project, abruptly divided into two groups, and a bit of tension entered the room. Every Chinese student knew about this event and had a clear story about it. In contrast, only one American student could produce a vague account of what had happened, and it was completely different from the Chinese version.

The fact that these American students had so little knowledge of this event not only surprised the Chinese students but also offended some of them. The Americans suggested that lack of knowledge on their part was a result of being too young in 1999 to know about world events, but the Chinese were the same age and found it hard to understand how such an important event, regardless of when it occurred, could be unfamiliar to anyone. Some of them speculated that this ignorance was due to U.S. government or media efforts to suppress information, but the Americans quickly showed that to be unlikely by pointing to information that was readily available on the internet in English, even as we sat there in Shanghai, where Facebook and Google were blocked.

As the group discussed the American version of the 1999 bombing, which is predicated on the claim that it was a mistake on the part of U.S. forces, the Chinese students became increasingly dismissive. The sole American student who knew about the event recalled that it had something to do with a targeting error by the Central Intelligence Agency, and the students' internet search revealed that this was the standard U.S. version of the event. For example, they found that a few days after the bombing, President Clinton said in a press briefing, "It's tragic, it's awful, but it was a tragedy, it was an accident. The NATO generals and pilots have worked very hard to avoid this. This will happen if you drop this much ordnance over this period of time."[5]

This all might have made sense for the American students, but for the Chinese students it was further evidence that the U.S. government and media had been successful in their efforts to distort or erase the truth about what really happened. For them, the bombing was no accident and was intended to remind China and the world of America's preeminence as a superpower, and the suggestion that it was a mistake was risible. But that is precisely what the American position asserted to be the truth. In short, the national memories for this event were not only different but also stood in stark opposition. This difference separated not only the Chinese and American

---

[5] https://www.bing.com/videos/search?q=clinton+apologizes+for+1999+attack+on+chinese+embassy+in+belgrade&&view=detail&mid=260EA16BF5A4F45C77A2260 EA16BF5A4F45C77A2&rvsmid=60C20C6D852E39950E2760C20C6D852E39950E27 &FORM=VDRVRV

students in our seminar but also citizens of the two countries more generally, including well-informed and experienced diplomats.

I return in more detail to this episode in chapter 6, but even at first glance, a few things stand out. First, the two sides brought very different narratives to the discussion, something reflected in their comments about the intentions of the actors, a hallmark of narrative texts. The American storyline was of an unintended accident by the American military, and the Chinese storyline was about an intentional, hostile act. Again, in this case, the students took these differences to be not about opinion or ideology, but about truth. When either side challenged the account of the other, this carried the implicit charge that those in the other group either did not have access to information, were brainwashed, or were lying, which of course made further discussion all but impossible.

Based on numerous conversations I have had with Chinese, it has become evident to me that if Americans remember the 1999 bombing at all, they remember it very differently than their Chinese counterparts. It is almost as if a clear gulf exists separating 300 million Americans from 1.3 billion Chinese when it comes to the truth of what happened. In an age of widely shared global access to information, we have to ask how this is possible.

1.5.3. Using Russian National Memory as a Lens for Interpreting the Current Events

National memory provides a lens through which current events can be viewed, something that becomes clear when one interpretive lens conflicts with another. Consider, for example, the lens used by Russian president Vladimir Putin in 2008 to describe the "Five Day War" with Georgia that had occurred just a few weeks earlier. The 2008 war was a brief but violent conflict in South Ossetia and Abkhazia, two contested regions of Georgia, but it spread to other areas of the country and Russian tanks almost reached the capital city, Tbilisi. It began on the night of August 7, 2008, with a bombardment by the Georgian army of Tskhinvali, a city in South Ossetia. This was followed within hours by a large-scale invasion by the Russian army into South Ossetia and Abkhazia and the rapid retreat of Georgian forces from these two regions. Russian airstrikes on these and other areas of Georgian territory ensued until a ceasefire was called on August 12 at the urging of the international community.

Russian interpretations of the 2008 war generally reject any suggestion that aggression or expansionism on their part was involved. Instead, these interpretations present a picture in which the underlying agenda for Georgia was to become a North Atlantic Treaty Organization outpost that could be a threat to Russia. From this perspective, the Russian incursion into South Ossetia at the outbreak of the conflict was in response to outside aggression. It was considered an act of legitimate defense against NATO. This interpretation was on display a few weeks after the 2008 war when Putin spoke to an international group of journalists and scholars.[6] There he asserted:

> One of the most difficult problems today is the current situation in the Caucasus: South Ossetia, Abkhazia and everything related to the recent tragic events caused by the aggression of the Georgian leadership against these two states. I call them "states,"[7] because, as you know, Russia has made a decision to recognise [sic] their sovereignty.

Following this statement by Putin, British journalist Jonathan Steele noted that the opening salvo of the war had indeed been fired

---

[6] "Russia Has No Imperial Ambitions—Putin," *Russia Today*, September 2008. Available at: http://www.russiatoday.com/news/news/30316

[7] Before the 2008 conflict South Ossetia was a part of Georgian territory, and it has not been recognized as independent by all the nations who are members of the United Nations General Assembly except for Russia, Nicaragua, Venezuela, Nauru, and Tuvalu.

by Georgian forces and that these forces had committed "atrocities" against South Ossetians. But Steele went on to say that the "moral high ground" then shifted to Georgia as Russian forces pursued their attack beyond South Ossetia. Putin responded to this with acerbic disbelief.

You know, your question doesn't surprise me. What really surprises me is how powerful the propaganda machine of the so-called "West" is. This is just amazing. This is unbelievable. This is totally incredible. And yet, it's happening. Of course, this is because, first, people are very susceptible to suggestion. Second, ordinary people usually don't follow world events that closely. So, it is very easy to misrepresent the actual course of events and to impose somebody else's point of view. I don't believe there is one person among us here who is not familiar with the facts. At least in this room, everybody knows perfectly well how the events unfolded in reality. I have given the true account on several occasions, including my recent interviews with CNN and ARD.

One might view this as mendacious bluster by Putin as an aggressive political rhetorician, but there is good reason to take his comments as reflecting sincere belief. His words and actions in other settings were consistent with a deep commitment to the truth of this account, so deep that he found it difficult to believe anyone could hold another view. For him, it was "amazing," "unbelievable," and "incredible" that people did so, and he explained it away as reflecting people's susceptibility to suggestion and the "propaganda machine of the so-called 'West.'"

When participants at this meeting in 2008 continued to question the need for the invasion of Georgia, Putin switched to another rhetorical line, this time invoking a Russian national narrative of World War II as a lens through which the short war should be viewed. At one point, he spoke as an exasperated teacher might speak to a slow student, revealing his frustration at others' inability to see an obvious truth:

> Now, let me explain why we went there. I have already explained the military aspect to you. Now let's remember how WW2 started. On September 1 [1939], Nazi Germany attacked Poland. Then they attacked the Soviet Union [in 1941]. What do you think the Russian Army should have done? Do you think it should have reached the border and stopped there?

Westerners listening to Putin's views often find them surprising and attribute them to his aggressive stance as an individual. They see his remarks as an attempt to refute accusations by Western leaders and journalists that the invasion of Georgia was an overreaction that reflects longstanding efforts to reestablish Russia's sphere of influence in the Caucasus, which had been part of the Soviet Union and the Russian Empire for centuries. In fact, however, Putin's comments reflect widely held views in his national community. In particular, the World War II narrative he invoked is a standard way of interpreting contemporary events. It is a narrative that enjoys sacred status for Putin and others and provides insight into Russian views in general today (Wood, 2011).

In short, this narrative can be taken as a sort of voice of the Russian nation, and it shaped what Putin said not so much as an individual, but as a member of this community. It is a narrative tool that could almost be said to be doing some of his thinking and speaking for him. It is noteworthy that he did not have to provide a full version of this narrative in order to make his point. Instead, he assumed that his audience could expand his shorthand mention of it into a more elaborate narrative if need be. This practice of using abbreviated expressions to point to a larger narrative rather than spelling it out is a feature of how national narratives function more generally and will be an issue discussed further in later chapters under the heading of the "narrative templates" and "privileged event narratives" that shape national memory.

Finally, it is worth noting the tenacity and emotion with which Putin used the World War II narrative. It served as a "cognitive instrument" (Mink, 1978) that grasps together information about events, actors, settings, and motives into a comprehensible whole, but it was more than that. It had strong emotional significance for Putin and for Russians more generally and provided him with a kind of moral authority that derives from the fact that this narrative positions Russia as a victim of attacks by alien enemies. For him, it was a narrative that was largely impervious to evidence or arguments that might be used to challenge it. Indeed, Putin's moral authority derived in large part from the narrative tool itself, something that was unlikely to be appreciated by non-Russians, but something that again highlights how members of different national communities can be guided by narratives that make it seem as if they live in different worlds.[8]

1.6. Narratives as "Equipment for Living" for National Memory

The three illustrations I have provided show that members of different national groups can have starkly different views of the past that make them seem to be living in different worlds. The illustrations are similar, however, when it comes to the source of the knowledge involved. Instead of coming from independent research based on historical archives or other evidence, many indicators[9]

---

[8] These two different worlds are in evidence in Russian and American films made about the 2008 war. *Olympus Inferno* was a Russian feature film that appeared only months after the war, and *5 Days of War*, directed by Renny Harlin, was an American action thriller that screened in 2011.

[9] I have not collected systematic evidence on this, but in all cases when asked about the source of their knowledge, students and others say it was what they learned in school and from the media.

point to what might be called "off-the-shelf technology" provided by others, including schools, the media, political leaders, and conversations at home.

In outlining his idea of "literature as equipment for living," Kenneth Burke (1998) provided useful insight into how such technology works. There he outlined how literature provides readers with a way to name, and hence to "size up," situations in everyday life. He noted a parallel with proverbs, which "seek to chart, in more or less homey and picturesque ways," types of social situations and thereby provide guidance in dealing with them. For Burke, works of literature can be viewed as "proverbs writ large" (p.594) that provide "*strategies* for dealing with *situations*" (p.595). Thus "*Madame Bovary* (or its more homely translation, *Babbitt*) can be taken to be the strategic naming of a situation. It singles out a pattern of experience that is sufficiently representative of our social structure, that recurs sufficiently often *mutatis mutandis*, for people to 'need a word for it' and to adopt an attitude toward it" (p.596). To call someone a Babbitt is to say the person follows the same storyline as the main character in Sinclair Lewis's 1922 novel about small-town and small-minded mercantile life in early 20th-century New England.

Burke's account of literature as equipment for living presupposes a sort of schematic version of works such as *Babbitt*, just as it would for, say, George Orwell's *Nineteen Eighty-Four* (1949) or Harriet Beecher Stowe's *Uncle Tom's Cabin* (1952). He was not suggesting that when sizing up a situation or actor, we must run through every page of a novel. Instead, an abbreviated version of the narrative that preserves a general storyline is involved, and this allows us to size up situations and people quickly, indeed almost instantaneously. One only needs to speak of Big Brother to index the whole plotline of Orwell's classic, and to call someone an Uncle Tom does the same for Stowe's book. If asked to do so, we can of course revisit the expanded text and specify how it provides a guide for sizing up a situation, but the abbreviated version is the usual version used in everyday life.

Burke's account of equipment for living reflects a few crucial assumptions. First, it is not something invented by those who use it. Instead, narrative tools and other equipment for living are off-the-shelf technology gathered from literature or other sources in a sociocultural context—which makes sizing up someone or something an inherently socioculturally situated effort. Second, Burke viewed the equipment for living as being efficient, both in the sense that a narrative reflected in a name like Babbitt provides a compact way to make sense of a great deal of information and in the sense that this can be done quickly. And third, Burke's account suggests that once we have sized up a situation by using a narrative tool, viewing it in a different way may take some effort. Questioning the relevance of a proverb or narrative to a situation is best done at the outset since once it is used, any arguments often occur within its confines.

Episodes of using narratives as equipment for living are part and parcel of everyday life, usually in an unconscious and unreflective way. The writer Flannery O'Connor (1993) provided a beautiful illustration of this in "The Comforts of Home." In this short story, Thomas, an aspiring historian of a small town in the American South, fights his mother's attempts to invite an unstable young woman, Star Drake, into their home as his mother attempts to save Star from a life of drunkenness, crime, and licentiousness. Thomas finds this "slut" repulsive as she flirts with him, and as part of an effort to get the local sheriff to arrest her, he plants a gun in her purse. The plan goes awry, however, and in an ensuing struggle over the gun, Thomas's mother steps between him and Star and is unintentionally shot.

The story ends with Sheriff Farebrother's entering the house unnoticed in the immediate aftermath of a shooting:

> The sheriff's brain worked instantly, like a calculating machine.
> He saw the facts as if they already were in print: the fellow had

intended all along to kill his mother and pin it on the girl. But Farebrother had been too quick for him. They were not yet aware of his head in the door. As he scrutinized the scene, further insights were flashed to him. Over her body, the killer and the slut were about to collapse into each other's arms. The sheriff knew a nasty bit when he saw it. He was accustomed to enter upon scenes that were not as bad as he had hoped to find them, but this one met his expectations. (p.404)

In O'Connor's account Farebrother instantly sized up the scene "like a calculating machine" by using a standard storyline for a sheriff familiar with characters and family quarrels in the American South of the time. Based on O'Connor's depiction of him in her story, once he had sized up the situation, it is very unlikely that Farebrother would be open to any other interpretation, regardless of the evidence. What he actually saw were three people and a gun, but the strategy he used for dealing with the situation led him to see "the facts as if they already were in print." This relied on a neat narrative that tied all the elements of the situation into an account that left no loose ends. It was a narrative about a murder committed to make room for forbidden love, but the conclusion he drew was actually false. In reality, Thomas had done everything he could to force his mother to give up her hopeless reform effort and expel the young woman from their home.

In short, O'Connor and Burke both provide insights about how narratives are ideal equipment for living. They both were dealing with temporally distributed events that would require an extended text to relay in an explicit way, but at the same time, they recognized an abbreviated form of mental representation that allows for instant judgment. As will be discussed in chapter 3, this is a property of narratives recognized by Aristotle in *Poetics* and has been explored in contemporary cognitive psychology as well.

This is not to suggest that every use of a storyline yields an identical way of understanding people and situations. Instead, the narratives used in literature and everyday life provide a more generic shared lens for understanding particular situations and individuals. Thus, *Nineteen Eighty-Four* is a narrative that provides a protean storyline for interpreting a range of situations, but the possibilities for using this plot—its "affordances" (Wertsch, 1998)—are not endless. Instead, they come with an accompanying set of "constraints." George Orwell's story might be useful for understanding the power of a totalitarian state to crush an individual, but it is less useful in sizing up the actions of Russians in a time of national crisis that calls for heroism and sacrifice. Instead, accounts of the experience of the Great Patriotic War such as Vasili Grossman's masterwork *Life and Fate* (2006) would be more relevant.

1.7. Summing Up

In developing his ideas about equipment for living, Burke focused on how individuals make sense of everyday situations that they encounter, but his line of reasoning can also be used to understand how members of national communities end up with shared ways of understanding larger historical events. This shared understanding reflects the use of shared narrative tools, which are the key to accounting for the stark differences that can arise between entire national communities' views of the past. These narrative tools "coauthor" what members of such communities think and say, and coupled with the assumption that our stories are true, can give rise to vexing and intractable mnemonic standoffs. The differences in such cases can be so great that groups appear to be living in different worlds, and the intractability of such standoffs suggests the operation of underlying codes or habits that are more general than particular narrative about particular events. These issues are taken up in the subsequent chapters, beginning with a proposal for an interdisciplinary approach in chapter 2.

2

A Conceptual Tool Kit

2.1. Introduction

In this chapter I outline a conceptual framework for studying how nations remember. I include it because the scholarship on national memory often produces isolated and inconsistent findings that confuse rather than contribute to a coherent account of national memory. The result can be a sort of "nonparadigmatic, transdisciplinary, centerless enterprise," which is the description once given to social memory studies by Jeffrey Olick and Joyce Robbins (1998, p.105). In order to get beyond that, I outline an approach that draws on the insights of figures such as Olick (2007), Aleida Assmann (2011), and Erll (2011) from a range of disciplines in the humanities and social sciences.

My goal in doing this is not to provide a comprehensive review of national memory. Instead, the focus will remain on questions raised in chapter 1, including: What makes it possible for members of one national community to agree so strongly among themselves and differ so starkly from others about the past? Why are communities so committed to the truth of their accounts of the past? and How do the cultural and mental processes that give rise to these patterns operate in ways that veil their impact, making it difficult to detect and manage them? I hope to formulate these questions in a way that provides insight into their connection to other parts of the larger picture of national memory. I begin with issues of methods and forms of evidence.

How Nations Remember. James V. Wertsch, Oxford University Press (2021). © Oxford University Press.
DOI: 10.1093/oso/9780197551462.003.0002

2.2. Methods and Forms of Evidence

The illustrations outlined in chapter 1 are similar in that they reveal differences between accounts of the past, but they diverge in methods and evidence, and this can be revealing about what national memory is taken to be in the first place. Consider the procedure of asking groups to list major events of a larger historical episode such as World War II. This seems like a straightforward method for gathering evidence, and it can yield useful insights. For example, the lack of overlap between the American and Russian lists noted in chapter 1 comes as a surprise to most people, including those who generated the lists.

But using this method in isolation suggests a particular vision of what national memory is—namely, knowledge about the past with little concern for context, especially the context of debate over contradictory views of the past. A different picture might emerge if we use other methods. The example of the confrontation between Vladimir Putin and Western journalists in chapter 1 is a case in point. Such confrontations may reveal aspects of national memory that do not emerge in a simple survey, and this points to the more general question of how varying forms of evidence suggest different ideas of what national memory is.

One issue that comes up in this regard is how to distinguish collective memory and collective remembering (Wertsch, 2002). Yadin Dudai (2002) has outlined this distinction in his discussion of collective memory "as a body of knowledge" versus collective memory "as a process" (p.51). The former is "a cardinal element of culture. It is characteristic of the given social group, yet changes over time" (p.51), whereas memory as process "is a constant dialogue between individuals and their social group" (p.51). The two visions of collective memory represent two different starting points and rely on different methods, suggesting a larger picture of complementary analytic efforts.

Sociological studies often focus on memory as a process, as reflected in Olick's observation that it can be understood as "public discourses about the past as wholes or . . . narratives and images of the past that speak in the name of the collective" (2007, p.33). In general, then, switching from one form of evidence to another can lead us down different paths for understanding what national memory is. This does not mean that one view is correct and others are wrong, but instead suggests the need for a framework that allows coordination among various methods and definitions.

This touches on a general issue that runs throughout analyses of nations and nationalism, namely whether the emphasis should be on top-down processes of the state and other institutions, or bottom-up processes in the form of mental and cultural factors. There is little doubt that states make great efforts at top-down control and in some cases have a powerful impact on national memory—at least as it is discussed in the public sphere. This impact may be most pronounced when it comes to events that *cannot* be part of public discourse. I return to this in chapter 4 in my discussion of events and personages who disappeared from national memory in the Soviet Union. And Louisa Lim (2014) has examined the issue in her book *People's Republic of Amnesia*, where she reports on the memory of young Chinese for the 1989 Tiananmen Square massacre.

In general, it is not unusual in trying to account for national memory to start with efforts by the state. When talking about why nations—at least *other* nations—remember or forget something, we often begin by saying things like, "They don't remember that event because the state controls everything they hear." As already noted in chapter 1, however, this overlooks two problems. First, it is what every group seems to think of other groups but is surprised to hear that it might apply to themselves as well. And second, there are bottom-up forces that limit the impact that state or other authorities have, especially when it comes to the codes and habits that underpin national memory.

In the end, therefore, both top-down and bottom-up forces need to be taken into account in the study of national memory. But emphasis on one or the other side of the picture continues to characterize many research efforts. This is something that Rogers Brubaker, Mara Loveman, and Peter Stamatov (2004) address more generally in their analysis of ethnicity and nation. They start with the observation that much of the existing research comes from "historical, political, and institutional studies of official, codified, formalized categorization practices employed by powerful and authoritative institutions—above all, the state" (p.33). This has yielded important insights, but in their view it is constrained by the assumption that top-down forces produce similar knowledge in members of a group, which they see as simplistic, mechanistic, and misleading. Specifically, they see it as missing insights about the cultural and psychological processes that shape the way institutional processes play out and have their impact.

In this connection Brubaker et al. discuss "circumstantialist" approaches that focus on moment-by-moment negotiation of knowledge in social context. Such knowledge creation is a bottom-up process that complements the top-down influences of authoritative institutions, and its study involves appropriate methods and evidence. Several efforts of this sort have come out of the "symbolic interactionism" of George Herbert Mead (1934) that led to studies of discourse analysis in the 1960s and 1970s. Figures such as Erving Goffman (1959) and Harvey Sacks, Emanuel Schegloff, and Gail Jefferson (1974) conducted fine-grained analysis of moment-by-moment discursive practices that shape human action, and they argue that such practices should be given analytic primacy when trying to understand either psychological or institutional processes.

The line of reasoning they proposed has been extended in several ways, including in studies of "conversational remembering" by David Middleton and Derek Edwards (1990). A starting point for Middleton and Edwards is that "people's accounts of past events, before they can be taken as data on the cognitive workings of memory, need to be examined as contextualized and variable productions that do pragmatic and rhetorical work, such that no one version can be taken as a person's real memory" (p.37). Together with the ideas of Sacks et al. and others, this amounts to a call to making circumstantialist discursive practices as part of the effort of the study of bottom-up processes involved in remembering.

Specifically with regard to national memory, circumstantialist analysis draws attention to ways that concrete discursive contexts can shape how the past of a nation is represented. For example, instead of simply being a matter of the presence or absence of national memory and national feelings, Prasenjit Duara (2000) has pointed to the "simultaneous superficiality and depth of national feelings" (p.35) whose strength varies greatly and sometimes rapidly, depending on circumstances. Thus, after a period of lying dormant, nationalism can sometimes be ignited almost at a moment's notice and surface in vibrant public discourse. By way of making his point, Duara outlined a picture of the Chinese reaction to the May 1999 bombing of the Chinese embassy in Belgrade: "Day 1: Eat at McDonalds [sic]; Day 2: Throw rocks at McDonalds; Day 3: Eat at McDonalds" (2000, p.35).

2.3. Avoiding Primordialism

For Brubaker et al. (2004), circumstantialist studies coming from sociology are just one way that the disciplinary reach can be expanded when dealing with ethnicity and national identity. In addition, they argue for the incorporation of ideas from cognitive and evolutionary psychology in analyzing bottom-up forces. This is part of understanding ethnicity, race, and nation "as perspectives on the world rather than entities in the world" (p.31). Their formulation reflects a discussion in American cultural anthropology that has been ongoing since its formulation by Franz Boas and others (King, 2019), namely the need to recognize the reality of cultural differences while at the same time not reducing cultures to primordial essences. This requires treating ethnicity, race, and nation not as preexisting entities, but as socially and psychologically constructed. In the terms of Brubaker at al. this involves avoiding the temptations of "analytical 'groupism'—the tendency to treat ethnic groups as substantial entities to which interests and agency can be attributed" (p.31). Their call to avoid this pitfall involves a seeming paradox, however, because along with eschewing analytic groupism in theory, they note the need "to explain the tenacious hold of groupism in practice" (p.31).

The evolutionary psychologist Pascal Boyer (2018) has explored a related set of concerns in his account of "intuitive inference systems" (p.20). These systems are sometimes referred to as "modules" or "domain-specific systems" in cognitive science and have been discussed in terms of rule-governed language processing systems that, for example, "turn sounds into meaning," where the system involved "receives a continuous stream of speech and turns it into a largely imagined stream of discrete words with boundaries between them" (pp.20–21). In addition to parsing sound and sentences, the list of intuitive inference systems that have been posited by researchers includes those involved in "understanding narratives" (p.21). In Boyer's account, intuitive inference systems share the properties that they (1) "operate, for the most part, outside consciousness," (2) are "specialized," and (3) are "evolved properties of our species, that is, ways of acquiring information that promoted the fitness of individuals that had them in their repertoire" (p.22).

For Boyer, a key part of a genuine science of humans is that "[t]he world is governed by physical laws, not by the intentions of agents" (p.23). But at the same time, paradoxically, we "treat people as whole and integrated persons. In other words, we anthropomorphize them." On the one hand, this is "just as wrong for a science of people as it was for the science of rivers and trees. Indeed, for centuries, being anthropomorphic about people has been the main obstacle to having a proper science of human behavior" (p.24). But on the other hand, Boyer argues, "There is of course nothing wrong in treating people as persons when we interact with them—quite the opposite. To construe others as unique agents with preferences, goals, thoughts, and desires is the basis for all moral understandings and norms" (p.24). In his account, then, scientific psychology and "intuitive psychology" (p.25) exist alongside each other, but they serve different spheres of application.

Along with intuitive psychology as applied to individuals' actions, Boyer notes that "folk sociology" (p.204) leads us to treat entire groups with preferences, goals, thought, and desires. Groups are treated like agents because "[t]his belief in groups being like agents is easily entertained by human minds, because of the over-whelming importance of intuitive psychology in our mental life" (p.222). The use of such metaphors when representing the social world is also motivated by the fact that "[t]he aggregation of myriad individual behaviors, many of which are prompted by other agents' behaviors, constitute [sic] complex systems, beyond what human minds can represent in consciously accessible form [, meaning] we are condemned to use folk sociology" (p.236).

Figures such as Boyer and Brubaker are part of a larger dis-cussion about the need for an interdisciplinary analysis of na-tional, ethnic, and other communities, and they both recognize the seeming paradox that even though "groupism" and "folk soci-ology" are misguided in strictly scientific terms, they retain a "te-nacious hold" on us in practice. My focus on symbolic mediation is motivated in part by a desire to address this paradox. The problems involved in not recognizing it can be seen in the case of stereotypes, which have been a topic in cognitive and social psychology for decades. Brubaker et al. note that existing research has provided insight about "the resistance of stereotypes to disconfirming in-formation; the dynamics of activation of stereotypes; the ways in which stereotypes, once activated, can subtly influence subsequent perception and judgment without any awareness on the part of the perceiver" (p.39). This research points to ways that stereotypes lead to ungrounded, if not false, conclusions, and society often condemns stereotypes as the source of prejudice and unethical action. Brubaker et al. and Boyer by no means dispute this. At the same time, however, they note that this form of reasoning, however flawed, needs to be accounted for rather than just criticized and dismissed.

In this vein, Brubaker et al. see the notion of "schema" as serving a useful role. The notion of a schema has a long history in philosophy extending back to Immanuel Kant, and in modern psychology it has been invoked by figures such as Jean Piaget (1953) and Frederic Bartlett (1932). It is a notion that is difficult to define in any simple way, but it is usually taken to be a general pattern of action or cognition of the sort Bruner alluded to when talking about how humans use "cookie cutters" in making sense of the world around them (chapter 1). For Piaget, early schemata in infants such as sucking and grasping are viewed as patterns of action that can assimilate an expanding set of objects in the environment and in so doing accommodate themselves into more variegated action patterns. These ways of interacting with the physical world are then viewed as providing the building blocks for patterns of cognition and memory at later ages, which were the main focus of discussions by Bartlett.[1]

Cognitive anthropologists such as Roy D'Andrade (1995) see the notion of schema as a point of collaboration for studying the mental processes involved in ethnicity and nation. And building on this line of reasoning, I propose that narrative schemata can play a particularly useful role. Specifically, narratives used as equipment for living provide a means for understanding the folk sociology that—however misguided and theoretically indefensible it may be from the perspective of a genuinely scientific account of human action—guides national memory in general and makes it possible

[1] I expand on Bartlett's notion of schemata in the section "The Debt to Bartlett" later in the chapter.

for different national communities to be so strongly committed to different accounts of the past.

To sum up, different methods for studying national memory tend to encourage different visions of what national memory is. Instead of suggesting the need for a single orthodox method, however, this suggests that different methods may be called for, depending on what one is trying to explain. But that still leaves us with the problem of how various results complement one another in larger effort. Ideally, this would take the form of a unit of analysis that allows us to operate at the crossroads where various disciplinary methods and claims can be coordinated. Brubaker et al. have suggested that the notion of schema can play a useful role in the study of ethnicity and nation, and in what follows, I expand on this by using the notion of narrative-based schemata and symbolic mediation to address key questions about national memory raised at the outset of this chapter. First, though, some reflections on the claim that national memory *is* memory.

2.4. Is National Memory Really Memory?

We routinely speak of how "America remembers the Vietnam War" or "Russia remembers World War II," but what sort of memory is this? Is it like memory in individuals, or are we just using loose metaphors? The answer touches on a problem that has long vexed the humanities and social sciences, namely how to account for differences between groups—with regard to memory or something else—without invoking some mysterious essence, biological or otherwise. This echoes the concern raised by Brubaker et al. about the "tendency to treat ethnic groups as substantial entities to which interests and agency can be attributed."

In the case of national memory—which I take to be a particular form of the more general category of collective memory—these are questions first raised nearly a century ago in the writings of Maurice Halbwachs. As a student of Emile Durkheim (1947 [1912]), Halbwachs took collective memory to be an inherently social phenomenon. But he was also a student of Henri Bergson (2014 [1896]), and this led him to be concerned with its psychological dimensions, which suggests that the study of collective memory had interdisciplinary leanings from the outset. It is not entirely clear how Halbwachs saw these perspectives fitting together, but at one point he made the telling comment: "While the collective memory endures and draws strength from its base in a coherent body of people, it is individuals as group members who remember" (1980, p.48).

At the same time that Halbwachs was outlining these claims, ideas about "individuals as group members" were also surfacing in psychology in the writings of Frederic Bartlett (1886–1969). Bartlett was a major figure of his era, but as is the case for Halbwachs, much of his impact was to come decades after his death (Roediger, 2000). Bartlett formulated his ideas about individual and collective processes in his classic 1932 volume *Remembering: A Study in Experimental and Social Psychology*, where he expressed skepticism about the "more or less absolute likeness [that] has been drawn between the social group and the human individual" (p.293). His comments were directed in part at Halbwachs, but as Olick (1999) has noted, Halbwachs's ideas of collective memory varied over his lifetime, making it unclear whether he was susceptible at all points to Bartlett's criticism.

Astrid Erll (2011) has discussed these same general issues in her formulation of "cultural memory," where she notes that Halbwachs "unites—albeit not explicitly—two fundamental, and fundamentally different, concepts of collective memory" (p.15). On the one hand is "collective memory as the organic memory of the individual, which operates within the framework of the sociocultural environment" (p.15). From this perspective, remembering, even when carried out by an individual in isolation from concrete social interaction, is collective in the sense that it draws on a social framework. It is what Halbwachs seems to have had in mind when saying that "it is individuals as group members who remember." On the other hand, Erll points to claims by Halbwachs about collective memory that concern "the creation of shared versions of the past, which results through the interaction, communication, media, and institutions within small social groups as well as large cultural communities" (p.15).

Erll's comments build on a 1999 article about the "two cultures" of collective memory studies by Olick. In his view, the "individualist understanding" of collective memory is "open to psychological considerations, including neurological and cognitive factors" (p.333), but it tends to "neglect technologies of memory other than the brain and the ways in which cognitive and even neurological patterns are constituted in part by genuinely social processes" (p.333). Conversely, the "collectivist understanding" of collective memory focuses on "the social and cultural patternings of public and personal memory, but neglects the ways in which those processes are constituted in part by psychological dynamics" (p.333).

Returning to Bartlett, it is possible to find an early formulation of the issues raised by Erll and Olick. As a psychologist, Bartlett resisted the idea that collectives *qua* collectives remember and argued that claims about "memory *of* the group" (p.296, italics in the original) were to be eschewed. At the same time, however, he recognized "memory *in* the group" (italics in the original) as a legitimate focus of inquiry. His concern on this score was the "social framework of memory" (p.294) and the assumption that "social organization" has a powerful influence on "both the manner and the matter of recall" (p.294). This was part of Bartlett's larger call for psychology to study remembering in social context in which he urged psychologists to go beyond using nonsense syllables and other stimuli stripped of cultural significance. He believed such materials systematically ignore the impact of group membership and hence memory *in* the group.

At bottom, Bartlett's concern was with how we can study remembering as a mental process of individuals while keeping in mind the social forces that shape their thinking and speaking. In this respect, his views sound similar to those of Halbwachs when the latter observed that "it is individuals as group members who remember" (1980, p.48). This perspective generally falls under the heading of what Erll discusses as "the organic memory of the individual, which operates within the framework of the sociocultural environment" (2011, p.15) and what Olick terms the "individualist understanding" of collective memory (1999, p.333), and it is my main focus in much of what follows.

2.5. Flashbulb Memories and Memory *in* the Group

A topic that provides a good illustration of how individual and social forces have been studied in tandem is "flashbulb memory" (FBM). This term was introduced by Roger Brown and James Kulik in their landmark 1977 article to describe the vivid, subjectively compelling recollection of occasions on which we first learn of important events such as the 1963 assassination of President John F. Kennedy. FBMs are not about a public event itself, but about the circumstances in which an individual first learns of it. In the case of the Kennedy assassination Brown and Kulik wrote, "Almost everyone [i.e., in the 1970s] can remember, with an almost perceptual clarity, where he was when he heard, what he was doing at the time, who told him, what was the immediate aftermath, how he felt about it, and also one or more totally idiosyncratic and often trivial concomitants" (p.73).

Brown and Kulik made several claims about FBMs that have been taken up in subsequent research. These include claims that FBMs derive from the surprising and emotional nature of the public event and that they involve unusually accurate recall supported by a special neurophysiological mechanism. Most important for my purposes were observations they made about "consequentiality," something measured by asking subjects, "What consequences for my life, both direct and indirect, has this event had?" This is a measure that is concerned with remembering as group members. For example, Brown and Kulik found that Black Americans in their study were more likely than Whites to have FBMs for the assassination of figures such as Malcolm X and Martin Luther King Jr.

In the decades since 1977, there have been numerous studies of FBMs. These have often been done in the wake of traumatic events such as the Challenger explosion in 1986 or the 9/11 attacks in 2001. Harnessing the basic definition of FBMs provided by Brown and Kulik, this research has continued to focus on autobiographical memory for the circumstances in which one learns of a public event rather the event itself. In a review of this research, William Hirst and Elizabeth Phelps (2016) have noted that some of the claims from the ideas proposed by Brown and Kulik in 1977 have come into question. For example, subsequent studies have not supported the idea that FBMs involve special "encapsulated mental processes" (p.37) tied to a specific neurophysiological mechanism. And despite the vivid nature and the high level of confidence associated with FBMs, they are not unusually accurate. Instead, they are "best characterized as involving both forgetting and mnemonic distortion" (p.36) that are not unlike memory for other events. Furthermore, research since Brown and Kulik's landmark article has often "failed to find any correspondence between emotional state and consistency" and has also suggested that that surprise "does not seem to be a necessary feature" (p.37).

All these revisions still leave a couple of areas of agreement about the unique nature of FBMs. First, it is widely recognized that the confidence attached to them distinguishes them from other autobiographical memories: "confidence in FBMs remains high, even as consistency declines [over time]" (p.41). Second, and of particular importance for my purposes, consequentiality continues to be viewed as an essential feature of FBMs and is taken to reflect group membership. Echoing the difference between Black and White subjects reported by Brown and Kulik, for example, Hirst and Phelps report on research showing that "French participants possessed FBMs for the death of French President Mitterrand, whereas French-speaking Belgian participants did not (Curci, Luminet, Finkenauer, & Gisle, 2001), indicating the consequentiality of Mitterand's death for French citizens, but not French-speaking Belgians" (p.8).

Consequentiality has intriguing implications for understanding the general issue of what Bartlett called memory *in* the group. Brown and Kulik may not have envisioned it in this way, but in essence it can serve as a method for shedding light on what it means for an individual to be a group member. In their original formulation, they speculated that consequentiality has to do with biological significance, pointing to the "high selection value [that] could account for the evolution of an innate base for such a memory mechanism" (p.73).

Such claims, however, are questionable on several grounds, starting with the fact that they are part of the now-discarded ideas about neurophysiology. Writing some four decades later, Hirst and Phelps suggest that we turn instead to ideas about social identity, and they go on to note that "on those rare occasions when FBMs are formed, because of their social consequentiality, they can play a substantial role in shaping social identity (Berntsen, 2009; Neisser, 1982)" (p.5). Thus, consequentiality is taken to be not only a matter of memory reflecting group identity, but of *creating* it and the borders that exist between one group and another.

2.5.1. A Narrative Approach to Consequentiality in FBMs

An interpretation of FBMs that takes claims about social identity into new territory was provided by the cognitive psychologist Ulric

Neisser (1928–2012). Writing a few years after Brown and Kulik's article appeared, Neisser (1982) proposed narrative as key to understanding the social forces involved in FBMs. When summarizing Neisser's lifetime of contributions to psychology, John Kihlstrom (2012) made special mention of this insight:

> Almost everybody else studying flashbulb memories focused on internal mental processes—like the "flashbulb" mechanism itself, or depth of processing, or the effects of emotion on encoding, or even just the effects of rehearsal gained by telling a story over and over again. But Neisser thought about the role of such memories in personal life and social exchange ("where were you when the Challenger exploded or the World Trade Center came down?"). Even more important, Neisser thought that flashbulb memories had their qualities because they served as benchmarks by which people divided up their autobiographies, and connected their personal stories to public history.

In developing his ideas, Neisser (1982) began by observing that "although the phenomenon [of FBM] itself is clear enough, its interpretation is not" (p.43) and then proceeded to explore new avenues for understanding it. He accepted the claim that in FBMs, "[p]lace, ongoing, activity, informant, aftermath, one's own affect and that of others . . . are important aspects . . . [and] appear again and again" (p.47), but instead of attributing these to "the uniform terms in which the event was experienced" or to "regnant brain processes at the time of the event" (Brown & Kulik, 1977, p.95), he pointed to something else. Specifically, he turned to "narrative conventions" (p.47).

As part of his general approach to cognition and memory Neisser (1967, 1976) had a deep interest in how schemata shape reconstructive memory processes. Expanding on ideas from Bartlett, he noted that "we have *schemata* for the arrival of important news as we have for other kinds of social transactions, and we apply these schemata when we try to remember how we heard about President Kennedy's assassination" (1982, p.47). This was more than a phenomenon of individual mental processes for Neisser. It also involves "narrative conventions" (p.47) shared by journalists, novelists, "mythmakers," and autobiographers in the social ecology as well as by those who read or see their accounts of a past event. These conventions guide us to include "*who, what, when, where,* and *why* in their stories, preferably with a little *human interest* thrown in" (p.47, italics in the original).

For Neisser, narrative conventions are useful for understanding the organization of FBMs because "*[w]hen* and *why* are self-evident," whereas "*who, what, where* and *human interest* remain, and generate the canonical categories of recall" (p.47, italics in the original). This is a way of formulating the point that FBMs are about an individual's experience of learning about an important event, not the event itself. Neisser went on to argue that "the notion of narrative structure does more than explain the canonical form of flashbulb memories; it accounts for their very existence" (p.47), and it is here that some of his most interesting claims appear:

> The flashbulb recalls an occasion when two narratives that we ordinarily keep separate—the course of history and the course of our own life—were momentarily put into alignment. All of us have a rough narrative conception of public affairs. Time runs on, events unfold, and occasionally there are "historical moments." History has to have such moments, because otherwise it wouldn't be much of a story. The death of a prominent person—or the resignation of a president—is a good place to end a chapter or to highlight a theme. This means that judgments of "importance" are . . . not so much judgments of the event itself as of how it has been or will be used by the media, by historians, and by ordinary people thinking about their experiences. How dramatic was the event, how central, how "big"? This, I think, is what Brown and Kulik's subjects called its "consequentiality." (p.47)

2.5.2. Big and Little Narratives

Neisser's interpretation of FBMs expands the discussion by taking into consideration social forces and narrative organization. However, it leaves one interesting question unaddressed: What are the criteria for deciding what a "big" event is, and why do only some big events elicit FBMs? Presumably, there are many events marked by historians and the media as big, dramatic, and "historical moments," but only some of them give rise to FBMs. For example, the passage of the Affordable Care Act in 2010 may be one of the most important events in American political history in the 21st century, and for many people it certainly had "consequences for my life, both direct and indirect." However, it is unlikely that it created an FBM for anyone other than a few policy and political activists. Hirst and Phelps make a similar point in observing, "It is probably the case that few American women remember the circumstances in which they learned of the confirmation of the first female Supreme Court Justice of the United States, Sandra Day O'Connor, but that event is surely consequential, especially for American women. FBMs are the exception rather than the rule, even for consequential public events" (pp.4–5).

So, what is it that makes some public events big in the sense that they give rise to FBMs in a social group, whereas other events are just big? Consider the prototypical cases considered in discussions of FBMs, cases that are the ones Neisser seems to have had in mind. Two things stand out in this regard. First, they are big in the sense that the event is experienced by large numbers of people. Although Hirst and Phelps have argued that "[t]he public does not need to be as large as a nation" and FBMs can be for "an event experienced within a family setting, such learning of the death of a parent" (p.37), events of national importance are at the center of discussions of prototypical FBMs. Second, the sort of prototypical events Neisser had in mind are not just big but involve some sudden reconsideration, almost an epiphany, about a collective's well-being or status. The standard cases in discussion of FBMs are traumatic events such as assassinations of leaders or attacks on the nation. In such cases, Neisser discussed the alignment of narratives in terms of how "we remember the details of a flashbulb occasion because those details are the links between our own histories and 'History.' We are aware of this link at the time and aware that others are forging similar links. We discuss 'how we heard the news' with our friends and listen eagerly to how *they* heard" (p.48). Neisser then goes on to propose that the resulting memories are "not so much momentary snapshots as enduring benchmarks" (p.48). Specifically, they are "the places where we line up our own lives with the course of history itself and say 'I was there" (p.48). He also suggests that this may affect not only the existence but also the content of FBMs. What Neisser says on this issue is consistent with an account of identity in which our life narrative is inherently linked to the narrative of nations or other communities, a claim that is consonant with Alisdair MacIntyre's argument that "the story of my life is always embedded in the story of those communities from which I derive my identity" (1984, p.221).

I have little disagreement with the line of reasoning proposed by Neisser, but it still leaves unanswered the question why some "big" events give rise to FBMs and others do not. Why is it that in the case of some events "little" autobiographical narratives are tied to "big" national narratives (Rowe, Wertsch, & Kosyaeva, 2002) in ways that produce FBMs and in other cases this does not occur? Again, I believe the answer is to be found in the notion that the big events that spawn FBMs are extremely significant and often traumatic for a national community, and this, in turn, suggests a somewhat different notion of how a personal narrative and a national narrative "line up." Namely, it suggests that FBM-eliciting events mark points in a national narrative where normally unchallenged assumptions about the national narrative come into question.

Many of these occasions involve a traumatic event on the national scene that leads us to wonder whether the background national narrative we had been assuming all along is valid. If part of the big national story of the United States is that the country is constantly making progress toward equality and justice, then the assassination of a figure such as Martin Luther King Jr. calls this underlying narrative into question. If another part of the big story is that the United States is powerful and hence safe, an attack such as the one on September 11, 2001, can call the narrative into question in other ways.

In such cases, it is almost as if the supporting structure of the big national narrative of "History" is shaken, much like the physical ground below our feet that is so taken for granted is shaken in an earthquake. This image, in turn, suggests the need to reconsider Neisser's comments about how "two narratives that we ordinarily keep separate—the course of history and the course of our own life—[are] momentarily put into alignment" in the formation of an FBM. Instead of being instances where "we line up our lives with the source of history itself and say 'I was there'" (1982, p.48), FBMs may reflect an unexpected *uncertainty* about a national narrative that usually underpins the narrative we are constantly creating and revising of our own life.

Most illustrations of FBMs involve such negative traumatic events, but before leaving the topic, it should be noted that they can also involve sudden, unexpected positive events. Ludmila Isurin (2017), for example, has reported on the FBM of citizens of the USSR associated with the launch of Yuri Gagarin into space on April 12, 1961. The announcement of this technological feat set off a wave of euphoria among Soviet citizens and a boost in national pride and patriotism that reflects a reassessment—in an upward direction in this case—of a national narrative.

Not all of these cases rely on the same evolutionary mechanisms about consequentiality proposed by Brown and Kulik when they mentioned "high selection value [that] could account for the evolution of an innate base for such a memory mechanism" (p.73). But at a functional level concerned with consequences for an individual that stem from a reassessment of the narrative of the larger group in which they are a member, the logic is the same.

2.6. The Debt to Bartlett

In his narrative-based account of FBMs, Neisser followed his general practice of appealing to the notion of schemata. He viewed FBMs as growing out of expectations based on regular patterns of narrative schemata found in society and in the mental life of members of a group. And in developing this aspect of his argument, Neisser (1967, 1976) was clear about his debt to Bartlett (1932), who is widely viewed as a crucial founding figure when it comes to this notion in the psychology of cognition and memory. Bartlett actually wrote relatively little about schemata, and at the time of his death, some of his students confidently predicted that it was a notion that would quickly disappear from discussions in psychology (Roediger, 2000). In fact, however, it continues to have outsized impact nearly a century later.

Perhaps the place where Bartlett's position on this issue plays out most clearly is not in his explicit claims, but in his methods, and it is here that one can gain further insight into his notion of schemata and of memory in the group. These methods brought social and cultural issues into the picture from the outset by focusing on how groups differ in the way that their members assign meanings to stimuli. Bartlett was concerned with what happens when the meaning system of one group comes into contact with meanings assigned by another. In one of his best-known studies, for example, he documented the difficulties that British university students encountered in recalling a Native American story "The War of the Ghosts" (1932, p.153). This was a story based on a meaning system that was quite different from that familiar to his British subjects, and the result was that his British subjects systematically distorted the text when they tried to remember it and pass it along to others. The whole interpretation of these results rests on the assumption that the schemata used by members of one group can garble narratives generated by another group.

The notion of schema suggested by Bartlett continues to shape psychology, sociology, and anthropology to the present day (Wagoner, 2017), and D'Andrade (1995) used it in his account of psychological anthropology concerned with how social forces are related to individual mental processes. One point on which discussions of schemata have generally not provided adequate answers, however, concerns their content and how this content might vary between groups. By definition, a schema is a general form of representation, but it must have some sort of group-specific content if it provides the foundation for distinguishing one community from another. Bartlett's experimental method hinged on the assumption that English and Native American communities bring *different* schemata to understanding stories, but he had nothing to say about of the content of this difference.

Other unanswered questions about schemata include: How do schemata come to be shared by members of a group? Bartlett clearly assumed that the British subjects in his experiments brought a particular set of schemata to his memory task, but how do members of a group come to share such mental structures? In addition, what is the role of schemata in the formation and maintenance of a group? What social function do they serve alongside their role in an individual's remembering and thinking? As noted earlier in the chapter, Hirst and Phelps touch on this issue, but much remains unanswered on this score.

Bartlett did not focus his efforts on answering questions such as these, which are crucial for understanding differences in national memory. However, his line of inquiry provides a starting point for addressing the question of whether national memory is really memory. In the case of collective memory, his answer was a qualified "Yes" as long as the focus remains on the mental functioning of *individuals as group members*. This line of reasoning guides what follows as I delve further into issues of national memory. The key issue remains how schemata, especially those built around narratives, play a central role in leading members of a national community to end up with similar accounts of the past.

2.7. Symbolic Mediation

To say that national memory is organized around narratives is hardly original, but focusing on how narratives serve as tools adds an essential dimension to the discussion. It means that they are part of an "irreducible tension" (Wertsch, 1998) in which human action is shaped by cultural tools, but individuals still have agency and can be assigned responsibility for what they say and do. It is an account in which narrative tools in and of themselves do not make agents do anything, but the affordances and constraints (Wertsch, 1998) built into them have a powerful impact in channeling their action.

My approach to these issues draws heavily on the scholarship of Russian figures such as Vygotsky (1896–1934), Luria (1903–1977), and Mikhail Bakhtin (1895–1975), all of whom viewed language as having a defining role in social and mental life. Their starting point is that we do not have direct or *im*mediate access to most objects in the world, including events from the past. Instead, our access is indirect because it is mediated by symbol systems, especially natural language. Vygotsky was quite explicit about the centrality of mediation (*oposredovanie*) in his thinking; for him, "[a] central fact of our psychology is the fact of mediation" (1982, p.166). In outlining "the instrumental method in psychology" (1981a), he listed several forms of mediation, including "language; various systems for counting; mnemonic techniques; algebraic symbol systems; works of art; writing; schemes, diagrams, maps, and mechanical drawings; all sorts of conventional signs" (p.137).

The main focus for Vygotsky and Luria, however, was natural language, one of whose crucial proclivities is to induce what Charles Taylor (1985) terms "articulation," a notion that has parallels with Burke's comments on how language is used to "size up" a situation. Taylor traces the idea of articulation to Johann Gottfried Herder (1744–1803), who along with Wilhelm von Humboldt (1767–1835) was an intellectual progenitor of Vygotsky and Luria. Instead of assuming that language simply expresses ideas we already have in mind, these figures represent a tradition that emphasizes how it serves a kind of creative function in providing a particular articulation of experience. In Taylor's account:

> Finding an adequate articulation for what I want to say . . . brings [something] in focus. To find a description in this case is to identify a feature of the matter at hand and thereby grasp its contour, to get a proper view of it . . . coming to articulate our sense of some matter is inseparable from coming to identify its features. It is these that our descriptions pick out; and having an articulated view of something is grasping how the different features or aspects are related. (1985, p.257)

This approach emphasizes the active, performative dimension of language, thereby making it a process that goes beyond describing the world and involves imagination or creation—Taylor's articulation. Similar ideas ran throughout the writings of Vygotsky (1986) and his colleagues. They can be found, for example, in the regulative potential of language that guides attention and thinking through the use of "egocentric" and "inner" speech, making it a matter of bringing features or aspects of objects into focus and grasping how they are related (Wertsch, 1985b).

These ideas were part of a larger intellectual discussion in Europe in the early 20th century involving figures such as Edmund Husserl (1859–1938), whose influence on Vygotsky flowed through Gustav Shpet (1879–1937), a student of Husserl's and one of Vygotsky's teachers in Moscow. In addition, the German philosopher Ernst Cassirer (1874–1945), whose major writings were on "the philosophy of symbolic forms," contributed to ideas of how language shapes mental life. Even though he was routinely dismissed by doctrinaire Soviet Marxists as an idealist, Cassirer's (1953, 1968) impact on figures such as Bakhtin (1986b) is clear. Going back still further Herder and Humboldt had much to say about the role of language in shaping nations (cf. Taylor, 1985), which brings the discussion full circle in understanding how the ideas of Vygotsky and Luria apply to national memory.

My personal effort to understand symbolic mediation started in the 1970s as a postdoctoral scholar in Moscow working with Luria (Figure 2.1). When I first encountered the ideas that he, Vygotsky, and others had developed, I assumed they could readily be transferred across intellectual and national borders, but this turned out to be naïve on my part, especially when it came to how social and individual processes are understood in Russian and Western traditions. I eventually came to realize that what was new to me had less to do with Marxism-Leninism than with differences in Russian and American cultural assumptions about the individual. Instead of starting with the atomistic agent, Vygotsky, Luria, and others began with a commitment to the social origins and residual "quasi-social nature" of individual mental functioning (Vygotsky, 1981b, p.164). In the past few decades these ideas have found echoes in Western research on "socially shared cognition" (Resnick, Levine, & Behrend, 1991) and "distributed cognition" (Hutchins, 1995), and these efforts provide a natural entry point for the study of national memory as a matter of individuals operating as members of a social group.

Figure 2.1. Alexander Romanovich Luria and author. Near Moscow, May 1976.
Photo in the author's collection

2.7.1. Literacy as an Illustration of Symbolic Mediation

In my discussions with Luria, I found one of his most striking claims to be that humans can live in different "realities" based on different symbolic systems. Following the lead of Vygotsky, he approached this issue from the perspective of what happens when a new form of mediation is introduced into social and mental processes and transforms existing patterns of thinking and memory. In this view, the appearance of a new form of mediation does not simply facilitate thinking or remembering by making it more efficient; instead, "by being included in the process of behavior, the psychological tool[2] alters the entire flow and structure of mental functions" (Vygotsky, 1981a, p.137).

Vygotsky and his students explored this claim in several ways. They observed how language acquisition in children transforms the ontogenesis of thinking, and they conducted "microgenetic" studies by introducing external memory aids into an ongoing lesson and observing how the flow of a student's mental functioning changed over the course of a single experimental session. They envisioned these studies as part of a more general research agenda, which also includes the transformations that occur in human history. Of particular importance for Luria in the "genetic domain" (Wertsch, 1991) of history was the transformation in human mental life that occurs with the emergence of literacy.

Historians (e.g., Havelock, 1976) and anthropologists (e.g., Goody & Watt, 1968) have examined the historical emergence of literacy for decades, and some have made claims about how the appearance of mass literacy in human history "transformed human consciousness" (Ong, 1982, p.78). Vygotsky and Luria contributed to this discussion (Vygotsky & Luria, 1993) by harnessing a natural laboratory setting provided by modernization efforts in Central Asia during the early decades of the Soviet Union. In this setting they were able to examine what transpires when formal schooling and literacy were introduced into a context where most people were nonliterate. This included crash programs in which Vygotsky and

---

[2] Vygotsky used "psychological tool" and "sign" [znak] in related ways in his writings. For my purposes, they fall under the more general term "symbol" in the present volume, which reflects the influence of Cassirer.

Luria participated to prepare large numbers of people to become teachers as part of a mass literacy campaign (Figure 2.2).

The research question in this case concerned how nonliterate people in Central Asia developed new forms of thinking and speaking with the appearance of formal education. Luria (1981) framed this question in terms of a distinction between the "practical thinking" based on directly experienced objects and events in everyday life and the "theoretical thinking" associated with the abstract reasoning that grows out of literacy practices. He and Vygotsky devised several measures to assess the abilities of nonliterate and newly literate people and traveled to Uzbekistan in the late 1920s and 1930 to examine subjects' use of abstract concepts and reasoning. In Luria's view, this was an effort to explore a "new level of consciousness" (1981, p.209) that emerges with literacy and allows people to operate in a different reality than had been accessible to them previously.

Figure 2.2. L.S. Vygotsky with students in Central Asia, 1929.
Permission to use photo provided by G.L. Vygodskaya

One of the measures of theoretical thinking that Luria and Vygotsky employed was syllogistic reasoning, using problems such as:

> In the far north, where there is snow, all bears are white.
> Novaya Zemlya is in the far north.
> What color are the bears there? (Luria, 1976b, p.108)

Luria (1976b, 1981) reported that nonliterate subjects responded in ways that are strikingly different from those who had been exposed to formal schooling. Instead of concluding that bears in Novaya Zemlya are white, they gave unexpected answers and often resisted engaging in the task altogether. Specifically, "many [nonliterate subjects] refused to accept the major premise, declaring that they 'had never been in the North and never seen bears'" (1976b, p.107), suggesting an unwillingness to operate in an abstract conceptual space not grounded in their practical perceptual experience. In response to repeated questioning in these studies, the subjects provided responses such as, "to answer the question you would have to ask people who had been there and seen [the bears]" (p.107).

Luria concluded that these subjects did not have access to the second reality of theoretical thinking associated with literacy practices. In contrast, adults who had been exposed to such education, even for as little as a few months, as in pedagogical institutes, responded to the syllogistic reasoning tasks in ways familiar to literate subjects everywhere, reflecting their mastery of "techniques of logical thinking that allow them to go beyond the bounds of direct experience" (1981, p.209).

Questions remain about whether the nonliterate subjects Luria tested in Central Asia were unable or simply unwilling to engage in such syllogistic reasoning tasks (Scribner, 1977; Wertsch, 1998), and there are other questions about the precise nature of the literacy practices involved (Scribner & Cole, 1981). For current purposes, however, the implications remain largely the same, namely that nonschooled subjects did not readily enter into the abstract reasoning space of theoretical thinking based on syllogisms that would allow them to draw conclusions about objects never encountered in practical activity. This reasoning space is something that comes into existence and can be used to draw logical conclusions because language is being used to operate in abstract problem spaces. This use of language is available in any language and is used in discursive practices at the core of mathematics and other abstract reasoning processes (Wertsch, 1985b). However, it did not guide the practical activities at the core of everyday life for the nonliterate subjects in Luria's study.

For Vygotsky and Luria, modernization efforts in Central Asia provided a natural laboratory for studying symbolic mediation in that it allowed them to address the question: How does the introduction of a new form of symbolic mediation alter the flow and structure of mental functioning? The new type of symbolic mediation in this case did not come in the form of a new national language such as Russian, Uzbek, or English. Instead, it relied on a "semiotic potential" (Wertsch, 1985b) available in any human language, namely the potential for theoretical thinking, which is harnessed in a widespread way only with the rise of the mass literacy of the past few centuries. By mastering syllogistic reasoning, we open up a different reality of abstract objects and theoretical thinking. Analogous issues arise in the case of narratives as symbolic mediation, but they follow a quite different path in human history.

2.7.2. Narratives as Symbolic Mediation

Narratives provide an essential part of the semiotic potential in any human language, and the same basic line of reasoning that Luria and Vygotsky used to examine literacy applies: Particular affordances built into a symbolic form channel mental processes in particular ways. But there are important differences between narratives and abstract symbolic means such as syllogisms in this regard. For starters, unlike abstract forms of language, narratives are "natural" in the sense that no special formal instruction is required to learn how to use them. Children in all cultures that have been studied seem to acquire the ability to tell narratives in their early years without formal schooling. Partly for this reason, narratives are so ubiquitous in everyday life that their presence and impact are easily overlooked. And in contrast to the transformative impact literacy has on thinking, where preliterate forms of mental life can be clearly described, it is difficult to document "pre-narrative" forms of thinking and remembering.

The existence of pre-narrative and non-narrative understanding has been a topic of debate in narrative studies. Building on ideas from Husserl and other phenomenologists, for example, David Carr (1986) has suggested that narrative tendencies structure human experience at such basic levels that it makes little sense to search for pre-narrative forms of understanding. Instead, human experience itself is already a storied reality, not some kind of raw, unorganized sets of events that have to be transformed into having a beginning, middle, and end by being subjected to narrative discourse. In Carr's account, narrative structure "inheres in the events themselves. Far from being a formal distortion of the events it relates, a narrative account is an extension of one of their primary features" (1986, p.117).

MacIntyre (1984) has outlined one of the strongest views of this sort by placing narrative at the foundation of human identity. For him, "conversations, . . . battles, chess games, courtships, philosophy seminars, familes at the dinner table, businessmen negotating contracts . . . human actions in general" (p.211) are marked by a beginning, middle, and end and hence constitute "enacted narratives" (p.211). MacIntyre emphasizes that "[n]arrative is not the work of poets, dramatists, and novelists reflecting on events which had no narrative order before one was imposed by the singer or the writer; narrative form is neither disguise nor decoration" (p.211). For him, "stories are lived before they are told" (p.212). The ensuing picture, then, is one in which "man is in his actions and practice, as well as in his fictions, essentially a story-telling animal" (p.216), and to make sense of what we or others do, we implicitly rely on narrative tools from the outset.

Views such as Carr's and MacIntyre's contrast with the stance that "human experience is in itself devoid of structure, or at any rate narrative structure" (Carr, 1986, p.45) and where "narrative imposes on the events of the past a form that in themselves they do not have" (1986, p.11). In Carr's telling this perspective is one that the philosophers of history Hayden White (1981) and Louis Mink (1978) assume. According to it, what exists before narrative form is imposed is a "mere sequence" of events with no sign of a beginning, middle, and end. Such an interpretation assumes that "structure in general and narrative structure in particular imposes upon human experience . . . something that is not 'natural' but forced, something which distorts or does violence to the true nature of human reality" (Carr, 1986, p.43).

In either of the two alternatives Carr presents, the inclusion of narrative tools into existing forms of discourse and thinking presumably involves some kind of the transformation Vygotsky envisioned. I shall return to these issues of pre-narrative understanding, but for now the point is that at the general level of symbolic mediation, claims on this issue have parallels with those that Vygotsky and Luria made about syllogistic reasoning. In both instances the issue is how symbolic mediation shapes mental realities. First, though, I turn to how narratives differ from abstract reasoning tools such as syllogisms in their inner logic, truth claims, and origins in human history.

2.7.3. The Inner Logic of Narrative Tools

In *Actual Minds, Possible Worlds*, Bruner (1986) outlined "Two Modes of Thought." These were what he called "paradigmatic" or "logico-scientific" thinking, on the one hand, and "narrative" thinking, on the other. His distinction corresponds with Paul Ricoeur's distinction between "the theoretical use of reason" (1991, p.23) and "narrative understanding," respectively, with the latter being associated with Aristotle's notion of "phronesis," or the practical wisdom involved in guiding one's life (Ricoeur, 1992, p.174). Starting with the assertion that there are "two modes of cognitive functioning, two modes of thought, each providing distinctive ways of ordering experience, of constructing reality" (1986, p.11), Bruner went on to claim that, although complementary, they "are irreducible to each other" because "the structure of a well-formed logical argument differs radically from that of a well-wrought story" (p.11). These two modes of thought have in common that each takes information and turns it into statements that imply causality, but "the types of causality . . . are palpably different" (p.11).

The syllogistic thinking studied by Luria and Vygotsky in the 1930s is an example of paradigmatic thought concerned with a "well-formed logical argument." The premises of the syllogism entail the conclusion that bears in Novaya Zemlya are white by virtue of the meanings of the statements and the logic that ties them together. In such cases a syllogism "attempts to fulfill the idea of a formal, mathematical system of description and explanation" (Bruner, 1986, p.12), and it yields truth strictly through formal deduction. In contrast, narrative thinking takes statements such as "The king died, and then the queen died" and leads us to search for "likely particular connections between two events—mortal grief, suicide, foul play" (1986, p.12). In such cases the conclusions we draw are a matter of verisimilitude rather than the necessary truths of paradigmatic thinking, and drawing these conclusion relies on narrative plot rather than logical deduction.

For Ricoeur (1984, 1984–1986, 1991), "emplotment" and "a synthesis of heterogeneous elements" (1991, p.21) are the key elements of narrative. At first glance, synthesizing heterogeneous elements might sound like what syllogisms make possible as well, but narratives differ because of their distinctive way of ordering experience, namely in terms of temporality and plot. Emplotment involves a process of taking a temporal sequence of event and "drawing a configuration out of a succession" (Ricoeur, 1991, p.22). As noted by Louis Mink (1978), this involves a Kantian judgment that "grasps together" temporally distributed events into a comprehensible storyline. In narrative thought there is a big difference between "The king died, and then the queen died," on the one hand, and "The queen died, and then the king died," on the other, but temporal order is simply not an issue when drawing the conclusion that bears are white in Novaya Zemlya.

As White (1981) has noted, plot is just one possible organizing principle for depicting past events. It is entirely possible to create an accurate account of the past by simply listing events in a timeline that is not organized around a narrative plot. Instead of picking out the years 1941 to 1945 as having special significance as the story of World War II, for example, it would be possible to list 1941, 1942, 1943, 1944, and 1945 in a timeline that variously records events such as hurricanes, the stock market prices, or epidemics of measles. As White has documented, such "chronicles," which have no discernible beginning or sense of an ending, have in fact been used to record life in past centuries. They are not, however, the tool of choice in historical analysis and, as will become evident, have even less of a role in national memory.

Understanding how the inner logic of narratives shapes their role as equipment for living requires going beyond narrative texts themselves and considering how they are embedded in the speaking and thinking of active agents. A figure who treats narratives from the perspective of a dynamic process involving an agent is the literary scholar Peter Brooks (1984). For him, the active, processual dimension of engaging with narratives involves "plotting," which "makes a plot 'move forward,' and makes us read forward, seeking in the unfolding of the narrative a line of intention and a portent of design that hold the promise of progress toward meaning" (p.xiii).

The whole process is shaped by a narrative logic in which "only the end can finally determine meaning" (p.22). Indeed, "the end writes the beginning and shapes the middle . . . [and] everything is transformed by the structuring presence of the end to come" (p.22). Throughout this process, an active agent is involved and can guide "plotting" in unique directions in any particular reading, but using narrative form means that in an important sense the procedure operates " 'in reverse' " (p.22). As Brooks puts it, "Perhaps we would do best to speak of the *anticipation of retrospection* as our chief tool in making sense of narrative, the master trope of its strange logic" (p.23). Brooks's formulation of this "strange logic" highlights ways that narrative form operates in a way that is quite distinct from that of the theoretical thinking found in syllogisms.

The importance of a sense of an ending and the anticipation of retrospection are key elements in the use of narrative in the telling of history. For example, they can give rise to the seeming paradox that historians writing long after an event occurred can offer insights that were not available to those who actually participated in it. Paul Cohen (1997) discusses this in the context of his "three keys" of history: event, myth, and experience. For him, experience bears some similarities to what White and Mink viewed as mere events that do not have a structure and stands in contrast to event and myth, both of which involve the "feat of redefinition" (p.xii). Cohen introduces these ideas in his account of the Boxer Rebellion in China from 1898 to 1900 and notes the striking difference between the experience of the participants, on the one hand, and the "redefinition" involved in creating events or myths, on the other:

> Individuals, in short, who didn't know whether they would emerge from their respective ordeal dead or alive, who did not have the entire "event" preencoded in their heads . . . therefore conceptualized what was happening to them in ways that differed fundamentally from the retrospective, backward-reading construction of historians. (p.xiii)

Once again, the inner logic of narrative can be seen at work. Those who are in the midst of experiencing human events do not know the outcome of the story of which they are a part and cannot operate "in reverse"; they do not have the possibility of making sense of what is going on by using Brooks's "anticipation of retrospection" that will be available to historians and mythmakers once a larger episode like the Boxer Rebellion is over.

Brooks also makes note of a further important feature of plot—namely, it must be "taken in by memory" (1984, p.11). This was part of a parallel Aristotle drew between visual arts and narrative, with the latter "conceived to be the outline or armature of the story, that which supports and organizes the rest" (p.11). The plot must be kept in mind while watching the various parts of the text unfold: "just as in the visual arts a whole must be of a size that can be taken in by the eye, so a plot must be 'of a length to be taken in by memory'" (p.11). It was in this sense of memory that it "is the key faculty in the capacity to perceive relations of beginnings, middles, and ends through time" that is required to read a novel, watch a play, or tell the past of one's nation. In Kenneth Burke's (1998) formulation, it is a crucial property of narratives as equipment for living that makes it possible for us to size up complex individuals or events in an instant by using a text that might take many hours to read in its entirety.

In his *Grammar of Motives* (1969) Burke outlined further claims about narrative organization based on his "pentad" for interpreting human action, a system comprising act, scene, agent, agency, and purpose. Similar to the factors Neisser used to examine flashbulb memories, Burke's pentad can be viewed as responding to standard journalistic questions to be answered in a news story: What? Where? When? Who? How? and Why? Bruner has noted the special importance of "Scene" in this regard. It is a sort of container within which the other elements play out, or "the background of an act, the situation in which it occurred" (Burke, 1969, p.4). For Burke, the key to understanding accounts of any kind of human action is not elements of the pentad operating in isolation, but their coordinated action in tandem—what he called their "ratios." One such ratio involves the beginning of a text (the scene) and its ending. It is only in certain settings provided by the beginning of a narrative that an ending can play out, and the retrospective view provided by an ending often gives insight into what the beginning means. All of these elements are part of what it means for a plot to be "taken in by memory."

An empirical study by Jeremy Yamashiro, Abram Van Engen, and Henry Roediger (2019) provides an illustration of how scene is reflected in the narrative tools involved in national memory. They asked 2,000 Americans questions about what they considered to be the origin story of their country and also questions about their political and religious leanings. What they found was that "conservative participants more frequently omitted foundational atrocities from America's origin story" (p.1), something that might reflect the view that America is somehow blessed with a divine mission. In contrast, secular respondents were more likely "to begin America with the independent state" (p.1), reflecting their view that the story of the country is of a nonreligious nature. In sum, "[o]rigin stories accord with varying images of America and American identity" (p.1). Such findings suggest that both the beginning (the opening scene) and the ending of narrative tools for telling the past are likely to shape national memory, making the two elements as well as their interaction core parts of the "strange logic" of national narratives.

2.7.4. Narrative Truth

In chapter 1 I observed that disputes over national memory are often different from those over opinion or ideology. In the latter, we can agree to disagree, whereas in the case of memory, we assume that truth is involved, leaving no room for compromise. This is the reason that we sometimes find ourselves at an impasse or mnemonic standoff and end up blurting out things like, "But that's just not true!" Given that stories are invariably at the heart of such disputes, this raises the issue of narrative truth.

As outlined earlier in this chapter, the conclusions we draw from syllogistic reasoning are true because they necessarily follow from the premises. If we accept the premises of Luria's syllogism, we know it is true that all bears in Novaya Zemlya are white. As in the case of mathematical equations such as $5 + 7 = 12$, the truth of this statement derives from the very meanings of the terms involved. It requires no external evidence. Such cases of "analytic truth" are distinct from "synthetic truth," whose verification requires empirical evidence beyond the meanings of the words or terms. We turn to external evidence, for example, to decide on the truth of the statement that water freezes at 0 degrees Centigrade or that the American Civil War began in 1861. These two cases of synthetic truth differ in that the former relies on the experimental method of natural science, whereas the latter requires archival or other forms of evidence used in the humanities. But they are alike in requiring external empirical evidence to verify the truth of a propositional utterance. This involves ways that evidence does or does not match a proposition, a topic that has long been discussed under the heading of correspondence theories of truth (cf. Russell, 1912).

At first glance, it might seem that assessing narrative truth would be a straightforward extension of assessing the synthetic truth of propositions and would involve a similar appeal to empirical evidence. After all, narratives are made up of propositions like "The American Civil War began in 1861," so this seems a good starting point for assessing the truth of the more extended text of which they are a part. However, the truth of a narrative is not something that can be reduced to the truth of the sum of propositions included in it. Instead, discussions of narrative truth involve something different stemming from the fact that a narrative has, as Mink (1978) wrote, "a unity of its own; this is what is acknowledged in saying that it must have a beginning, middle, and end" (p.197). This unity exists at a level above and beyond the propositions that go into a story, and the result is that "the *form* of the narrative, as well as its individual statements of fact, is taken as representing something that may be true or false" (p.197).

For Mink, this was part of a larger discussion of how narrative description differs from theoretical reasoning, where he noted:

Narrative has in fact been analyzed, especially by philosophers intent on comparing the form of narrative with the form of theories, as if it were nothing but a logical conjunction of past-referring statements; and on such an analysis there is no problem of *narrative truth*. The difficulty with the model of logical conjunction, however, is that it is not a model of narrative form at all. It is rather a model of *chronicle*[3] . . . [In contrast] a historical narrative claims truth not merely for each of its individual statements taken distributively, but for the complex form of the narrative itself. Only by virtue of such form can there be a story of failure or of success, of plans miscarried or policies overtaken by events, of survivals and transformations which interweave with each other in the circumstances of individual lives and the development of institutions. (1978, pp.197–198)

In coming up with a narrative about the past, this means that the account "is a product of imaginative construction, which cannot defend its claim to truth by any accepted procedure of argumentation or authentication" (Mink, 1978, p.199). And in contrast to propositional truth, "there are no *rules* for the construction of a narrative as there are for the analysis and interpretation of evidence" (p.199) that would support a statement.

To illustrate how this plays out concretely, I turn again to the statement that the American Civil War began in 1861. The truth of this proposition (i.e., whether or not it corresponds with reality)

---

[3] See comments by White on chronicles earlier in this chapter.

can be defended by an "accepted procedure of argumentation or authentication" based on analyzing archival materials such as newspaper accounts. But matters are different when it comes to the larger narrative of which this proposition is a part. This becomes apparent when one considers arguments that have raged for decades over whether the story of the Civil War is one about ending slavery or about preserving the Union. These arguments have been the topic of a heated debate in America from the Civil War until the present, and at core they revolve around narrative truth—what the right, real, or true narrative of the war is.

An important site where this mnemonic struggle has played out is the motives behind the words and deeds of Lincoln and other major figures in the Civil War. In collective memory, this debate has often been formulated as a stark opposition between a desire to preserve the Union or a desire to eliminate slavery, often with attempts to show that Lincoln always did or did not believe in one or the other of these alternatives. In such cases there has been little patience for ambiguity. By contrast, historical scholarship has been more likely to consider a complex mix and evolution of motives, often by tracing the existence of both sides of the opposition to an earlier point and documenting their evolution. For example, David Blight (2001) writes, "The Northern postwar ideological memory of the conflict as a transformation in the history of freedom, as an American second founding, was born in the rhetoric of 1863 fashioned by Douglass, Lincoln, and others whose burden it was to explain how the war's first purpose (preservation of the Union) had transfigured into the second (emancipation of the slaves)" (p.15). In such cases, the debate in both memory and history has not been driven by the discovery of new archives and propositional truths. Instead, it has been over narrative truth.

A similar conclusion stems from the research of sociologist Barry Schwartz (1997), who has provided a general picture of American collective memory for Abraham Lincoln in the century following the Civil War. Again, this research points to struggle over the real or true story of Lincoln's motives rather than propositional truths. Schwartz views the evolution of memory of Lincoln in the context of broader political and cultural forces in society, suggesting a kind of mutual reinforcement between these forces and collective memory in the decades following the Civil War. Using this approach, he documents how Lincoln was "transformed . . . from a conservative symbol of the status quo during the Jim Crow era into the personification of racial justice and equality during the New Deal and the civil rights movement" (p.469).

The analyses of Blight and Schwartz support the idea that different narrative truths reflect broader political forces at work in society, and this raises a broader question: What determines this truth? If, as Mink said, "there are no *rules* for the construction of a narrative as there are for the analysis and interpretation of evidence" (1978, p.199), and if a narrative account "is a product of imaginative construction, which cannot defend its claim to truth by any accepted procedure of argumentation or authentication" (p.199), what grounds are there for coming up with narrative truth?

The folksy wisdom of Harry Truman is not usually consulted in such discussions, but it provides a starting point for addressing this question. Reflecting on a lifetime of reading history, Truman opined in an interview, "No two historians ever agree on what happened, and the damn thing is they both think they are telling the truth. But you had to find that out for yourself and that somebody with authority has to make them understand that their viewpoint and the other viewpoint can be brought together and agreement can be reached" (Miller, 2018).

Truman's conclusion that authority is often involved in formulating accounts of the past is a starting point that will be agreed to by many. However, his comments on the sources of this authority leave many questions unanswered. His observation that "you had to find out for yourself" suggests that some sort of rational reflection based on evidence is part of the answer. This might take the form of weighing the evidence in support of one narrative as opposed to another, something similar to what takes place in a court of law that pits one lawyer against another in the attempt to convince the jury of what the true story of an event is. The philosopher Stephen Toulmin (1958) proposed such trial procedures as an analogy for how inquiry in the natural sciences occurs, and its applicability to deciding between narratives about the past would seem to be even more appropriate.

But Truman seemed to believe that authority is often based on something other than evidence and rational argument when he said "someone with authority" needs to be involved. Reflecting his lifetime of political deal-making, this appears to involve a procedure in which someone steps in to "make [people] understand that their viewpoint and the other viewpoint can be brought together and agreement can be reached." This view takes us beyond evidence and rational argument into another form of authority, and it raises a host of questions. What authorties should we turn to in such cases—politicians, professors, cult leaders, Big Brother?

This is an issue to which I return in later chapters, but at this point I would note that my approach takes me back to comments by Brubaker, Loveman, and Stamatov (2004) about social science accounts that are overly focused on top-down forces. Their criticism was aimed at "historical, political, and institutional studies of official, codified, formalized categorization practices employed by powerful and authoritative institutions—above all, the state" (p.33). Like Brubaker et al., I believe that top-down forces are important, but the sort of mechanistic influence of top-down forces they note often gives short shrift to bottom-up cultural and psychological processes involved in areas such as national memory.

In the following chapters, I address this issue by considering some of the discursive and mental processes involved in national memory. This touches on issues that Brubaker et al. raise in connection with both circumstantialism and mental schemata. In particular, I shall be concerned with how narrative forms and the mental habits associated with them shape national memory. This involves

taking into account what Olick (1999) calls an individualist understanding of collective memory—which does *not* amount to a call
for methodological individualism or the claim that individual psychological processes can by themselves explain group processes.
Instead, it is a call to recognize how mental habits such as those involved in national memory both reflect and support the social and
political forces at work in a society. For example, I shall argue that
they can provide a sort of braking force that thwarts or otherwise
shapes top-down efforts to rewrite the past. In the end, my point is
that taking mental processes and other bottom-up forces into account does not displace but complements other efforts to understand struggles over narrative truth.

2.7.5. The Origins of Narrative in Human History

Perhaps because emplotment appears to be so natural and provides
such a powerful and efficient means for organizing large amounts
of information, it is hard to imagine human understanding without
it. As noted earlier, the historian David Carr (1991) wrestled with
this issue, and it has been discussed in evolutionary psychology as
well. Merlin Donald (1991) speculates that narratives have been in
the cultural tool kit of humans for millennia and were "fully developed . . . in the Upper Paleolithic" (p.257), leading him to conjec-
ture that "a gathering of modern postindustrial Westerners around
the family table, exchanging anecdotes and accounts of recent
events, does not look much different from a similar gathering in a
Stone Age setting" (p.257).

Even though the claim that narrative is "*the* basic product
of language" (Donald, p.257) may make it difficult to imagine
"pre-narrative" life, this has not kept scholars from searching for
evidence and engaging in thought experiments in an attempt to understand what that life might have been like. Their line of reasoning
often parallels that used by Vygotsky and Luria as they searched

for how the introduction of a new form of symbolic mediation transforms an existing form of mental life.

In discussing findings from laboratory studies, for example, the cognitive neuroscientist Jeffrey Zacks (2017) proposes that narrative functioning is an overlay on older processes he calls "event models" (p.184) whereby humans (and other animals) automatically fill in the bits of information needed to take in events in the world. He argues that event models have evolved "over a long period of time, well before the emergence of language or of pictorial depictions" (p.184) and that they serve as a base for our ability "to comprehend depictions of events in pictures or movies" (p.184). These are part of a larger framework in which our ability "to understand stories about events is built on top of our systems for representing events from perception" (p.184). In this view human perception of stories, pictures, and films "parasitizes...our evolved mechanisms for representing unmediated events" (p.184).

Other approaches to the origins of narrative thinking can be found in studies of human evolution. Erin Wayman (2012) and Yuval Noah Harari (2011), for example, suggest that transformational events of some 70,000 years ago played a crucial role in this regard. Harari argues that a "Cognitive Revolution" at that point made the "ability to speak about fiction ... the most unique feature of Sapiens language" (p.24). For him,

the truly unique feature of our language is not its ability to transmit information about men and lions. Rather, it's the ability to transmit information about things that do not exist at all. As far as we know, only Sapiens can talk about entire kinds of entities that they have never seen, touched or smelled. Legends, myths, gods and religions appeared for the first time in the Cognitive Revolution. (p.24)

Harari's claims build on the assumption that the evolutionary accomplishments he lists would not exist "outside the stories that people invent and tell one another" (p.29). They are accomplishments that presumably build on the event models described by Zacks.

It is significant for the study of national memory that along with transforming cognitive capabilities in individuals, Harari sees the appearance of narratives as having major social consequences. Namely, in contrast to other apes such as chimpanzees, who rely on personal acquaintance and face-to-face interaction to form social groups that are limited to about 50 individuals, the use of narratives by *Homo sapiens* makes it possible to create communities of almost unlimited size.

> [F]iction has enabled us not merely to imagine things, but to do so *collectively*. We can weave common myths such as the biblical creation story, the Dreamtime myths of Aboriginal Australians, and the nationalist myths of modern states. Such myths give Sapiens the unprecedented ability to cooperate flexibly in large numbers. (p.25)

Harari's claims are based on indirect evidence and speculation about what must have happened to account for the breakout of *Homo sapiens* involved in moving from being an "unexceptional ape" to taking a dominant place among all human species. In his essay on "making stories," Bruner (2002) proposed a similar line of reasoning.

> I doubt that such collective life would be possible were it not for our human capacity to organize and communicate experience in a narrative form. For it is the conventionalization of narrative that converts individual experience into collective coin which can be circulated, as it were, on a base wider than a merely interpersonal one. Being able to read another's mind need depend no longer on sharing some narrow ecological niche but, rather, on a common fund of myth, folktale, "common sense." (p.16)

Research in another genetic domain—ontogenesis—has relied on other forms of evidence to make the analogous case that narratives reshape human cognition. Psychologists such as Robyn Fivush and Catherine Nelson, for example, have documented that between two and five years of age, "children's developing language and narrative skills allow them to understand and represent events in more complicated ways than they did earlier in life" (2004, p.494). On the basis of extensive empirical studies they conclude that "narratives bring a new form of organization to events [and add] layers of comprehensibility to events above and beyond what is available from direct experience by linking events together through causal, conditional, and temporal markers" (p.494).

Such research often builds on evidence about pre-narrative, indeed pre-linguistic, motor and perceptual skills. Piaget (1953) and others have produced a rich set of findings on early "sensorimotor" development that underlies subsequent stages of mental life, and scholars such as Bruner have argued that grammatical and narrative structures often overlay these early forms of sensorimotor intelligence. One upshot of this is that the roots of narrative thinking appear quite early in childhood, again making it difficult to disentangle them from motor and perceptual processes. In principle, however, the appearance of narrative tools can be expected to alter "the entire flow and structure of mental functions" (Vygotsky, 1981a, p.137) by introducing meaning-making in the form of the "strange logic" of narrative.

In sum, scholars from several disciplines have made claims about how narrative use transforms human mental life in human evolution and ontogenesis. These claims rely on various forms of evidence, but a common thread is that narrative thinking emerges at very early phases of human development. In the case of children, it seems to be tied to infants' abilities to track moving objects and distinguish between agent-like and other objects, and in human history it appears so far back in the past that we can only speculate about precursors and early development. This means that it is difficult to disentangle narrative use from other aspects of mental development, an observation that is consistent with the transparency of narrative tools in thinking and memory.

2.7.6. Two Levels of Narrative Analysis

Up to this point, I have focused on specific narratives about concrete events. As noted in chapter 1, however, the narratives that "coauthor" national memory often seem to have a more general form. In addition to countless discrete narratives, each about a particular event, I shall argue that the "rich legacy of memories" envisioned by Renan (1990) is shaped by schematic storylines. These do not contain detailed information about particular dates, places, and actors but are a more general narrative form that yields habits shared by members of a national community.

This line of reasoning is consistent with numerous findings in psychology and cognitive science showing that human memory is weak on details but good at retaining general outlines of past events. It is also consistent with viewing human memory as a matter of active reconstruction that organizes and reorganizes information into larger wholes and preserves the gist of information at the expense of details (Schacter, Gutchess, & Kensinger, 2009). Research has yielded a picture of humans as "cognitive misers" (Fiske & Taylor, 1991) who favor efficiency by organizing information into larger, more general units even if this involves sacrificing specifics. Once again, these are claims that can be traced back to Bartlett (1932), who presented memory as an active "effort after meaning" guided by schemata.

From this perspective, instead of being united only around specific narratives about discrete, concrete events, members of a mnemonic community may be bound together by schematic forms extracted out of the countless narratives they encounter from early childhood on. Formulating things in this manner requires two levels of analysis: a surface level of narratives having concrete form and content—what I term "specific narratives"—and a deeper level of "schematic narrative templates"[4] (Wertsch, 2002). In addition to approaching these levels as part of semiotic or linguistic analysis, they can be viewed in psychological terms, where the counterparts of the underlying codes are mental habits and unconscious "fast thinking."

Specific narratives are surface texts that include concrete information about the particular times, places, and actors involved in an event. An illustration of a specific narrative is:

> On June 22, 1941, German forces invaded the USSR without warning. After massive losses in the fall of 1941, the Soviet army stopped the Germans in Moscow, and they went on to defeat the German invaders in Moscow, Stalingrad, Kursk, and elsewhere leading up to the March to Berlin and total defeat of Germany in 1945.

This text qualifies as a specific narrative because it names concrete actors (Germans, Soviet army), dates (June 22, 1941), and places (Moscow, Kursk). Specific narratives may be very brief, or they can go on for thousands of pages. It is not length that makes them specific; it is the mention of definite, concrete information about times, places, and actors.

Whatever their length, specific narratives typically include detailed descriptions of multiple characters engaged in complicated plot twists, issues that have been the subject of extensive research in linguistics, psychology, and anthropology. A well-known analysis of the inner complexity of narratives was provided by the Russian philologist and folklorist Vladimir Propp (1895–1970).

---

[4] This distinction bears some resemblance to others such as that between "explicit" and "implicit" national narratives as outlined by Aleida Assmann (2008), but it often draws from different theoretical traditions and has somewhat different implications.

In the *Morphology of the Folktale* (1968 [1928]), he analyzed 100 Russian folktales that exemplified 31 basic structural elements, or "functions," and formulated how they are part of an elaborate, highly structured typology. The functions he identified include items such as "Departure," in which "the hero leaves home," and "Designation" in which "the hero is tested, interrogated, attacked, etc., which prepares the way for his receiving either a magical agent or helper" (p.39). In addition to defining these functions, Propp formulated an account of how they appear in linear sequences in stories and how the 31 functions are related to one another— what have come to be termed "syntagmatic" and "paradigmatic" relationships in writings by figures such as A.J. Greimas (1966) and Claude Lévi-Strauss (1955).

In contrast to the detailed complexity of interaction among elements and functions in specific narratives, narrative templates are largely devoid of concrete detail about the time and place of events and about most actors. And especially when they are the shared forms of symbolic mediation that bind members of a national community together, they can be quite simple in nature. To be sure, elements in them can still be categorized as functions, but these elements are so generic and content-free that Propp's definitions of functions are largely superfluous.

Another point of contrast with specific narratives, which exist in directly observable surface texts, is that narrative templates exist as posited underlying codes to be unearthed through the analytic efforts of researchers. The underlying forms in this case can have multiple instantiations in the form of specific narratives— something that is implied by the very term "template." In this regard, narrative templates have parallels with schemata as described by Brubaker et al. (2004), which "are of course not directly observable" but rather are "posited to account for evidence—experimental, observational, historical—about how people perceive and interpret the world and about how knowledge is acquired, stored, recalled, and extended to new domains" (p.41). These are issues to which

I return in chapter 3 as I examine particular narrative templates in particular national memory projects.

2.8. Habit

The final item in the conceptual tool kit outlined in this chapter is habit. This may appear to be such a simple, everyday notion that it requires no special consideration, but it has been a topic of discussion in philosophy, psychology, and sociology for over a century, suggesting it is more complex. A key topic in this discussion has been the relationship between habit and memory. The two are sometimes set in opposition, but in the study of national memory there is much to be gained by understanding how they are connected.

An important early figure in this discussion was Henri Bergson (1859–1941), who formulated a distinction between habit and memory in terms of "motor mechanisms" and "independent recollections" (2014, p.40). Motor mechanisms take the form of repeated actions based on automatic, embodied processes and involve no direct representation of the past. In contrast, independent recollection registers the past in the form of "image-remembrances," which Bergson assumed to involve ideation not found in the motor mechanisms.

Bergson illustrated this distinction by using a lesson devoted to memorizing a text such as a poem. An essential property of habit in such cases is that it loses track of its origins and exists only in the present. As Bergson put it: "the lesson once learnt bears upon it no mark which betrays its origin and classes it in the past; it is part of my present, exactly like my habit of walking or of writing; it is lived and acted, rather than represented" (p.42). From this perspective, a habit reflects the past, but it does not reflect *on* the past. As in Neisser's account of schemata, the efforts involved in its formation involve "a great number of individual experiences, but they do not reflect these experiences separately" (Neisser, 1967, p.287). In contrast to habit, Bergson considered memory to be concerned with some image or verbal account of the lesson itself—its setting, who was present, what they said, and so forth. For Bergson, then, memory is about the past in a way that habit is not.

In the hands of other scholars, habit encompasses a broader set of issues than those considered by Bergson. For example, the philosopher and psychologist William James (1890) laid out a vision of habit that included, but was not restricted to, exact replication of an action such as reciting a poem. At one point in formulating this more general account, James noted a parallel between habit and a crease in a sheet of paper, writing, "It costs less trouble to fold a paper when it has been folded already" (1890, p.106). For James this reflects the fact that habit "*simplifies the movements required to achieve a given result, makes them more accurate and diminishes fatigue*" (p.112, italics in the original).

Here and elsewhere in his account of habit, James gave motor mechanisms a central role, and in this respect his account overlaps with Bergson's, but he went on to create a more expansive view that touched on social and ethical issues. Indeed, he imagined habit as "the enormous fly-wheel of society" (p.121), which suggests the powerful inertia that habit can impart to social processes and also how it can impede change. In this latter respect James noted that habit is society's "most precious conservative agent" (p.121) and can serve to preserve a social order even when we see aspects of it that are undesirable and in need of change.

> [Habit] alone is what keeps us all within the bounds of ordinance, and saves the children of fortune from the envious uprisings of the poor. It alone prevents the hardest and most repulsive walks of life from being deserted by those brought up to tread therein. It keeps the fisherman and the deck-hand at sea through the winter; it holds the miner in his darkness, and nails the countryman to his log-cabin and his lonely farm through all the months of snow;

it protects us from invasion by the natives of the desert and the frozen zone. (p.121)

James summed up this discussion with the sobering claim that habit "dooms us all to fight out the battle of life upon the lines of our nurture or our early choice, and to make the best of a pursuit that disagrees, because there is no other for which we are fitted, and it is too late to begin" (p.121). Again, this is a much more general picture of habit than that proposed by Bergson, not only in going beyond motor mechanisms but also in its implications for society.

Although James and Bergson differ on several points, one point on which they generally agree is that habit is to be distinguished from memory (or is a distinct form of memory in Bergson's case), and this is a point that continues to characterize discussions in psychology today. In a review of contemporary research on memory, for example, Henry Roediger, Elizabeth Marsh, and Stephanie Lee (2002) note the lasting impact of the related distinction between "knowing how" and "knowing that" used by the philosopher Gilbert Ryle (1949). And using other terminology, the psychologist Larry Squire (1987) distinguished "procedural" and "declarative" forms of memory, with the former including skills and abilities of the sort that would fall under the heading of what Bergson and James termed habit. In contrast, declarative memory includes both episodic memory for events such as the specifics of a lesson to memorize a poem and "semantic" memory for "relatively permanent knowledge of the world" (p.4), such as the fact that iambic pentameter is a common poetic form. Both procedural memory and semantic memory are not concerned with representing events from the past, and this sets them apart from episodic memory, whose very definition is based on remembering past events.

Distinctions such as those used by Squire have been important when mapping out the massive body of research on memory in psychology from the past several decades. Roediger et al. (2002) note that a more complete list of categories that have been proposed would include procedural, declarative, explicit, implicit, conscious, and unconscious memory. They also note that when these are put to work in empirical studies, it is often difficult to maintain distinctions that may seem clear in the abstract. As in the case of national memory, part of the problem in psychological studies of memory stems from the plethora of methods and evidence used by various scholars. In providing just a short sampling of these, for example, Roediger et al. note the use of standard tests of memory for words or pictures, cued recall, and serial recall, which raises the possibility that different methods might entail different definitions of what memory is.

In their review, Roediger et al. make an important comment in passing that has major implications for national memory. Namely, they write that there may be "a procedural component to all acts of remembering, even on supposed declarative or episodic tests" (p.5). This suggests that some of very interesting unanswered questions remain about how distinct forms of memory are related—especially how procedural memory might be a part of other types. The implication for the study of national memory is that habits play an important role in just about all accounts of the past.

Up to this point, the issues I have raised come from philosophical and psychological studies of the individual. One exception is the comment by James about habit as the "conservative agent" behind the "enormous fly-wheel of society." In elaborating on this point, he built on two commonsensical observations about habit. First, many of our most powerful habits are formed in early years of life and are very hard to change later. Rather than leading to despair, this led him to point to the opportunities of education "to *make our nervous system our ally instead of our enemy*" (p.122, italics in the original). And second, he was pointing to how membership in a collective is heavily determined by habits that do not change even if people are dissatisfied with their station in life. This provides insight into the massive social coordination problem underlying any large-scale community. Rather than pointing to top-down forces from the state or other authorities, James was pointing to unconscious habits as an essential key to what holds a large collective together. This social dimension of habit has also been a focus for sociologists such as Pierre Bourdieu (1977). Addressing a puzzle posed by Leibniz centuries earlier about how large social entities can be coordinated, Bourdieu outlined a notion of "habitus" that allowed him study the "conductorless orchestration which gives regularity, unity, and systematicity to the practices of a group or class, and this even in the absence of any spontaneous or externally imposed organization of individual projects" (p.80). Without such a notion, Bourdieu argued that analysts are likely to be "condemned to the naïve artificialism which recognizes no other principle unifying a group's or class's ordinary or extraordinary action than the conscious co-ordination of conspiracy" (p.80). Like James's claims about how habits are inculcated at an early age, Bourdieu asserts, "The habitus is precisely this immanent law, *lex insita*, laid down in each agent by his earliest upbringing" (p.81).

My account of how habit shapes national memory is inspired in no small part by the ideas Paul Connerton (1989) outlined in his compact, masterful volume *How Societies Remember*. Connerton framed his argument in terms of distinction between "*inscribing* practice" and "*incorporating* practice" (pp.72–73). The former focuses on how "we preserve versions of the past by representing it to ourselves in words and images" (p.72). Commemorative cere-monies provide examples of how we can depend on "re-enactments of the past, its return in a representational guise which normally includes a simulacrum of the scene or situation recaptured" (p.72). In contrast, incorporating practices can be used to "preserve the past deliberately without explicitly re-presenting it in words or images" (p.72). In cases of "habitual memory the past is, as it were, sedimented in the body" (p.72).

Connerton draws on Bergson, among others, to explore these issues and is motivated by many of the same concerns that are of interest to me. The distinctions that he ends up drawing are not the same as the one I shall outline between narrative mediation and the habits that grow out of it, but the motivation behind such distinctions is similar. Both cases point to the need in collective or national memory studies to transcend boundaries between the individual and society and between one discipline and another. Connerton seeks to address this by expanding the study of memory beyond inscribing practices, and my approach relies on symbolic mediation in the form of narrative tools and the mental habits that ensue.

2.9. Summing Up

The conceptual tool kit I have outlined in this chapter involves the claims that (1) human communication and mental life are fundamentally shaped by symbolic mediation, (2) narratives play a leading role in the symbolic mediation of national memory, and (3) the study of narrative tools must address underlying codes and associated habits as well as surface form.

From this perspective narratives are assumed to transform collective memory when they are incorporated into human discourse just as syllogisms transformed the theoretical reasoning of the nonliterate subjects in the Central Asian study that Luria and Vygotsky conducted. The symbolic mediation in this case brings with it a "strange logic" organized around plot rather than the formal logic of syllogisms or other deductive forms of thinking. Furthermore, differences in the stock of stories used by different national communities yield quite divergent views of the past, views that end up in the form of shared habits in a community that guide our thinking in unconscious ways.

Of course, it is always possible, at least in principle, to resist using the cultural tools that have been given to us by the powerful institutions of a state or other authority. That would be something like what Luria's nonliterate subjects did in refusing to engage in the language game of syllogistic reasoning. But once we begin to use a set of narrative tools, it becomes quite difficult to avoid the grooves of thinking that are built into them. A crucial task for the study of national memory, then, is to understand where the equipment for living comes from and how it shapes our mental habits in the hope that we can gain some reflective distance and even find ways to manage it.

Running throughout this line of reasoning is the idea that different forms of symbolic mediation give rise to different mental habits, a conclusion that provides the groundwork for understanding how nations can differ so profoundly in their accounts of the past. These types of mediation often escape our notice because they operate as underlying codes rather than explicit surface form, and this raises the issue of how to conceptualize these underlying forms along with their psychological correlates in the form of transparent habits and fast thinking. These are issues to which I turn in more detail in the chapters that follow.

3

National Narratives

3.1. Introduction

Building on the claims about narrative mediation outlined in chapter 2, I now turn to particular ways that narrative tools shape national memory. At several points I use illustrations that provide reminders of how national memory can overpower other voices in political discourse, sometimes with negative consequences. These illustrations also provide the background for understanding some key characteristics of national memory, namely how it differs from analytic history and requires consideration of both surface and deeper levels of narrative functioning. The focus throughout remains on individuals as members of a group.

I write these words in St. Louis, a city that 50,000 Bosnian Muslim refugees have come to call home. They arrived after the bloody implosion of Yugoslavia in the early 1990s that forced them to flee the violence led by Slobodan Milošević, the Serbian nationalist leader, sometimes called the "Butcher of the Balkans." Between 1992 and 1995 tensions between Serbs and Bosnians exploded into full-blown conflict in the Bosnian War. People from these two groups— as well as others—who had coexisted peacefully for decades, indeed centuries, turned against one another with unexpected violence. In some cases, combatants living in the same village or even members of the same family faced off along national lines. The cycle of torture, rape, and killing culminated in July 1995 when 8,000 Bosnian men and boys were executed by Serbian forces at Srebrenica. This is the largest genocidal massacre on European soil since World War

How Nations Remember. James V. Wertsch, Oxford University Press (2021). © Oxford University Press.
DOI: 10.1093/oso/9780197551462.003.0003

II, and it has been the topic of commemorative events and museum exhibits in St. Louis.

A crucial means that the Serbian leader Milošević used to stoke conflict was national memory. This turned out to be an extremely effective means for fueling resentment not only against Bosnian Muslims for humiliations from centuries ago but also against Croatians and others for deeds of a few decades earlier. In such cases, national memory seems to be packed with incendiary material ready to be set off by nationalistic leaders.

Serbian hostility toward Bosnian Muslims stemmed back some six centuries to the expansion of the Ottoman Empire into their territory, a point used repeatedly by Milošević when he mentioned the Battle of Kosovo in 1389 in which Ottoman Muslims defeated an army led by a Serbian prince. This humiliating defeat was part of national memory for many Serbs, kept alive through oral histories and a famous painting depicting the battle's carnage that could be found in many Serb homes throughout the 20th century. National memory for such events had a powerful hold over Serbs and proved to be a major impediment to efforts by Western diplomats trying to negotiate an end to the violence.

As another example of conflict animated by national memory, consider the violence between Armenia and Azerbaijan that broke out in the early 1990s. These two republics in the USSR became independent states when the Soviet Union collapsed, and they soon fell into brutal conflict over the disputed territory of Nagorny Karabakh. The ensuing struggle peaked in 1993 and resulted in more than 25,000 deaths and 1 million displaced persons. Sporadic violence fueled by differences over national narratives in this case has gone on for decades.[1]

Thomas de Waal (2003), a long-time observer of the Caucasus, writes that "To hear leaders on either side talk about the origins

---

[1] The intractability of this dispute is evidenced in major new fighting more than a quarter century later at the time this book is being written.

of the Armenia-Azerbaijan conflict is to hear two narratives, each hermetically sealed from the other" (p.125). According to one Azerbaijani political leader, "the Armenian side . . . began to make territorial claims on Azerbaijan, and they stood behind the beginning of the separatist movement in Nagorny Karabakh. So there is no doubting the responsibility of the Armenian ultranationalists in this question" (p.126). But an Armenian leader told de Waal, "this problem was always there and it was completely obvious that when central authority weakened or ceased to exist [i.e., with the breakup of the Soviet Union], then we would get what we now have. . . . There was no doubt about that—and it seems to me that it was obvious to the Azerbaijanis too" (p.126).

Not only are these narratives hermetically sealed, but the members of each group are also certain that the truth of their story is "obvious" and would be admitted as such by their adversaries if they were only honest. Strong confidence in one's own story and the inability to believe that anyone could believe anything else are core ingredients of what it means to live in different mental realities grounded in different national narratives. Political scientist Roger Petersen (2011) notes these factors in his account of escalating cycles of violence that rely on "strategic use of emotions" among warring parties driven by the dynamics of anger, fear, contempt, resentment, and hatred. The historian Timothy Snyder (2010) elaborates the picture of toxic forces in his examination of the rabid nationalism involved in the mass killing of Jews in the "bloodlands" in Eastern Europe in World War II, where he argues that the disappearance of state authority is an invitation to unchecked brutality.

Introducing national narratives into the discussion does not suggest that they can explain the strategic use of emotions or the deterioration of state authority. If it were simply a matter of national narratives, for example, the turmoil in Yugoslavia would have broken out before Milošević made his 1987 populist speech at a rally that launched his career of rabid nationalism. Instead, the strategic use of emotions and weakened state authority may be best viewed as providing necessary but not sufficient conditions for national narratives to have their incendiary effect. As is the case for most issues in the study of national memory, any single item in the conceptual tool kit needs to be viewed as part of a larger picture.

With these caveats in mind, I turn to a few key distinctions in an effort to provide additional insight into how national narratives play a role in national memory. The first involves national memory and analytic history; the second is between specific narratives and narrative templates, where I will provide a more elaborated account of a topic I introduced in chapter 2; and a third distinction is between "fast" and "slow" thinking. In all cases, narratives as symbolic mediation remain the core issue, and the concern is with how they have their surprising impact.

3.2. National Memory and Analytic History

National memory typically claims to provide a true account of the past, but it also inevitably serves the needs of an identity project, and when the pressures for truth and identity clash, the latter often wins out. Paul Cohen describes this in terms of "myth," with its tendency for "impressing of the past into the service of a particular reading of the present" (1997, p.xii). In contrast, what I term "analytic history"[2] is, or at least strives to be, "a reasoned reconstruction of the past rooted in research" (Blight, 2009, p.242). It is more likely to retain a primary commitment to rational procedures for pursuing truth and accuracy—even if they yield outcomes that are unpopular with members of a national community. In Blight's account, "History is what trained historians do," and it "asserts the authority of academic training and rules of evidence" (p.242),

---

[2] I include the modifier "analytic" in order to emphasize that the form of history I have in mind is one branch of efforts to address the past and is distinct from oft-criticized notions of a universal history as envisioned by Halbwachs. I am grateful to an anonymous reviewer for helping me clarify this.

whereas "memory carries the more immediate authority of community membership or family experience" (p.243).

The distinction between these two ways of relating to the past is often relative instead of absolute, and the difference between them has been a point of extended debate. In his classic 1882 article "What Is a Nation?" Renan (1990) argued that national memory is not simply different from history but exists in tension with it. He made a particular point of noting that "Forgetting, I would even go so far as to say historical error, is a crucial factor in the creation of a nation, which is why progress in historical studies often constitutes a danger for [the principle of] nationality" (p.11). A few decades later, the founder of collective memory studies, Halbwachs, noted that the goals of "formal history" (1980, p.78) stand in opposition to those of memory. And in recent decades the historian Pierre Nora has set forth an even stronger version of how history and memory exist in an adversarial relationship. For Nora, "Memory and history, far from being synonymous, appear now to be in fundamental opposition ... History is perpetually suspicious of memory, and its true mission is to suppress and destroy it" (1989, pp.8–9).

Over the past century, this is a discussion that has witnessed claims ranging all the way from asserting that history and memory cannot be differentiated to viewing them in fundamental opposition. Mink (1978) has examined the first of these alternatives in his account of how history differs from fiction. He was concerned with the dilemma that historical narrative "claims to represent, through its form, part of the real complexity of the past, but as narrative it is a product of imaginative construction, which cannot defend its claim to truth by any accepted procedure of argument or authentication" (p.199). For Mink, the dilemma reflects the larger fact that "History and fiction are alike stories or narratives of events and actions" (p.183), which means that "narrative history and narrative fiction move closer together than common sense could well accept" (p.203). In the end, however, he concludes that a crucial distinction does exist between historical and fictional narratives. Indeed,

"It would be disastrous . . . if common sense were to be routed from its last stronghold on this point" (p.203).

An incisive formulation of this distinction can be found in an illustration Jan Assmann provides of the two ways of relating to the past. In the early pages of *Moses the Egyptian* (1997) he writes:

> Unlike Moses, Akhenaten, Pharaoh Amenophis IV, was a figure exclusively of history and not of memory. Shortly after his death, his name was erased from the king-lists, his monuments were dismantled, his inscriptions and representations were destroyed, and almost every trace of his existence was obliterated. For centuries, no one knew of his extraordinary revolution. Until his rediscovery in the nineteenth century, there was virtually no memory of Akhenaten. Moses represents the reverse case. No traces have ever been found of his historical existence. He grew and developed only as a figure of memory, absorbing and embodying all traditions that pertained to legislation, liberation, and monotheism. (p.23)

Assmann warns that the distinction between history and memory is not ironclad, and we should not assume an "all-too antiseptic conception of history as 'pure facts' as opposed to the egocentrism of myth-making memory" (p.14). Instead, he proposes that they are related because "history turns into myth as soon as it is remembered, narrated, and used, that is, woven into the fabric of the present" (p.14), echoing Cohen's comment about how in myth the past is impressed into the service of a particular reading of the present.

Weaving history into the fabric of the present is usually part of self-serving identity projects, making the past into *our* past, to paraphrase William James. It also makes the past seem less distant and separated from the present. The historian Peter Novick (1999) noted this in his comment about collective memory's tendency to deny the "pastness" of events and "insist on their continuing presence" (p.4). For him, this is one of the points that distinguishes it from history, which "by its nature, focuses on the historicity of events—that they took place then and not now, that they grew out of circumstances different from those that now obtain" (p.4). In this view memory turns out to be "in crucial senses ahistorical, even antihistorical" (p.3), whereas history aspires to more objective rational analysis that encourages us to recognize the possibility that there are competing ways to emplot events.

In contrast to an objective analysis of the past that separates it from the present, national memory tends to assume a "continuing presence" of the past, often with strong emotional overtones. In an analysis of memory of the slave trade in America, for example, Bernard Bailyn (2001) asserted that memory's appeal is based on the fact that "Its relationship to the past is an embrace ... ultimately emotional, not intellectual" (quoted by Blight, 2009, p.243). This is coupled with the fact that the forces behind memory are seldom part of a conscious, reflective strategy and do not rely on careful analysis but instead are built on off-the-shelf narrative tools that introduce perspective and emotion in unconscious ways and make it possible, if need be, to ignore or override inconvenient facts. The result is that collective memory "sees events from a single, committed perspective; is impatient with ambiguities of any kind; reduces events to mythic archetypes" (Novick, pp.3–4).

In formulating his version of the difference between history and collective memory, Novick asserted that the former is more inclined to acknowledge the complexity of the past and must have "sufficient detachment to see it from multiple perspectives, to accept the ambiguities, including moral ambiguities, for protagonists' motives and behavior" (p.4). This detachment requires a form of conscious, analytic thinking that encourages us to follow evidence wherever it leads, including in directions that run counter to claims of a national identity project. As a result, historians sometimes map out accounts of the past that differ sharply from what we believe as members of a national community. To be sure, historians do not always live up to their own standards, and they do retain biases, but these standards nonetheless remain at the core of historians' aspirations.

The most crucial difference between national memory and analytic history is not their content or even accuracy but the forms of discourse they involve, especially when it comes to giving precedence to established narratives or to objective information and argument. To engage in historical analysis is to agree to work in accordance with the socially evolved norms for collecting and weighing evidence, addressing or rebutting competing accounts, and rationally defending one's overall conclusions in response to challenges from others, including when this leads to overturning an existing narrative interpretation. In this respect it is like the adversarial procedures of a court case noted in chapter 2. Engaging in historical analysis also means not being overconfident in one's account or dismissing others' versions out of hand. Instead, if other analysts come up with different conclusions, one is obligated to consider these conclusions, and one can criticize and rebut them only by operating in the same framework of norms. These procedures emerge in the form of institutionally legitimated forms of reasoning such as those tied to the professionalization of historical research.

Blight (2001) has examined this in his account of the efforts to train new generations of American historians in the 1920s to bring objective analysis to bear on events of the Civil War that had been part of the "Lost Cause" mythic storyline favored in the South. The roots of this effort can be traced to the 1890s with "the training of scholars in 'scientific' seminars under Herbert Baxter Adams at Johns Hopkins University or William A. Dunning at Columbia" (p.297). With this, "new forms of Lost Cause dissent came on the scene [that] countered the control that veterans and the Daughters exercised over historical memory" (p.297).

In contrast to the neat distinction that scholars sometimes draw between analytic history and national memory, historiographers and philosophers such as Louis Mink (1978) and William Cronon

(1992) have emphasized the difficulties in maintaining it, and for some, this might seem to suggest that in the end it is indefensible and simply collapses. The view taken here is that while sometimes difficult to maintain, the distinction in fact is not only possible but necessary—both for analytic and ethical reasons. Without it, we run the risk of finding ourselves in a situation where we must accept an account of the past simply because it has the most authority or brute force to back it up, and this robs us of one of the few strategies we have for managing conflicts, something to which I shall return in chapter 6.

By way of summary, here is a schematic outline of the distinction between memory and history:

Memory	History
Reflects a subjective narrator	Aspires to be objective
Reflects the single committed perspective of a mnemonic community	Acknowledges multiple perspectives
Is overconfident and impatient with ambiguity	Is open to doubt, recognizes complexity, ambiguity including moral ambiguity
Relies on unconscious, unreflective thinking	Relies on conscious, reflective thinking
Is not open to rational, deliberative adjudication	Relies on rational deliberation based on logic and rules of evidence
Denies pastness of events, links past to present	Views events as then and not now
Requires no special training	Part of a professional discourse with its own norms of evidence and logic
Preserves narrative at expense of evidence	Preserves evidence at expense of narrative

Given the focus on narrative tools in my account of national memory, the final opposition in this list may provide the best shorthand way of summarizing the distinction between national memory and analytic history. When acting as members of national communities, we are likely to be quite resistant to giving up a national narrative, even in the face of strong contradictory evidence. As Rogers Smith (2003) notes, it may take social revolution or crushing and total military defeat to make people willing to give up "stories of peoplehood." In contrast, trained historians often make it a point to challenge existing narratives of the past— both those of other historians and those from collective memory. One of their primary aims is to critique and overturn established narratives, and this often involves bringing evidence to bear in such a way that the need to revise and refute a narrative becomes obvious. For historians, this is one of the measures of professional accomplishment.

An illustration of how this plays out in historical scholarship can be found in *Operation Barbarossa and Germany's Defeat in the East* by David Stahel (2009). Stahel's study is based on an extensive re-examination of German archives and other sources, and it challenges existing accounts in scholarly history and popular memory that tell a story of how the German army was overwhelmed by Russian weather and the seemingly endless masses of Soviet troops. In formulating his argument, Stahel recognizes the claims of others, but he also provides extensive evidence that points to hubris and ineptitude on the part of the German military leadership as major causes of their defeat. He sums up his 500-page tome by saying:

> Far from the picture presented in many publications, which in the early years of World War II laud the German field marshals as grand operators and the panzer commanders as dashing innovators of a revolutionary military concept, this study

presents a contrasting image. In addition to the complicity of the field commanders in the many planning and conceptual blunders inherent in Barbarossa, these same men compounded their initial oversights with an enduring blindness towards the difficulties encountered during the summer campaign . . . The fatal inability to recognise [sic] the limitations of the forces under their command was inherent to the campaign itself, but what is more surprising is the slow learning curve among the generals at the front who were confronted with day-to-day problem of the advance. (p.444)

Stahel's effort to overturn the prevailing narrative of Operation Barbarossa does not dispute many of the facts included in other accounts, but it draws on archival evidence to show that a narrative about "dashing innovators of a revolutionary concept" captured only a part of the larger story, and a misleading one at that. Instead, the real story, or narrative truth, is of how "the men who led the German armies in Operation Barbarossa were functionally competent, but strategically inept" (p.447), and Stahel's point is to present this story as an alternative, a sort of corrective response in a dialogue based on evidence and rational argumentation. In his view, there is more than ample reason to "forestall the ingratiating descriptions which have previously defined German operations in the summer of 1941" (p.448).

The argument Stahel presents in *Operation Barbarossa* is just one illustration of how an account that had come to be widely accepted can be challenged by relying on archives and logical argumentation. This is standard procedure for historians as they seek to contribute to their profession by preserving evidence at the expense of a narrative, and in this respect it is a case of historical discourse that contrasts with the tendencies of collective memory to preserve a narrative at the expense of evidence.

3.3. A Russian Narrative Template: "The Expulsion of Alien Enemies"

I now return to the distinction between specific narratives and narrative templates outlined in chapter 2, using an illustration from Russia. In this instance, the power of the narrative template to shape national memory is so strong that it is reflected in the very appellation of events. Specifically, the expression "Patriotic War" (*Otechestvennaya voyna*) is used to refer to two defining events in Russia's past that are separated by more than a century and are told using different specific narratives. These are the war between Russia and Napoleon in 1812 and the epic conflict with Germany between 1941 and 1945. Westerners may not automatically see any parallel between these two events, but for Russians the "Patriotic War" (*Otechestvennaya voyna*) of 1812 and the "Great Patriotic War" (*Velikaya otechestvennaya voyna*) of 1941–45 have clear parallels. In such instances, history may not repeat itself, but for the members of one mnemonic community, it rhymes, as Mark Twain was reputed to have said.[3]

The term "Great Patriotic War" surfaced in Russia soon after the German invasion in 1941, suggesting that Russians were quick to recognize the familiar storyline of events unfolding before their eyes. For them, the war with Germany was a case of the same story with different characters. People from other nations are certainly capable of seeing the parallel between the war of 1812 and the conflict of 1941–45 when it is brought to their attention, but it is not built into the standard equipment for living that they employ. For the Russian mnemonic community, though, the parallel between the two wars is evidenced in multiple ways. In addition to being reflected in the titles of the two wars, for example, the phrase "Hitler

---

[3] It turns out that there is no definitive evidence that this originated with Twain, but it is often attributed to him. For a discussion, see: https://en.wikiquote.org/wiki/Talk:History.

as a second Napoleon" is a widely known expression for members of this community. Thus, events that are separated in time, place, and characters—and depicted by unique, specific narratives—have come to be viewed as instantiations of the same underlying storyline.

At first glance this might be taken to be a case of analogic thinking, a topic that has long been of interest in psychology (Duncker, 1945). Standard accounts of analogy, however, do not appear to cover all the aspects of the cases considered here. For starters, these accounts are not necessarily tied to narrative form. Furthermore, analogies are usually viewed as involving a relationship between one event or object and another. In the Russian case, the Great Fatherland War and the Fatherland War are just two of a larger set of events, *all* of which are connected by what Neisser (1967, p.2987) would call the same schematic, "nonspecific but organized representation." A third way that this case extends the notion of analogy envisioned by Duncker and others in psychology is that parallels between the Fatherland War and the Great Fatherland War are automatically detected by members of one national community but not by members of others. Instead of assuming that the analogy at issue is something that individuals of all groups could come up with and have equal access to, a national narrative template is something that helps define one group and set it off from communities.

As just noted, the Patriotic War and Great Patriotic War are just two of many events that reflect a narrative template shared by Russians. A more complete list begins in the 13th century with the Mongol invasion along with another historical figure of the same era, the Russian prince and national hero Alexander Nevsky, who also fought against German invaders, and it goes on from there. Russians, for instance, routinely speak of other iterations of the same story involving invasions by Swedes, Poles, Turks, and Germans.

It was because the Russian national community was familiar with specific narratives about these events and the general code

underlying them that Stalin could call his nation to action in a famous radio speech in July 1941 after the devastating invasion by
Germany. He exhorted his fellow citizens: "Let the heroic images of
our great ancestors—Alexander Nevsky, Dmitri Donskoi, Kusma
Minin, Dmitri Pozharsky, Alexander Suvorov, Mikhail Kutuzov—
inspire you in this war!" The power of this appeal to Russians had
nothing to do with Marxism-Leninism, the official ruling ideology
of the time. Instead, it stemmed from shared knowledge in the
Russian mnemonic community of specific narratives about battles
against Teutonic knights in the 13th century, Mongols in the 14th
century, Poles in the 17th century, Turks in the 18th century, and
French in the 19th century. But it also pointed to an underlying
code that links these episodes in Russia's past.

What the various specific narratives that Stalin alluded to have in
common for the Russian mnemonic community is the "Expulsion
of Alien Enemies" narrative template, which I posit takes the following nonspecific, but organized, form:

1. An "initial situation" in which Russia is peaceful and not in-
   terfering with others
2. "Trouble," in which a foreign enemy viciously attacks Russia
   without provocation
3. Russia comes under existential threat and nearly loses everything as the enemy attempts to destroy it as a civilization.
4. Through heroism and exceptionalism, against all odds, and
   acting alone, Russia triumphs and succeeds in expelling the
   foreign enemy.

Appreciating the power of this narrative template should not be
taken to suggest that the events recounted in the specific narrative instantiations of it are fabrications or figments of the imagination of the Russian mnemonic community. Russia obviously *has*
suffered at the hands of foreign enemies on numerous occasions. At
the same time, however, the narrative template at issue sometimes

"controls the fate of stored information" (Neisser, p.287) in ways that can be surprising to non-Russians. All this indicates that a particular emplotment of events is shaping memory in a way that is peculiar to members of a particular national community. To appreciate the overriding power of this narrative template, consider an interpretation of Soviet communism that surfaced in post-Soviet Russia. Whereas communism is typically viewed in the West as an ideology whose aggressive tendencies required containment, Soviet communism came to be interpreted by Russians as an alien enemy in the form of Western ideas that invaded and victimized *them* and had to be defeated and expelled if Russia were to survive as a civilization.

This interpretation was reflected, for example, in the ideas of the Russian author and nationalist Alexander Solzhenitsyn (1978). His account of socialism, communism, and Western Enlightenment ideas more generally was based on the idea that socialism and materialism had been invading and destroying the spiritual tradition of Russian civilization. And to those used to seeing a fundamental antagonism between communism and capitalism, it comes as a further surprise that Solzhenitsyn saw *both* as ideological enemies of Russia because both were manifestations of the same general set of Western ideas, values, and threats.

This is a line of reasoning that is hardly new; it has been part of the Russian national community for centuries. Dostoevsky's novels, for example, are replete with the theme of alien ideas like materialism and socialism invading Russian society, ideas that many of his characters believe must be expelled in order to avoid descending into the nihilism and atheism that would doom their civilization. These underpinned, for example, the amoral actions of the character Nikolai Vsevelodovich Stavrogin in *Demons* (1994).

The overriding fixation of this novel is with what Richard Pevear (1994) calls the "isms that came to Russia from the West: idealism, rationalism, empiricism, materialism, utilitarianism, positivism, socialism, anarchism, nihilism, and underlying them all, atheism" (p.xvii). The characters in Dostoevsky's writings experience these as demons that can invade Russia, especially when introduced by someone who has been exposed to the West. And as Pevear notes, the antidote and means for casting out these demons is to be found in "the Russian earth, the Russian God, the Russian Christ, the 'light from the East'" (p.xvii).

This struggle between national cultures comes into sharp focus in an epiphany that one of the characters in *Demons* experiences on his deathbed. Dostoevsky, who viewed epiphanies as revealing genuine truth, used a sudden, clear insight by Stepan Trofimovich Verkhovensky to reveal Russia's susceptibility to being afflicted with dangerous, diseased Western ideas. Using a passage from the biblical book of Luke, Verkhovensky burst out with the recognition, "you see, it's exactly like our Russia. These demons who come out of a sick man and enter into swine—it's all the sores, all the miasmas, all the unclean-ness, all the big and little demons accumulated in our great and dear sick man, in our Russia, for centuries, for centuries!" (Dostoevsky, 1994, p.655). Again, it is the same basic story of expelling alien enemies but with different characters—this time in the form of foreign ideas.

In sum, the Russian Expulsion of Alien Enemies narrative tem-plate routinely shapes specific narratives about the past. This provides common grounding for the Russian mnemonic community and can also be the source of disputes between Russians and other mnemonic communities. It plays a role in the conflicting accounts of Russians and Georgians about the 2008 war (Wertsch & Karumidze, 2009), in the conflicting accounts of Russians and Estonians about moving the Bronze Soldier statue commemorating World War II dead in Tallinn in 2007 (Wertsch, 2008b), and in other cases as well.

3.4. Fast and Slow Thinking About the Past

Recent studies of the "new unconscious" in cognitive psychology and neuroscience can provide useful insights into the psychological dimensions of national memory. Talk about unconscious processes might appear to be a return to the psychoanalytic tradition of Freud and others, but something quite different is involved. Instead of being concerned with repressed thoughts and unconscious emotions and drives, the claims are about rapid, largely automatic cognitive processes that occur in the "blink" of an eye (Gladwell, 2007) in perception and decision making. It is as if our bodies make a decision before our minds begin to become engaged.

The unconscious thinking studied in this research is related to research on "implicit" memory (Jacoby & Kelley, 1987), "intuition" (Haidt, 2012), and "fast thinking" (Kahneman, 2011), and early versions of it can be found almost a century and a half ago in the writings of William James (1884) on how emotional states such as happiness that enter our awareness follow, rather than precede, behaviors like smiling. Drawing on findings in neuroscience and related fields, psychologists have returned to these issues, and over the past few decades increasing weight has been given to the unconscious side of the ledger.

In an image that echoes one of Plato's famous allegories, for example, Jonathan Haidt (2012) has written about a rider atop an elephant. As Haidt sees it, the "rider is our conscious reasoning—the stream of words and images of which we are fully aware. The elephant is the other 99% of mental processes—the ones that occur outside of awareness but that actually govern most of our behavior" (p.xiv). He goes on to note that even though the "rider serves the elephant" (p.xiv) most of the time, the rider "can see further into the future [and] can help the elephant make better decisions. It can learn new skills and master new technologies, which can be deployed to help the elephant reach its goals and sidestep disasters" (p.46).

In analyses of national memory, the habits associated with narrative templates are the rough counterpart of the elephant. Although narrative-based habits may have great power and operate in ways that sometimes suggest we aren't aware of the forces that guide what we think and say, the image laid out by Haidt suggests that we also are capable of acting as reflective agents who can make better decisions and "sidestep disasters." Even if this involves just the 1% of our mental processes, it can spell the difference between the rational discussion needed to adjudicate, say, national disputes about the past. All this suggests the need to delve further into both unconscious decision making and rational reflection on it.

The study of national memory takes the distinction between unconscious and conscious processes in cognitive psychology into new territory. This is so first of all because cognitive research typically takes mental functioning of humans in general as its topic, whereas the focus in national memory studies is on individuals as members of distinct mnemonic communities. And second, the account of national memory outlined here focuses on symbolic mediation in the form of narrative tools, something that is not part of standard accounts of unconscious thinking. Psychologists such as Amos Tversky and Daniel Kahneman (1974), for example, address issues such as how rational decisions based on laws of probability can lead to overcoming fast but misguided decisions and allow us to arrive at more accurate predictions of empirical outcomes, an approach in which little attention is given to how membership in particular groups or the use of symbolic mediation peculiar to those groups might influence these processes. Nonetheless, insights from research on conscious and unconscious thinking can contribute to the understanding of how narrative tools are employed by national communities and can be put to use in elaborating these claims.

Several ideas that Kahneman outlines in his 2011 book *Thinking, Fast and Slow* are relevant in this regard. Drawing on a wide range of empirical studies in cognitive psychology and neuroscience, Kahneman develops a story involving two main "characters" (p.19) in mental life: System 1 and System 2.

System 1 operates automatically and quickly, with little or no effort and no sense of voluntary control.

System 2 allocates attention to the effortful mental activities that demand it, including complex computations. The operations of System 2 are often associated with the subjective experience of agency, choice, and concentration. (pp.20–21)

Kahneman goes on to note that even though "System 2 believes itself to be where the action is, the automatic System 1 is the hero" (p.21) of the story—a view similar to Haidt's image of the elephant and its rider. In Kahneman's account, the "automatic operations of System 1 generate surprisingly complex patterns of ideas, but only the slower System 2 can construct thoughts in an orderly series of steps" (p.21). Whereas the former unfold effortlessly and unconsciously, the latter require focused, conscious reflection. System 2 can sometimes step in and check the work that System 1 is doing in its automatic, unconscious way, but this requires effort and concentration, whereas one of System 2's properties is its "laziness, a reluctance to invest more effort than is strictly necessary" (p.31).

This laziness can be a serious problem because System 1 decisions are sometimes misleading or even clearly wrong. We tend to be unaware of this, however, and to make matters worse, Kahneman reports that extensive research shows that "many people are overconfident, prone to place too much faith in their intuition" (p.45). We often make do with impressions and decisions from System 1 mental processing when it would be better to subject them to System 2 reflection.

To the extent that Kahneman touches on the issue of narrative in his analysis, he does so in connection with System 1, where he mentions "narrative fallacies," a notion he takes from Nassim Taleb's bestseller *The Black Swan* (2007). In Taleb's view the narratives that guide our decisions are often hopelessly superficial, oversimplified, and misleading, the result being that "we humans constantly fool ourselves by constructing flimsy accounts of the past and believing they are true" (Kahneman, 2011, p.199).

In their passing discussion of narrative, Kahneman and Taleb focus on simple stories that we construct to make sense of events, something that we do effortlessly, suggesting it is a System 1 process. The line of reasoning they follow is consistent with the picture I have been outlining here, with one possible exception. Namely, it says nothing about narrative tools and how they might be provided by a community. Instead, they seem to suggest that we construct "flimsy accounts of the past" on our own rather than by relying on off-the-shelf narrative tools provided by others.

Kahneman discusses how narratives and narrative fallacies operate within the confines of System 1 thinking as part of a broader concern with the basic rule of "what you see is all there is" ("WYSIATI").

> An essential design feature of the associative machine is that it represents only activated ideas. Information that is not retrieved (even unconsciously) from memory might as well not exist. System 1 excels at constructing the best possible story that incorporates ideas currently activated, but it does not (cannot) allow for information it does not have. The measure of success for System 1 is the coherence of the story it manages to create . . . When information is scarce, which is a common occurrence, System 1 operates as a machine for jumping to conclusions. (p.85)

Along with encouraging us to jump to conclusions, the WYSIATI rule leads to overconfidence. In this form of mental functioning, "neither the quantity nor the quality of the evidence counts for much" (p.87). Instead, "We often fail to allow for the possibility that evidence that should be critical to our judgment is missing—what we see is all there is" (p.87). This is part of the widely documented tendency toward "confirmation bias" (Mynatt, Doherty, & Tweney, 1977), which is a tendency to "seek data that are likely to be compatible with the beliefs they currently hold" (Kahneman, 2011, p.81). It involves a failure to detect and address information that contradicts and poses problems for our views, and it results in a proclivity to overlook or dismiss such information and focus on information that confirms what we already believe.

For Hugo Mercier and Dan Sperber (2017), the implication of this line of reasoning is that:

> [H]uman reasoning is both biased and lazy. Biased because it overwhelmingly finds justification and arguments that support the reasoner's point of view, lazy because reason makes little effort to assess the quality of the justifications and arguments it produces. (p.9)

Confirmation bias has been studied extensively in the context of decisions in logical problem-solving studies conducted in laboratory settings. Mercier and Sperber take this a step farther by noting that it can be a source of dysfunction and conflict in the everyday life of collectives as well. Indeed, it has been called the "bias most pivotal to ideological extremism and inter- and intra-group conflict" (Lilienfeld, Ammirati, & Landfield, 2009, p.391). And in the view of Raymond Nickerson (1998):

> The bias can contribute to delusions of many sorts, to the development and survival of superstitions, and to a variety of undesirable states of mind, including paranoia and depression. It can be exploited to great advantage by seers, soothsayers, fortune tellers, and indeed anyone with an inclination to press unsubstantiated claims. One can also imagine it playing a significant role in the animosities and strife between people with conflicting views of the world. (p.205)

Fast thinking, intuition, implicit attitudes, and confirmation bias are all notions that have been developed as part of an effort to understand the mental functioning of human individuals in general.

Only rarely do discussions of these topics stray into how group membership shapes performance. The account of narrative mediation I am outlining does nothing to undercut existing findings from such research. Instead, my point is to extend these findings to examine group differences in thinking and memory. The focus may still be on the individual, but in Bartlett's useful dictum, it is the *individual as a member of a group*. Expanding on Kahneman's ideas, we might ask how the System 1 "machines for jumping to conclusions" that guide the members of one mnemonic community might differ from those guiding the members of another.

In this elaborated perspective, what is involved are narrative-based habits for making quick, almost automatic judgments that are not usually subject to the effortful conscious reflection of System 2 thinking. Rather than deliberately and consciously selecting an item from a stock of stories to make sense of an event, the influence of narrative templates is so automatic and powerful that they almost seem to take the lead and encourage members of a group to act in similar ways with overconfidence in how they size up events in a predictable manner. Taken to an extreme, this suggests that it may be more appropriate to speak of how narrative templates engage an agent (take the agent for a ride on the elephant?) rather than how an agent uses them. However, that is where System 2 can come in, making it possible for the active agent to re-enter the picture through conscious reflection and do a more diligent analysis of evidence than would derive from jumping to the conclusions suggested by a narrative template. Because System 2 tends to be lazy and require significant effort to become engaged, however, the sort of critical reflection required to bring a narrative template's interpretation into question often is not undertaken.

What sort of experience would encourage us to undertake "effortful mental activities . . . associated with the subjective experience of agency, choice, and concentration" (Kahneman, 2011, pp.20–21)? In the case of national memory, one good candidate is encountering an account of the past that clearly contradicts our own. This alternative version of what happened may surprise—and on occasion even offend—us. To be sure, our first response is likely to be to stick with our fast, nearly automatic interpretation provided by System 1, and because of the overconfidence associated with System 1 thinking we may simply dismiss our interlocutor as misguided, stupid, lying, or brainwashed. Such responses are precisely what lead to mnemonic standoffs, but given the laziness of System 2 this is a path we all too often take.

At least on some occasions, however, humans seem capable of slowing down and doing the effortful conscious reflection that System 2 entails, and this brings me back to the distinction between national memory and analytic history. Rather than the confident snap judgments of the former, analytic history involves institutionalized practices governed by consciously recognized norms of a specialized professional group. When engaged in these practices historians are held to account by the need to consider all relevant evidence and alternative explanations of past events, and this can lead them to question the basic narrative plotline that grasps events together in a familiar and comforting picture. As figures such as White, Mink, and Cronon have argued, the practices of analytic history can never yield a completely satisfactory and final check on the biases involved in national memory because of the "moralizing impulse" (White, 1981, p.22) of narratives. But these practices remain one of the best systematic antidotes we have to the incomplete or false conclusions we often make so confidently about the past.

3.5. By Way of Summing Up: A Visual Illustration

In this final section, I draw on one of the great forms of Soviet popular culture to illustrate fast thinking and the Expulsion of Alien Enemies narrative template. Specifically, I turn to a propaganda poster that comes from the dark days of the Great Patriotic War

Figure 3.1. Poster by the Kukryniksy group. The wording reads, "Courageously and irresistibly we fight and stab. We are Suvorov's grandchildren and Chapaev's sons."
Everett Collection Inc./Alamy

when the German invasion of the USSR was at its most alarming point and Soviet citizens were in need of inspiration (Figure 3.1). The poster was created by the Kukryniksy group, a collective named for three artists whose caricatures, especially their satirical depictions of Fascist leaders, were extremely popular at the time.

The poster depicts angry, determined Red Army soldiers and tanks advancing against the enemy with the encouragement of three ghostlike figures looming over them. These figures, from left to right, are Alexander Nevsky (1221–1263), Alexander Suvorov (1729–1800), and Vasily Chapaev (1887–1919). Nevsky and Suvorov were revered military leaders from early chapters of Russian history who expelled alien invaders. Nevsky defended Russia against Germanic Teutonic knights and also managed to negotiate with Mongol groups sweeping in from the east in the 13th century. Suvorov was a renowned military leader who never lost a major battle against the Ottoman Empire, the Poles, and others in the 18th century. In addition to fighting invaders, he helped Catherine the Great expand the empire into territories such as Crimea, Belarus, and Lithuania, a practice Catherine explained as a way to protect the nation from alien enemies.

At first, Chapaev may appear to be the odd man out in this case because he did not fight against an enemy from outside of Russia's borders: He was a Red Army commander during the Russian Civil War from 1917 to 1922 who fought on Russian soil. But anyone resisting the Soviet state then, let alone during the Great Patriotic War, was considered to be an alien enemy. Indeed, during the Great Patriotic War Russian defectors were categorized as "former Russians." Another undoubted reason for Chapaev's appearance in this poster was that exploits of his heroism seem to echo those of Stalin, whose role in the Civil War was well known to Soviet citizens at the time.

The decision to feature Nevsky, Suvorov, and Chapaev in the poster built on three popular Soviet films of the time. In his 1938 masterpiece *Alexander Nevsky*, director Sergei Eisenstein presented the medieval Russian prince as a strong, brilliant leader who destroyed German invaders in 1242 at the "Battle of the Ice," depicted in an unforgettable concluding scene. After the 1941 invasion, *Alexander Nevsky* played almost nonstop to enthusiastic audiences in the USSR. The 1941 film *Suvorov* featured General Suvorov as a brilliant and headstrong military figure during the reign of Catherine the Great. And *Chapaev*, which came out in 1934, depicted a hero of the Civil War who was both a member of the humble proletariat and a committed warrior against capitalist and land owner enemies. In all cases the heroes of these films were unflinching in their fight against enemies and well aware of their historical mission on behalf of Russia.

The visual depictions of Nevsky, Suvorov, and Chapaev came from actors in the three films rather than from portraits we have from history, but Soviet citizens at the time could also be depended on to know who Nevsky, Suvorov, and Chapaev were. And if the stories and images of these three heroes required any further reinforcement, it was provided by the text at the bottom, which reads: "Courageously and irresistibly we fight and stab. We are Suvorov's grandchildren and Chapaev's sons." All this information would have been instantly and effortlessly processed by Soviet citizens.

In general, this poster can be taken as a visual illustration of the claims of this chapter. First, it points to the importance of national memory rather than analytic history in mobilizing a population. We have little empirical evidence about how the poster was received in Soviet society during the Great Patriotic War, but from historical accounts, it appears that such propaganda was popular and probably effective as well. Second, the poster reflects the Expulsion of Alien Enemies narrative template that plays such a central role in Russian national memory. Stalin and other Soviet authorities had actually downplayed this narrative template in the official Marxist ideology during peacetime, but they reverted to calling on this underlying code in the emergency context of wartime. This suggests that the narrative was a deep source of agreement in the Russian national community that went beyond anything offered by Marxist-Leninist ideology.

Third, the narrative template in this case served to unite the Russian population and set it apart from other national communities. What was immediately obvious and moving to Russians in the poster would have to be explained to Americans or others if they were to understand anything of the poster because they did not have access to the narrative that shaped so much of the Russian worldview. And even if non-Russians understood the factual content of the poster, they would be unlikely to experience the emotional impact because the stories depicted are not part of their national identity project.

And fourth, fast thinking was involved in Russians' understanding of the poster. The images and the overall message were likely to be immediately obvious to most Soviet citizens at the time. Any sort of slow, reflective thinking was not only unnecessary but might not have been encouraged in any event, given that it could lead to wondering why Suvorov, a military genius who never lost a battle in his long career, was in the poster when German forces had inflicted one devastating blow after another on the Red Army up to that point in the Great Patriotic War.

4

Selectivity and Emplotment
in National Memory

4.1. Introduction

One of the hallmarks of national memory is selectivity. Memory includes certain events and actors and ignores others, and it does so systematically. Discussions of how this is done often start by focusing on decisions made by leaders about history instruction, monuments, and the media. In his bestseller *Lies My Teacher Told Me*, for example, James Loewen (2018) outlines how school systems have cooperated with textbook publishers to come up with an account of the past that celebrates certain aspects of American history and keeps others under wraps. Similar ideas routinely surface in discussions of why historical monuments are erected or dismantled or how media outlets such as *The History Channel* decide what to include in its programming.

To be sure, political leaders and institutions are involved in shaping national memory, but focusing on conscious top-down efforts by the state and the media yields a picture that is incomplete at best. This is especially so when it is assumed that they have anything like complete license in representing the past. The key to understanding why this is so concerns narrative form and function. As noted by historian William Cronon (1992), "the very authority with which narrative presents its vision of reality is achieved by obscuring large portions of that reality. Narrative succeeds to the extent that it hides the discontinuities, ellipses, and contradictory experiences that would undermine the intended meaning of its

How Nations Remember. James V. Wertsch, Oxford University Press (2021). © Oxford University Press.
DOI: 10.1093/oso/9780197551462.003.0004

story" (pp.1349–1350). Thanks in part to these proclivities, "A powerful narrative reconstructs common sense to make the contingent seem determined and the artificial seem natural" (p.1350).

This suggests that top-down efforts by state authorities and others are constrained by narrative tools, especially narrative templates and the mental habits associated with them. The first thing to recognize in this regard is that media or state authorities who seek to control national memory typically rely on the same basic set of narrative tools as those used in the community itself. If leaders in a society stray too far from the narrative resources of the larger mnemonic community, their efforts are likely to be artificial and short-lived. To have staying power, official accounts must rely on negotiation between authorities and the population rather than the imposition of any desired version of history from on high, and this involves negotiating within a framework of shared narrative resources.

This is not to say that negotiations between state authorities and members of a community are always smooth or easy or involve anything like the ideal forms of communicative rationality envisioned by Jurgen Habermas (1984; McCarthy, 1984). Indeed, efforts by the state and media often meet with resistance. Perhaps the best-known account of such resistance—at least attempted resistance—to official accounts of the past can be found in George Orwell's (1949) classic novel *Nineteen Eighty-Four*, where the protagonist Winston Smith tries to carve out a small space for his own ideas as he works for a state devoted to thought control. In his public life, Smith spends his time at the Ministry of Truth tossing documents down the "memory hole" to be incinerated. These are newspaper articles and other items no longer accepted as true by authorities as they continually revise and update collective memory in the service of the present, making Smith's work an extreme version of "impressing the past into the service of a particular reading of the present" (Cohen, 1997). In the hidden recesses of his private life Smith does engage in small acts of opposition, but in the end, these are futile because the state in Orwell's ominous account had the power to collapse any distinction between public and private. The ensuing picture is one of how an ever-present, all-powerful state can stamp out resistance by individuals, relying on brutal coercion if need be.

Heroic, and often tragic, lone actors like Winston Smith may make for good fiction, but most actual cases of bottom-up resistance to official history involve group efforts. In her discussion of "memory activists," for example, Carol Gluck (2007) examines groups who coordinate their efforts to keep alternative accounts of the past alive even when they conflict with efforts by the state. She reports that for the first several decades following World War II the official Japanese narrative of the conflict was controlled by national authorities, who sought to promulgate preferred narratives—usually heroic ones—and silence competing accounts. In the face of this, however, bottom-up efforts to maintain "vernacular memory" continued, led by "countless groups dedicated to preserving the memory of their own particular experience and seeking a place for that experience within the larger field of public memory" (p.7). Indeed, in many places "an entire civil society of . . . 'memory activists'. . . tirelessly lobbied for recognition, compensation, and commemoration—in short, for inclusion in an expanded heroic narrative" (p.7).

In the case examined by Gluck, the measures used to suppress vernacular memory are quite determined, but they pale by comparison to heavy-handed efforts in totalitarian regimes. In these settings, unwavering, indeed heroic, efforts may be required to preserve vernacular memory. Tulviste and Wertsch (1992), for example, report on the unofficial histories that existed during of the Cold War in the Soviet republic of Estonia, where nearly all ethnic Estonians learned *two* histories—one official, state-sponsored version and another underground unofficial version. This was part of the Soviet context more generally, where, in fact, doubt about the official state history could be so strong that at least some citizens actually believed that anything appearing in the official media or textbooks was prima facie evidence of its being *false* (Wertsch, 2002). Such views had to be kept strictly private, however, because the consequences of revealing them could be dire, including lengthy prison sentences. Even in this setting, however, resistance to state-sanctioned official history continued. In Estonia, groups operated in deeply private settings, and in Moscow networks of memory activists worked in their homes to type and retype copies of lengthy texts about Soviet prison camps such as Alexander Solzhenitsyn's (1985) *Gulag Archipelago*.

An entire set of procedures and a special vocabulary emerged in the Soviet setting to keep criticisms of the state and party secret. People were cautious about discussing many issues over the telephone, leading to Soviet jokes (*anekdoti*) about the practices they used. Such anecdotes were told (in private) and in some cases reflected on the very practice of keeping secrets. One that was circulating in 1985 was about a phone conversation between the new leader of the USSR, Mikhail Gorbachev, and his recently deceased mentor, Yuri Andropov (1914–1984) over a mythical red telephone in the Kremlin that connected living leaders with their deceased forerunners in the imagined Great Communist Beyond:

In a frenzy of anxiety and anger, Gorbachev calls Andropov on the red phone and says, "Yuri Vladimirovich! I can't believe this! I opened the central safe in my office in the Kremlin and discovered from secret documents how bad things are in our workers' paradise. The economy is collapsing, the youth are restive, the Red Army is corrupt and weak, and our missiles don't work! How could you leave me with such a mess and not even tell me?"

After a silence, the resonant voice of Andropov comes over the line and says, "Misha! Misha![1] You have always been such a good Communist. You were outstanding in the Red Pioneers and the

---

[1] A Russian diminutive of Mikhail.

Komsomol.[2] You were simply brilliant as you ascended through the Communist Party. With your great mind and wisdom, you arc the hope of the Party. You should know this is not something we can talk about over the phone."

This anecdote reflected a serious issue that confronted people in their everyday life in Soviet society, namely how to keep things out of view of the KGB[3] and other authorities. It meant endless discussions "in the kitchen," a form of whispered conversation around the kitchen table that was hopefully not being picked up by hidden microphones or nosy neighbors. Such discussions were a version of the private "backstage" performance outlined by Erving Goffman (1959) in his dramaturgical analysis, and they stood in stark opposition to "front regions" such as school or political meetings where quite different, official forms of discourse were required. Among the pressures of living in such settings was the need to monitor children to make certain that no part of backstage performance was allowed to make its way into public life. Soviet parents had anxious discussions about when it would be safe to let their children know about certain books, photos, or manuscripts they had at home and how to warn their children about when and where they could mention them.

Practices of this sort play out in extreme form in totalitarian societies where the punishment for getting it wrong could be severe, but to some degree backstage and front regions are part of American or any other society. Students from minority groups in American society, for example, often have doubts or even learn alternative accounts of the past that they refrain from discussing in public. When asked whether he knew the American history taught in school, for example, a distinguished African American

---

[2] The Soviet youth corps.
[3] Committee for State Security, the secret police force and main security agency in the USSR from 1954 to 1991.

colleague once told me, "Of course," and when I asked him whether he believed everything in it, his response was, "Of course not!", reflecting the fact that he also had learned two histories and belonged to two distinct mnemonic communities in America.

In sum, modern states go to great lengths to promulgate an official account of the past, with all the selectivity that such an account entails. I shall argue later in the chapter that these efforts are more likely to succeed when authorities build on the narrative resources that they share with the larger mnemonic community. In some cases, however, state authorities do try to override these narrative resources. In the Soviet case, for example, authorities went to great lengths to promulgate an official Marxist narrative about the heroic class struggle of all workers and peasants, regardless of national identity. For reasons I have already noted, however, the effort was often unsuccessful and was supplanted by mental habits based on Russian national narratives.

4.2. Resources for Selectivity in National Memory

Selectivity in national memory takes many forms, and once selections are made, much of the work for creating a view of the past has already been already done. It is easy to overlook this, but when we are surprised by others' account of the past, it is often because we and they have failed to notice how choices about what should and should not be included in an account are built into the narrative tools that co-author what we say.

The selectivity that comes with narrative tools is part of a larger discussion of what Eviatar Zerubaval (2003) calls the "time maps" of mnemonic communities. In his account, communities follow *"norms of historical focusing* that dictate what we should mnemonically 'attend' to and what we can largely ignore and thereby forget" (p.27, italics in the original). These norms provide the foundation for dividing up the past into "historically 'significant'" periods, on the one hand, and those that are "'irrelevant' and thereby essentially relegated to social oblivion" (p.27), on the other.

Before going further into how norms and narratives influence the selectivity of memory, it is worth noting that other forces can shape what is included in and left out of a group's account of the past. For starters, there is the simple fading of memory over time. This is something that Roediger and DeSoto (2017) have examined with regard to memory for U.S. presidents. They report a pattern of collective memory by Americans that is generally characterized by high recall for recent presidents and declining memory the further back in time one goes. This occurs in such a regular fashion that Roediger and DeSoto suggest it is possible to predict when a president today is likely to disappear from collective memory tomorrow.

But this only works for presidents who are in living memory. Going back further in time introduces elements of historical focusing tied to narrative tools because it involves switching from what Aleida Assmann (2008) calls social memory to cultural memory, which relies on the mnemonic resources a community provides. In this notion of cultural memory, historical events and figures often don't simply fade with time. If they did, figures such as President Chester Arthur should occupy a larger place in national memory than George Washington or Abraham Lincoln. Instead, memory for U.S. presidents from earlier periods is influenced by a national narrative about the nation's overall past, yielding an uneven picture with high points at the beginning (Washington, Adams, Jefferson, Madison) and other points for figures like Lincoln who were at the center of crucial turning points in the American story. Between these spikes, the national memory for presidents involves entire decades of presidents who have disappeared from memory, having been "essentially relegated to social oblivion."

In what follows I examine two basic ways that narrative tools shape the historical focusing of national communities. First, they include certain events and actors and leave out others, and second, they emplot these events and actors in particular ways. These two forms of narrative mediation are interrelated, but they can function independently. As laid out in chapter 1, for example, it is possible for two mnemonic communities to pick out the atomic bombings in 1945 as part of historical focusing but to emplot the event in very different ways.

An essential difference between the two ways that narrative tools shape mnemonic focusing concerns the level of consciousness involved. A decision to focus on an event or actor is relatively explicit and can be the topic of public debate. The decision to make Martin Luther King's birthday an official holiday in the United States, for example, followed years of contentious debate and votes by state legislatures. Narrative emplotment, in contrast, often goes unnoticed because it is more subtle and transparent, making it sometimes appear that no decision was involved at all.

4.2.1. Selecting Events and Actors for Mnemonic Focusing

When it comes to selecting events to be included in national memory, one of the most commonly employed means is holidays. The declaration of a new holiday involves public debate and pronouncements, usually followed by widespread observance, all of which is shaped by national narratives operating in the background. The declaration of a holiday routinely includes claims that the nation will never forget the event or individual, but in fact the trajectory of many holidays is one of declining interest.

To some degree this reflects the recency effect noted by Roediger, wherein a holiday becomes less widely celebrated and sinks into oblivion over time. In the United States, for example, President Woodrow Wilson declared November 11 as a holiday in 1919, a year after the armistice that ended World War I. What started out as solemn observance on the 11th hour of the 11th month morphed into the more generic Veterans Day in 1954 as the "Greatest Generation" (Brokaw, 1998), who were veterans of World War II, took center stage in America and then received less and less notice as the veterans of both world wars passed from the scene.

As in the case for presidents, however, something more than simple fading over time is often at work for national holidays. Namely, the way that a nation's life is emplotted in national narratives shapes the process. This is part of what Zerubavel calls a collective's "commemogram" that recognizes "the uneven chronological distribution of historical 'eventfulness'" (p.31). Such commemograms reflect the larger grand narrative of a nation, where a nation's origins are typically important. It is for that reason that Independence Day on July 4 retains its central place in the American commemogram. As noted by John Bodnar (1992), the celebration of Independence Day has taken on different form over time and has become highly commercialized, but it remains firmly in place in the national calendar and in times of national crisis serves as a rallying point for Americans to come together in patriotic fervor. In contrast, other holidays, such as Armistice Day and Columbus Day, have faded from the calendar and are no longer taken to be sufficiently important to merit time off from work or school.

Similar trends can be found in Russia, where remembering the Soviet Union has gone through several phases, especially since the collapse of the USSR in the early 1990s. One of the most important places where this has played out is the origin story of the USSR as commemorated by the Day of the Great October Socialist Revolution. During the Soviet period, this holiday occurred on November 7 and was the most zealously observed state holiday of the year. It celebrated the Russian Revolution in 1917 that led to the rise of communism and the Soviet state, and as I observed firsthand in the 1970s, the celebration of this holiday took on massive proportions across the country and involved countless official events extolling the Great October Revolution as well as widespread revelry. When the Soviet Union collapsed, however, a new chapter in "symbolic politics" (Bourdieu, 1992) emerged in the form of competing narratives about Russia and the meaning of the 1917 revolutions.[4]

In her account of "the embarrassing centenary" of this event in 2017, Olga Malinova (2018) outlines how the official Russian historical narrative of the 1917 revolutions has changed since the collapse of the Soviet Union. She identifies two conflicting approaches to the memory politics that emerged in this context: one based on a "critical 'working through' the memory of a traumatic and criminal past" and one geared toward "consolidation of the nation/ nation-building" (p.272). These two approaches have competed for "discursive hegemony" (p.272) and each "fits into the symbolic landscape created by various social actors" (p.272)—a process reminiscent of the "memory activists" described by Gluck (2007).

The first approach, which prevailed in the early years following 1991, involved a group of Russian elites trying to reframe the Russian Revolution "as a great, though tragic, episode of the national past" (Malinova, 2018, p.272). It was while this vision was in its ascendency that the Russian government canceled November 7 as a public holiday in 2004. In this phase of the debate President Boris Yeltsin and his team "relied on a discourse about 'the crimes of the Soviet regime' to establish the narrative that emphasized the contrast between the 'new' and 'old' Russia" (p.276).

Eventually, however, this contingent of mnemonic activists did not succeed in the symbolic battle, which came to a head as the country approached the centenary of the 1917 revolution. In place of a narrative based on the process of working through the memory of a traumatic and criminal past, the "elite seem to have come back to the idea of 'reconciliation and accord' that was coined by Boris

---

[4] Two revolutions occurred that year in Russia, one in March after the abdication of the tsar and the emergence of a provisional government, and a second one in October with the Bolshevik takeover led by Lenin. The latter came to be celebrated in November with the change from the Julian to the Gregorian calendar in 1918.

Yeltsin's team in the mid-1990s" (p.272), and this is a path that has been followed during the administration of Vladimir Putin. The analyses provided by Malinova (2015, 2018, 2019) touch on several additional issues in this complex story, such as discussions about whether the real focus of a working-through effort should be the March or November revolution in 1917, but the larger story is about the fate of the Great October Revolution. It is a story that began with an effort to get the national community to work through the memory of a traumatic and criminal past but eventually came to settle for an account based on the need for reconciliation and accord. The tortuous path this followed suggests just how difficult it can be for a national community to come to terms with dark chapters from its past.

This effort of trying but failing to address dark chapters from the past and then moving on to a narrative of reconciliation and accord is reflected in the treatment of November 7 as a public holiday. Malinova sees this as part of the post-Soviet effort to deal with the Russian Revolution that distanced itself from working through a traumatic and criminal past and moved toward "the apologetic narrative of 'the 1000-year Russian state'" (2018, p.272). The form of commemoration that was left was the watered-down Day of Accord and Reconciliation, whose very title suggests that the Great October Revolution has sunk into oblivion and is no longer taken to be a defining point in Russia's national narrative.

In general, dealing with a dark chapter from the past is very difficult for national communities, and it is an exercise that seems to be initiated only in times of major crises. As Rogers Smith (2003) notes, attempts to carry out such fundamental reassessment occur in the rare instances of a social revolution or crushing and total military defeat. It seems to be only then that people are able, at least temporarily, to give up or revise crucial parts of their "story of peoplehood." The Russian discussion analyzed by Malinova took place in such a setting, namely the collapse of the USSR, an event

Vladimir Putin labeled "the greatest geopolitical catastrophe of the century."[5]

In *Race and Reunion* David Blight (2001) outlined an analogous pattern in American memory of slavery and the Civil War, where he describes a "tormented relationship between healing and justice" (p.57). In the wake of the crushing and total military defeat of the Confederacy, he identifies competing visions about the meaning of what had happened. In particular, he focuses on a "reconciliationist" vision and an "emancipationist" vision and documents how they struggled for hegemony in American memory in the decades after the Civil War. Initially, the call for justice dominated, but in the end it gave way and "the forces of reconciliation overwhelmed the emancipationist vision in the national culture" (p.2).

The cases mapped out by Malinova for Russian national memory of the 1917 revolutions and by Blight for the Civil War in America differ in many obvious respects. However, they both can be taken as demonstrations of how hard it is for national communities to deal with traumatic events from their past. Both struggles involve intranational conflict or even civil war, which may be the most traumatic of all events and the darkest of all chapters to build into national memory. The pattern they have in common is one in which an effort to address traumatic and criminal episodes head on comes to the fore in early stages, but the pain and discord this generates eventually become so great that members of the community give up and turn to an account that focuses on reconciliation and harmony rather than justice.

In contrast to the demise of November 7 as the celebration of the Day of the Great October Socialist Revolution, May 9 as the Day of Victory in Russia has risen to the top of important holidays in the nation's commemogram. Of course it was always known in Russia that May 9 marks the official end of the Great Patriotic War in 1945,

---

[5] http://www.nbcnews.com/id/7632057/ns/world_news/t/putin-soviet-collapse-genuine-tragedy/#.XVGw01BOlKc

but significant official celebrations of this day started only in 1965. The holiday came to be widely celebrated during the Soviet period but less so than November 7. During the Putin era, however, the prominence of May 9 has risen to unparalleled heights, and today the 1945 triumph of the Soviet Army has become a centerpiece in what Oleksii Polegkyi (2016) has termed a "new religion" that worships the "cult of the great victory."[6]

As in other cases of official state holidays, the rise of May 9 as a Russian holiday benefited from efforts by the state, which devoted massive resources to celebrating it, providing a reminder of the importance of top-down forces. Again, however, these should not be overestimated. The elevation of May 9 to the status of a major holiday relied heavily on preexisting dispositions in the national community, and chief among these is the mental habits of the Expulsion of Alien Enemies narrative template. The Russian leadership was able to harness the power of this underlying code, making it a sort of co-author of their effort, a development that stands in striking contrast to what happened to the Day of the Great October Revolution, which had no real underlying support in the form of a narrative template.

4.2.2. Blank Spots and Forgetting in National Memory

As is the case for events, the individual and group actors included in memory are routinely the object of concern for state authorities, who have a strong interest in selecting certain items for mnemonic focusing and seeing others left out of the picture. Just as the Day of the Great October Socialist Revolution was downgraded and then largely neglected in post-Soviet Russia with the rise of the Day

---

[6] http://www.neweasterneurope.eu/articles-and-commentary/2004-russia-s-new-religion-the-cult-of-the-great-victory

of Victory on May 9, the memory (as well as statues) of Vladimir Lenin and others who were leading personages in the revolutionary narrative has fallen away in the post-Soviet period, providing a powerful illustration of an adage by Bernard Kaplan (1990) that memory and narratives always involve "neglection" as well as selection.

In certain telling instances the forces that lead to neglecting an actor can be quite active and involve the "silencing" of information that must be relegated to social oblivion. Of particular interest are cases of "refusing to remember overtly while remembering covertly" (Stone, Coman, & Brown, 2012). During Soviet times, a veritable industry devoted to this created what came be known as "blank spots" in history (Wertsch, 2008a). The consequences of not knowing what was included on the latest list of such blank spots could be very serious for Soviet citizens. Constant self-vigilance was required to avoid mentioning or even acknowledging the existence of certain actors in public who were, in fact, widely known in private.

Consider the case of a Soviet photograph from 1937 that included Nikolai Yezhov, who was the notorious People's Commissar of Internal Affairs (NKVD) at the time. Yezhov presided over the most brutal years of the Great Purge, in which thousands of civilian and military leaders of the USSR were stripped of their positions, imprisoned, or executed, and hundreds of thousands of ordinary citizens suffered similar fates. In a 1937 photo (Figure 4.1) taken at the Moscow-Volga Canal embankment he was included along with Stalin and two other high Soviet officials, Marshal Kliment Voroshilov and Premier Vyacheslav Molotov (left-hand photo). Unlike the other three, who died natural deaths, Yezhov was a victim of the very system he oversaw and was himself executed in 1940, at which time he disappeared from the official Soviet account by being airbrushed out of the photo (right-hand photo).

Selectivity of this sort is so blatant that some have seen it as humorous. Armando Iannucci's macabre comedy *The Death of*

Figure 4.1 Left: Kliment Voroshilov, Vyacheslav Molotov, Joseph Stalin, and Nikolai Yezhov walking along the banks of the Moscow-Volga Canal, in April 1937. Right: Yezhov was later removed from this photograph.
Original photo: TASS via Getty Images. Manipulated photo: AFP via Getty Images.

Stalin (2018), for example, depicts numerous characters who were relegated to becoming blank spots in history upon their arrest and execution. Not surprisingly, the film quickly become an object of derision for Putin and was virtually banned in Russia. But during the Soviet period, the activities depicted in the film took on deadly consequences for individuals and entire groups who were "liquidated" both in reality and in memory. Among the practices this entailed were airbrushing photos (King, 1997) and instructing elementary school students to strike out passages in their textbooks about individuals who had been heroes and the next day were deemed "enemies of the people" (Wertsch, 2002).

4.2.3. Selectivity of Narrative Emplotment

Picking out events and actors deemed worthy of remembering serves as a starting point in a national memory project, but how they are emplotted is often of equal or even greater importance. Russia and the United States may be similar in selecting World War II as an event worth mnemonic attention, but the two national communities emplot it in quite different ways. Even the beginning and ending dates are different. People in both countries know that the German invasion of Poland occurred on September 1, 1939, but in Russian national memory this pales in comparison with the German invasion of the Soviet Union on July 22, 1941. Just as this marks the beginning of the Great Patriotic War for Russia, the Japanese attack on Pearl Harbor on December 7, 1941, marks the beginning of the real story for most Americans. And whereas May 9 marks the end of the Great Patriotic War for Russians, many Americans would point to August 15 as Victory in Japan Day after the atomic bombings of Hiroshima and Nagasaki.

Along with shaping what events are included in an account of the past, emplotment relegates certain episodes to social oblivion. Consider an episode that has long been a source of anger for many Eastern Europeans: the secret protocols of the Molotov-Ribbentrop Pact signed on August 23, 1939. The announcement of the pact between Germany and the USSR came as a shock to countries such as Great Britain and France who had assumed they would be fighting on the same side as the USSR—which, in fact, they eventually did. But what was not immediately known was the existence of the secret protocols of the pact, which divided up territories in Poland, Ukraine, and the Baltic countries that lay between Germany and the Soviet Union. Estonia, Latvia, and Lithuania, for example, were ceded to the Soviet Union, resulting in their being annexed in 1940.

From the outset, Soviet leaders went to great lengths to turn the secret protocols of the Molotov-Ribbentrop Pact into a blank spot in history. They did this first of all by simply denying that such protocols existed, making them disappear from history. But information about the protocols leaked to the populations of the small Baltic countries and to the Western media within weeks of their being signed in 1939. From then until late in the Soviet era, what Estonia, Latvia, and Lithuania viewed as the onset of brutal occupation was presented in official Soviet history as the results of an uprising of workers and peasants who wanted to join their socialist

"big brothers" in the USSR. The Soviet authorities' longstanding refusal to admit the existence of the secret protocols of the Molotov-
Ribbentrop Pact was motivated by the fact that they contradicted
an official narrative in which the USSR was a victim of Nazi aggression and then went on to rescue the world from German Fascism.
In this view the Red Army liberated, rather than occupied, countries in Eastern Europe, and any claims that this liberation was not
welcomed were heresy.

For many of those on the receiving end of this "liberation," however, such Soviet claims were false and gave rise to smoldering
anger. It was not surprising, then, that memory activists struggled
for decades in private settings to educate people in their community about the secret protocols. During Soviet times in Estonia
these activists did all they could reasonably do to ensure that an
unofficial history (Tulviste & Wertsch, 1992) about an independent Estonia continued to exist in the face of efforts by Soviet
authorities to stamp it out. During the darkest years of Soviet occupation, Estonians were sometimes sentenced to years in prison
for simply displaying three balloons with the colors of the banned
Estonian national flag, let alone the flag itself, yet every Estonian
seemed to be familiar with the unofficial history of how their independent country became part of the USSR in the 1940s. They all
knew both an official and unofficial history of their country, but
they largely remained committed to the truth of only one, which
quickly re-emerged in public as Soviet oppression began to weaken
in the 1980s.

After decades of steadfastly denying the existence of the secret
protocols of the Molotov-Ribbentrop Pact, Soviet authorities did
an abrupt about-face in 1989 when Mikhail Gorbachev admitted to
the world that the documents had shown up in Soviet archives after
all. This gave rise to excited expectations among ethnic Estonians
and other members of national minorities that Soviet authorities
would have to admit the lies in official history and be forced to recognize the falsehoods in Russian national memory as a whole. They

were to be disappointed, however, because Gorbachev's announce-ment simply signaled a shift to new tactics based on emplotment. Russian authorities in the post-Soviet years never retracted the admission that the protocols exist. However, the former of-ficial Soviet narrative of the protocols has slipped into social ob-livion, something that can again be chalked up to the resilient counterforce of the Russian narrative template. Textbook writers and other keepers of national memory did this by acknowledging the existence of the protocols but arguing that they were part of a clever strategy by Stalin to expand Soviet borders westward and extend the time for preparation for the impending attack from Germany. This line of reasoning had actually surfaced be-fore the collapse of the Soviet Union, but it took on new standing when the protocols were openly acknowledged and had to be accounted for in the official account of events leading up to the Great Patriotic War.

As a result, Estonian anticipation of how damaging the secret protocols would be for the Russian view of the past did not pan out. This did not require overt suppression of a specific narrative by Russian authorities. Instead, the story of the secret protocols that emerged in Russian textbooks and other official sources took the form of a re-emplotment based on the Expulsion of Alien Enemies narrative template, which again demonstrated its flexible, protean properties as a schema. The result was that this narrative template was not seriously threatened in the Russian mnemonic community.

Isaiah Berlin's (1991) comparison of nationalism to a bent twig is apropos in this regard. In his view, even if held down for extended periods by external forces, nationalism has a strong tendency to snap back into place. The site where this occurs in symbolic medi-ation is in a national narrative template. As an underlying code, it makes it possible for members of a national community to preserve a basic story even in the face of strong contradictory evidence. In the case of the Molotov-Ribbentrop episode, there may be no amount of evidence that would shake the habits of thinking in the

Russian community tied to the Expulsion of Alien Enemies narrative template. This suggests that analytic history, which aspires to preserve evidence even at the expense of a narrative, may be a weak antidote to the unconscious mental habits associated with a narrative template. Such habits—which, again, are part of every national community—can make it unnecessary for authorities to airbrush a photo or use other top-down efforts to relegate an event or actor to social oblivion. Instead, they are part of a protean capacity of a narrative template to re-emplot information, making it a subtle means that provides less of an obvious target to resist—and hence all the more powerful.

4.3. Privileged Event Narratives

Much of my discussion so far has been about narrative templates. Operating as underlying codes, they give rise to habits and fast thinking that direct our attention to certain events and actors and relegate others to social oblivion. This might seem to suggest that there is little reason to consider the role of specific narratives, but that would be to overlook some crucial issues in the symbolic mediation of national memory. For starters, it would overlook the fact that it is through specific narratives that members of a mnemonic community have access to narrative templates in the first place. Narrative templates are, again, posited underlying codes, and hence our direct experience is not with them but with countless specific narratives in daily life, education, the media, and elsewhere. It is through these encounters that we develop the habits associated with narrative templates and become members of mnemonic communities. This reflects Neisser's observation that "cognition is constructive, and . . . the process of construction leaves traces behind" (1967, p.287). Narrative templates are the traces left behind by countless efforts to construct the meaning of past events using specific narratives.

In addition to playing this role in the formation of narrative habits for members of a national community, specific narratives are what analysts rely on for empirical evidence about narrative templates. As an American who has spent decades trying to understand Russian views of the world, for example, I have encountered thousands of stories about the past, but no one ever took me aside and said, "Look, Jim, here is the schematic form that underlies all that you have been hearing." Instead of having some kind of direct access to the underlying code, my understanding emerged through encounters with specific narratives. After formulating the Expulsion of Alien Enemies storyline, I checked its validity by asking Russian colleagues whether it sounds familiar and reasonable, and for the most part they report that it does, suggesting that my analysis of countless specific narratives to come up with a narrative template is on the right track. But again, my access had to come via these specific narratives.

The main reason that specific narratives deserve our attention, however, has to do with the power they have in their own right in a mnemonic community. In contrast to narrative templates, with their abstract account of the past, specific narratives are about actual people and events that make it possible for them to pack more of an emotional punch than a schematic form. Purveyors of national memory understand this very well and for that reason base their rhetorical efforts on detailed stories about real individuals and events. It is the fact that the Great Patriotic War story includes concrete actors (e.g., Stalin, Hitler), places (e.g., Leningrad, Stalingrad), and events (e.g., the German invasion of the USSR in 1941) that makes it possible to emplot these items in a vivid and visceral story of intrigue, heroism, suffering, and victory against all odds. To be sure, the impact of this specific narrative is given additional energy in the Russian national community by the fact that it instantiates an underlying code, but its emotional appeal still relies on the heroism and heartbreak of real people with whom listeners and readers can identify. This formidable combination of a particular specific narrative and a narrative template creates the conditions for what can be termed a "privileged event narrative" (PEN).

4.3.1. The Great Patriotic War as a PEN in Russia

For the Russian national community in the 21st century, the narrative of the Great Patriotic War is an obvious PEN. It is simultaneously a specific narrative about a concrete event and an instantiation of the Expulsion of Alien Enemies narrative template. As Masha Gessen (2017) writes, the Great Patriotic War is so prominent in Russian national discourse that it sometimes appears to be the *only* noteworthy event of the 20th century. Part of its power of course stems from the fact that the event occurred in the recent past, but countless other events did as well without attaining the status of a defining event for the community.

The standing of the Great Patriotic War as a PEN makes it a preferred lens through which other events can and should be viewed and hence for making rhetorical appeals to a mnemonic community. When Putin sought to justify the Russian invasion of Georgia in 2008 (chapter 1), for example, he used the German invasion of 1941 as the lens through which the attack—or counter-attack from his perspective—should be viewed. If just the Expulsion of Alien Enemies narrative template were at issue, he could have made his appeal by invoking Napoleon's invasion of 1812 or even the invasion of Western ideas in the form of Marxism. But when defending Russian actions, he harnessed the Great Patriotic War, and this points to the particular power it enjoys as a PEN.

Members of a national community share a tendency to accept a PEN as an obvious lens for viewing the past, present, and future. To people outside this community, this can be jarring, and they may find themselves asking: Why do they always bring up X (an event from the past) when talking about current events? Such choices can easily lock in mental realities in ways that escape a national community's notice but strike people from other communities as puzzling. Hence Putin's invocation of World War II when talking about threats of NATO may seem obvious and compelling to Russians but seem to outsiders as strange, if not paranoid.

In discussions where this comes up, we can find ourselves struggling not only to understand but also to avoid giving offense. If Americans challenge Russians over why they constantly bring up World War II in discussions of current events, they can be met with a curt response that it is, after all, the most important event of the 20th century, so why wouldn't it hold lessons for the present? Taking the story of the Great Patriotic War as a lens through which other events should be viewed, then, also comes with the assumption that its privileged status involves not being open to question or criticism, especially by those outside the Russian national community. It has a sacred quality, meaning that for outsiders to question it can be offensive and for members of the mnemonic community itself to question it can be heretical.

In trying to account for PENs, it is often tempting to begin by turning to the power of living memory, the implication being that each generation will have its own candidate for PENs, based on a life-forming experience. Discussions in the United States, for example, often begin with the observation that someone is a member of the Depression generation, the Vietnam War generation, or the "Greatest Generation" of World War II (Brokaw, 1998). This is an issue that has been studied in sociology for decades (Corning & Schuman, 2015; Mannheim, 1952;). Collective experiences during the "critical period" of young adulthood are remembered in particularly vivid ways later in life and serve to distinguish one generation's political perspective from that of others. In some cases, these experiences can be personal and searing and give special authority to the statements of those involved. In discussions in America about terrorism, for example, a statement like "I lost my father on 9/11" can bring the discussion to an abrupt end—even though it might not be clear how it is relevant to the issue at hand.

Again, however, this is not just a matter of direct personal experience. Instead, it often stems from being a member of a collective that has had particular experiences during the formative years of its generation. Many Americans feel strongly about an event like 9/11 even if they experienced no direct personal loss. It is part of what Aleida Assmann (2008) terms "social memory," which is grounded in lived experience and "vanishes with its carriers." If a major event occurs within a generation's social memory, it can provide particularly powerful support for its candidacy as a PEN. At the same time, however, symbolic mediation in the form of Assmann's "external symbols and representations" that operate on a longer timeline to underpin cultural memory can create vivid accounts of the past. Many Jews, for example, take the Holocaust to be a lens for viewing other events even if they were born several decades after 1945.

The relationship between social memory for such an event and the long-lasting cultural memory of following generations is something Vamik Volkan (1998) addresses in his account of a "chosen trauma." He defines this as "the mental representation of an event that caused a large group to face drastic losses, feel helpless and victimized by another group, and share a humiliating injury" (p.8). As a psychiatrist, Volkan emphasizes the emotional dimensions of groups' experiences and argues that individuals who have been traumatized can end up struggling "to mourn the loss or reverse the humiliation" (p.8). Furthermore, this struggle can extend beyond a single generation. It is often not possible to complete the psychological work needed to come to terms with these feelings, and hence they can end up being "'deposited' into the developing self representation of children in the next generation" (p.8).

Volkan uses these ideas to explore why certain episodes from the past are the focus of attention—or even obsession—while other events, including some that might have had greater objective consequences, have little impact on a collective's worldview. As an example, he points to the success that the Serbian nationalist leader Slobodan Milošević had in mobilizing Serbs' actions toward Bosnia-Herzegovina after the breakup of Yugoslavia in the 1990s. Milošević's frequent use of the 1389 Battle of Kosovo in his virulent brand of nationalism meant that he skipped over more recent bloody chapters of Serbian history such as those from World War II.

Observations such as this by Volkan have obvious implications for the study of national memory, but from the perspective of symbolic mediation outlined in this volume, the term "chosen trauma" can be problematic for a couple of reasons. First, not every PEN involves all the dimensions of trauma that Volkan outlines. While fully recognizing that the Great Patriotic War was a traumatic event for Russia, it does not entail the sort of feelings of helplessness and humiliating injury that Volkan includes in his description. If anything, Russians are justifiably proud of their victory and have developed an account of it that does not focus on unresolved psychological issues. An even more important reason for questioning the term "chosen trauma" has to do with the term "chosen," which suggests a conscious decision to focus on a particular traumatic event, perhaps after considering alternatives. In contrast, a perspective grounded in symbolic mediation focuses on how the selection of a particular event often is built into the narrative tools we inherit as unconscious equipment for living.

This is more than just a terminological issue, especially when it comes to understanding and managing intergroup conflict. Recognizing the power of national narratives to shape our thinking and speaking in unconscious ways can help us avoid the temptation to jump directly to chalking up different viewpoints to ignorance, brainwashing, or ill will. We find it all too easy to discount or dismiss others' accounts of the past by saying, "Of course they are saying that to make themselves look good, but they really know better" or "It's natural that they want to glorify their past." To be sure, members of groups can be fully capable of being instrumental or manipulative in these ways, but to start with this attribution assigns a kind of conscious, instrumental intent to them that overlooks the role of unconscious narrative habits and fast thinking and often results in putting ourselves into rhetorical corners that are hard to escape.

Returning to Russian memory of the Great Patriotic War, it would seem only natural that the shock and pain it brought would lead to its emergence as a privileged event narrative, and not just for the generation who fought in the conflict. Indeed, the Great Patriotic War seems to have been on track to emerge as a PEN even before 1941. Sergei Eisenstein's film *Alexander Nevsky*, for example, came out in 1938 and provided a sort of "preview" of the looming threat from Fascist Germany by deploying earlier episodes of history in which alien enemies had to be expelled from Russia. In the film, the invading Teutonic knights from the 13th century are referred as "the German"[7] and were depicted in the very helmets that were used by the invaders in the impending conflagration in 1941. Eisenstein anticipated this vision a bit too early for Stalin, who ordered the film not to be shown while he was negotiating with Germany before its 1941 invasion, but after June 22, 1941, the film became a wildly popular staple of Soviet moviegoers.

In sum, the status of the Great Patriotic War story as a PEN for Russia derives from a list of forces that goes well beyond the usual suspect of top-down efforts by state authorities to invoke the past in service of the present. For starters, the PEN builds on the groundwork that was already in place in the form of the Expulsion of Alien Enemies narrative template. This is precisely what makes it relatively easy for leaders to elevate a story to near cult status. The power of the Great Patriotic War story also owes something to recency and the lived experience of the generation that participated in the event, and the inertia of this lived experience seems to have been passed on to the children and grandchildren of those who survived the war, reflecting the force of trauma as outlined by Volkan. All these forces come together in the case of a PEN in this

---

[7] The Russian term was "*nemets*," which also means an alien or foreigner.

case, and their confluence made Russian authorities' decision to focus on the Great Patriotic War seem almost preordained. In such cases the underlying code of a narrative template is crucial, but the visceral power of a specific narrative also plays a role.

4.3.2. The Century of Humiliation as a PEN for China

For members of the Chinese national community, the Century of Humiliation story serves as a privileged lens in ways similar to how the Great Patriotic War does for the Russian community. It is a story about the humiliation of China in the Opium Wars with England and other European powers in the 1840s and includes other chapters of humiliation at the hands of the West and Japan, including the first Sino-Japanese (1894–1895), the Boxer Rebellion (1900), the dismemberment of Chinese territory in the wake of World War I, and the Japanese invasion of China in the 1930s. This century came to an end in 1949 when Mao Zedong announced that China was finally able to rise up off its knees.

Zheng Wang (2012) has documented the relentless efforts in schools and other settings to ensure that Chinese citizens "never forget national humiliation," and as a result, the slogan is known to virtually every Chinese citizen. It is part of the "historical consciousness and its complex of myth and trauma [that] are the dominant ideas in Chinese public rhetoric" (p.xiii). Wang argues that this is part of a rhetoric of "chosen glory" (p.37), a framework in which "Chinese view themselves as possessing both a strong sense of both cultural and moral superiority" (p.47), which makes the events of 1840 to 1949 seem particularly humiliating by contrast. Indeed, it might be argued that assumptions about cultural superiority are what make it possible for the Chinese to be secure enough to talk about humiliation in the first place and include it in the title of this national narrative. It is a term that virtually no other modern country makes overt in its account of the past even though national communities invariably can point to at least one humiliating episode.

This combination of moral superiority and humiliation has been a focus of intense discussion for decades in China. It can be found in the writings of Lu Xun (1881–1936), for example, a writer whose powerful impact on Chinese society remains to this day. In *A Madman's Diary*, Lu (2014) recounts the shock of being awakened to China's weakened state when he saw a photo of a Japanese soldier beheading a Chinese captive from the Russo-Japanese War of 1904–1905. What he found particularly disturbing was the passive, indeed apathetic, state of the Chinese witnesses in the photo. For him, this was a starting point for anguished self-criticism and a call to action by the Chinese. His unforgiving criticism of the slavish mentality, timidity, and passivity by the Chinese was the topic of many of his essays and short stories that are part of the curriculum of China's schools today and are widely known in the general public.

These and other efforts by the Chinese state have contributed to a set of habits around the Century of Humiliation story, making it into a PEN. Wang (2012) points to elements of the schematic nature of this narrative when writing of how historical memory "functions at a preconscious or subconscious level" (p.36) and constitutes a sort of "national 'deep culture' [that] is not objective knowledge and very often cannot be explicitly learned" (p.36). The length of the event in this case and the inclusion of several distinct sub-events distinguish it from the Great Patriotic War that serves as a PEN for Russians, but it serves much the same function based on a combination of a specific narrative and a narrative template.

The resulting habits of discourse and thought have been discussed by historians and other intellectuals concerned with how the Chinese population goes through brief episodes of recognizing its humiliation and then having the episodes sink from consciousness for longer periods. During the Republican period, for example, Paul Cohen (2002) argues that "after being subjected to acts of national humiliation, [the Chinese] erupted in anger for a short time but then promptly forgot the source of their anger and retreated to their original condition of indifference" (p.1). All this, however, has not stopped Chinese authorities from harnessing the population's memory of the Century of Humiliation and using it as a lens for viewing other events.

The Century of Humiliation narrative is routinely invoked in debates about current events, sometimes in ways that can surprise a Western audience. Just as Americans may wonder why Russians are so quick to cite the Great Patriotic War when explaining contemporary events, they can be surprised at the frequency and fervor of Chinese invocations of the Century of Humiliation. In this connection, Paul Cohen (2002) writes, "Patriotic Chinese in the twentieth century referred endlessly to the humiliations (*guochi*) their country had experienced at the hands of foreign imperialism beginning with the Opium War" (p.1).

The template-like qualities of this PEN surface in observations the Chinese make about how a current event is another chapter in a long list of humiliating episodes from the past. The Chinese leader Deng Xiaoping, for example, made a point of noting in 1990 that the decision by a group of industrialized countries to impose sanctions after the 1989 Tiananmen Square massacre had parallels with how world powers punished China during the Boxer Rebellion:

> I am Chinese, and I am familiar with the history of foreign aggression against China. When I heard that the seven Western countries, at their summit meeting, had decided to impose sanctions on China, my immediate association was to 1900, when the allied forces of the eight powers invaded China. (cited in Wang, 2012, p.183)

And during the massive 1999 demonstrations in China following the Belgrade bombing (see chapter 1), a student was reported by CNN to have said, "It's the same old story, when hegemonist powers unite to bully China, it's always the same" (from Wang, 2012, p.185). This formulation of the same story with different characters points to the presence of a narrative template, this time in the form of the Century of Humiliation plot.

Over the past century the Chinese government has announced official days of national humiliation or shame (*gouchi ri*) to mark the anniversary of particularly painful episodes. In recent years, September 18 has been designated as a nationwide Day of Humiliation to commemorate the beginning of Japanese occupation in 1931, but this is just one of many events during the Century of Humiliation that are covered in school textbooks, the media, and other sources. Again, reflecting the template-like quality of this storyline, a Wikipedia article[8] on Day of Humiliation includes the following items. They constitute a long list of the same underlying story played out with different characters:

Defeat in the First Opium War (1839–1842) by the United Kingdom

The unequal treaties (in particular Nanking, Wampoa, Aigun, and Shimoneseki)

The Taiping Rebellion (1850–1864)

Defeat in the Second Opium War (1856–1860) and the sacking of the Old Summer Palace by British and French forces

Defeat in the Sino-French War (1884–1885) by France

Defeat in the First Sino-Japanese War (1894–1895) by Japan

The Eight-Nation Alliance suppressing the Boxer Uprising (1899–1901)

British invasion of Tibet (1903–1904)

The Twenty-One Demands (1915) by Japan

Japanese invasion of Manchuria (1931–1932)

The Second Sino-Japanese War (1937–1945)

[8] https://en.wikipedia.org/wiki/Century_of_humiliation

Further parallels between the Century of Humiliation and the Great Patriotic War as PENs can be found in their function. In both cases, their use rises and falls, depending on the needs of the state, and they are especially likely to be called forth as lenses for viewing contemporary events when state authorities need to foster patriotism in the face of a foreign adversary. They can also be useful in distracting attention away from domestic complaints in times of trouble. In this vein, Wang (2012) argues that the leaders of the Chinese Communist Party "have creatively used the content of historical memory to generate new theories and explanations to redefine the party's membership and mission in the post-Tiananmen era" (p.224). Instead of serving as the "vanguard of the Chinese working class" the Party recast itself as "'the firmest, most thoroughgoing' patriot" (p.224). Similarly, Cohen (2002) observes that with the loss of faith in communism in the 1990s, Chinese authorities decided "to fill the minds of the young with narratives of the suffering and humiliation of the imperialist interval in China's history and entreat them to 'not forget'" (p.1).

Along with similarities, there are some differences that separate the Century of Humiliation PEN from the Great Patriotic War. For starters, it was an event that occurred over the course of a century rather than just a few years. Indeed, the repeated episodes of humiliation noted in the earlier list are cases of the same story with different characters *within* this PEN. This is one reflection of how the mental habits tied to this narrative function in China, but over the long course of Chinese history, this century is also considered to be just one episode alongside others. In this account, it instantiates a general storyline or narrative template that traces its history to more than two millennia ago. As Cohen (2002) notes, this "was nothing new in China. It lay at the very heart of the well-known Spring and Autumn period saga of Goujian, King of Yue, who, after being defeated at Mount Kuaiji (in modern Zhejiang) by his arch-rival Fuchai, the king of Wu, was forced into servitude by the latter" (p.2).

In sum, the Century of Humiliation story serves as a PEN for China much as the Great Patriotic War does for Russia. In both cases, the visceral power of the story derives from the fact that real people, events, suffering, and so forth are recounted in a specific narrative, and a deeper cultural resonance of the story derives from the fact that a narrative template is involved. The combination provides an ideal foundation for mental habits of group members that automatically select crucial pieces of information and neglect others as part of narrative emplotment.

4.4. Selective Memory and Nation Narcissism: A Comparative Study of Remembering World War II

I have argued that PENs combine the strengths of a narrative template with those of a specific narrative. In the Russian case these properties combine to form a Great Patriotic War PEN that shapes the norms of historical focusing for the mnemonic community. In addition to dealing with the Great Patriotic War and other events of the past, this PEN provides a lens for viewing events in the present, something that is evidenced in Putin's view of the 2008 Russo-Georgian War and his confident assertions about why Russia had to respond in the way it did (chapter 1).

World War II was of course fought by many countries, raising the question of how Russian norms of historical focusing compare with those of other places. Is World War II a major event in national memory for other countries, or is this just the case for Russia? Results from cross-national survey studies about world history by James Liu and colleagues (Liu et al., 2005) indicate that World War II ranks high on the list of important events of the past millennium, even in nations that were not directly involved in it. This would seem to suggest that it could serve as a PEN in many countries, but as will be outlined in this section, other factors intervene to make this less likely. In the United States, to be sure, certain parts of the war seem to serve as a lens for viewing other events: The 1941 surprise attack on Pearl Harbor is often used in discussions of the 9/11 attack on New York in 2001, and President George H.W. Bush and others have compared Saddam Hussein to Adolf Hitler.

But when it comes to the entire war, it is harder to find a narrative template in the United States or other countries that would qualify the World War II narrative as a PEN as it does in Russia. To be sure, in the United States, World War I and World War II are sometimes interpreted as reflecting a City on a Hill narrative template. In this interpretation, America entered these conflicts as part of an effort to introduce or reintroduce freedoms to people everywhere in the world; Europe twice fell into chaos and the United States intervened to restore democracy. In the end, however, this is not a widely or deeply shared part of American national memory, and even if it is recognized, it is not a pattern that can be applied to multiple other specific narratives about the past. Instead, it acts more like a weak analogy in the American mnemonic community between the two world wars and not a narrative template of the sort that guides Russian memory.

Another reason that the World War II story fails to qualify as a PEN in the United States and elsewhere has to do with the visceral nature and salience of the specific narrative at issue. World War II was obviously an important event for America and involved tragic loss for many individuals and communities, but it lacks the ubiquitous and authoritative presence that it has in the Russian national community. In America the war shares the limelight with the Great Depression, the Vietnam War, and other events from the 20th century. The greater impact of the war on Russia, as compared to America, should perhaps come as no surprise, given that Soviet deaths in World War II outnumbered U.S. deaths by a factor of at least 50 to 1.

The power of the Great Patriotic War as a PEN for Russians also stems from the fact that this narrative assigns them the role of the core actor that drove the whole story forward. As will become evident in what follows, other nations appear to have similarly high estimates of their importance, and this raises the issue of "national narcissism" (Abel et al., 2019 Zaromb et al., 2018) that seems to be part of every national memory everywhere. And finally, its status is reflected and reinforced by rich and detailed knowledge of the details of the story. These points are supported by cross-national empirical studies conducted by Roediger and his colleagues that have explored two related issues: (1) estimates of a nation's contribution to the war effort and (2) knowledge of events within World War II.

4.4.1. Estimates of Nations' Contribution to the World War II Effort

In a 2019 survey study by Roediger and colleagues, participants were asked to estimate their country's contribution to World War II. The investigators collected data from over 100 respondents in each of 11 countries.[9] After providing basic demographic data (age, gender, national identity), respondents were asked to complete several tasks, including estimating their country's contribution to the war. In this last item the respondents from the eight Allied countries were asked, "In terms of percentage, what do you think was [your country's] contribution to the victory of World War 2? In other words, how responsible was [your country] for the victory of the war?"

The results are striking in that respondents from many countries provide very high estimates of their nations' contribution. People

---

[9] The countries (with numbers of respondents in parentheses) were Australia (107), Canada (121), China (105), France (106), New Zealand (112), Russia (133), United Kingdom (118), United States (135), Germany (133), Italy (146), and Japan (122). The total sample size for the study was 1,338 with a mean age of 35.5 years, and 56.5% of the participants were female.

from three Allied countries assigned more than 50% of the victory to their own country's efforts: Russia (75%), the United Kingdom (51%), and the United States (54%). The total combined percentage effort estimated from the eight Allied countries was 309%. This well over the 100% mark, which would be the objective maximum, and it is even more striking considering that several other Allied countries were not included in our survey. In an effort to get respondents to look at the larger picture and take other countries' contribution to the war into account, they were also asked to provide estimates for the eight Allied countries (including their own), alongside a ninth listing of "Other countries." Following this procedure, the respondents were forced to come up with a total of 100% for the nine countries. When faced with the partial list of Allied countries, people in four Allied countries cut the percentage of their country's contribution by half or more. The four others whose estimates dropped less were Russia (going from 75% to 64%), the United States (from 54% to 37%), the United Kingdom (from 51% to 29%), and France (from 30% to 18%), although the latter two were close to cutting by half.

In general, Russian respondents stood out from all other groups in this study. They believed that the former Soviet Union was largely responsible for the victory in World War II, and they largely stuck with their estimate when pushed to consider Russia's contribution in the context of other nations. Participants from the United States, Britain, and France adjusted their estimates downward to a greater extent when comparisons were included, and other countries did so even more. These results point to unusually strong certainty among Russians of how much they contributed to the war effort, and it makes another finding reported by Roediger et al. about estimates of other countries' contributions to the war effort all the more striking. This finding concerned the percentage of credit for victory given to each country by people from the *other* countries. For example, for the United Kingdom, the average of the estimates provided by participants from other Allied and Axis countries, but omitting ratings from people in the United Kingdom, was 19%. In general, the values for other countries were much smaller than the percentages people assigned to their own countries.

The most striking finding using this procedure is that participants assigned the United States a significantly greater percentage of the victory in World War II (27%) than they did for the Soviet Union (20%). This runs counter to just about any objective measure of the damage inflicted by the USSR on the Axis powers or the losses they suffered in World War II. The widespread idea that America played a bigger role in winning the war may have some grounding in the industrial might the United States brought to bear, but it is hard to reconcile with the fact that around 25 million Soviet citizens lost their lives in World War II compared to 416,800 U.S. soldiers and sailors; or with the fact that the Soviet Union lost more troops in each of several individual battles than the United States did in the entire war; or that 600,000 Red Army troops died in the first months of the German invasion in 1941 before the United States entered the war.

The quantitative picture provided by such statistics can be usefully supplemented by other, more qualitative measures of Russia's contribution to the Allied victory. Hitler and other German leaders viewed Russia as being populated by primitive, "Asiatic" people who had to be exterminated. The racism against Jews is well known, but it was also aimed at Slavs, and the result was that the German invaders treated the Soviet population much more brutally than they did the countries in Western Europe. One result was that every segment of Soviet society was called on to fight the German invaders in an all-out struggle that required massive sacrifices by women and children as well as men. Some 800,000 women served in the military, usually in medical and other support roles, but also as pilots, snipers, machine gunners, tank crew members, and partisan fighters.

The surprising underestimation of Soviet contributions to World War II by respondents other than Russians may reflect the impact of Hollywood and Western popular culture. This is suggested by the analysis Viet Thanh Nguyen (2016) provides of the "industry of memory" that has shaped so much of the world's perception of America's war with Vietnam. In the case of World War II, these sources place much less emphasis on the Eastern Front in Europe than on the Western Front and the war in the Pacific. In stark contrast, the Russian respondents were clear in their estimate of the central importance that the Soviet Union played in World War II, a finding that is consistent with the outsized role that the Great Patriotic War plays in the Russian cultural imagination. In contrast to other countries, where it exists alongside other events, this war is by far the most important event over the past century for Russians, and this could be expected to encourage high estimates of Russia's role in it.

Overall, these results from Roediger et al. (2019) reflect general tendencies that have variously been described as "the ethnocentric bias of group self-centeredness" (Sumner, 1906), collective narcissism (de Zavala et al., 2009), national narcissism (Zaromb et al., 2018), or the tendency of people in groups to see themselves and their group in a positive light and minimize or derogate outgroups (Assmann & Czaplicka, 1995; Paez & Liu, 2011; Wertsch & Roediger, 2008). Claims about ethnocentrism and narcissism in these studies are not tied to the individual pathology referred to as "narcissistic personality disorders." Instead, they point toward bias in memory that guides discourse and thinking, and in the narrative approach proposed here, these forms of selectivity are assumed to reflect national narrative equipment for living used to make sense of the past.

4.4.2. Knowledge of the Events in World War II

Along with the outsized importance that Russians attribute to their country in winning World War II, they stand apart from other national groups in terms of the extent and sophistication of knowledge. It is not clear that such detailed knowledge is always part of a PEN, but in this case, it is striking and is reflected in a 2019 study by Abel and colleagues. These investigators examined data from the same 100 respondents in each of 11 countries[10] who participated in the study reported in the previous section. In this case, respondents were asked to list "the 10 most important events" of World War II. In addition, they completed a multiple-choice general knowledge test about World War II and a recognition test involving actual and made-up events from the war.

The results once again reveal major differences between Russia and other countries. This is evident in subjects' responses to the request to list the 10 most important events of World War II. The 1,338 participants from all countries generated a total of 11,491 items in response to this request. Using a cutoff of 50% agreement within each national sample as a criterion indicating significantly shared collective memory, the number of "core events" listed by groups ranged from two in the case of Japan to seven in the case of Russia. This large number for Russia was higher than any other country and indicated a level of detailed knowledge about the war that is consistent with having it as a PEN.

Furthermore, it is not just a matter of having generally more knowledge about World War II. The Russian respondents produced a list of events and an image of the war that differed from all the other groups in the study. These other groups showed striking similarities among themselves in contrast to Russia. Nine of these 10 groups agreed (again, at 50% or more) on three key events in their list of core events: the attack on Pearl Harbor, D-Day, and the atomic bombings of Japan. The only country that did not reach the 50% cutoff for one of these events (D-Day) was Japan. Furthermore, 8 of these 10 groups included the Holocaust, as did about a third

---

[10] Again, the countries were Australia, Canada, China, France, New Zealand, Russia, United Kingdom, United States, Germany , Italy, and Japan.

of the respondents in the two remaining groups (32% for China, 31% for Japan). In general, then, all the groups in this study *except Russians* had a pronounced tendency to include four basic items in their list of most important events:

Attack on Pearl Harbor (December 7, 1941)
D-Day (June 6, 1944)
Atomic bombings of Japan (August 1945)
The Holocaust (extending for several years and ending in 1945)

This list of events may appear familiar because it is the same one presented in chapter 1 based on numerous presentations to college students and other audiences in the United States. Abel et al. (2019) report that a few other items showed up in the list of one group or another as core events. For example, the Australians and Germans included the four events in the list above plus the German invasion of Poland, those from the United Kingdom included these four plus the invasion of Poland and the Battle of Britain, and the French respondents included these four plus De Gaulle's radio address to the French nation of June 18, 1940. Thus, for all countries except Russia, there was a tendency to include the four core events (and, in a few cases, additional ones as well).

In contrast, the Russian respondents presented a strikingly different picture. This was so first of all because their list of agreed-upon items extends to seven events—more than any other group. Furthermore, the Russians generally displayed a higher level of agreement on core events than the other groups did. The lowest level of agreement for an event in the Russian group was 59%, and it usually was much higher, whereas agreement on several items by the other 10 groups often barely reached a majority. There is no simple metric for "how collective" collective memory is, but it is noteworthy that the Russian list of events in World War II reflects strikingly higher within-group agreement than any other group in the study.

Furthermore, several of the items included on the Russians' list differed from those of the other groups. Indeed, there is only *one* event on the Russian list that is also on that of the other groups— D-Day, and as noted in chapter 2 the very term and meaning of "D-Day" (or "opening the second front") are quite different for Russians than for others. For Americans this meaning evolved from what General Eisenhower called a "great crusade" into "a symbol of the triumph of good over evil, a standard against which to judge patriotism, duty and war."[11] In 2019 it was still being touted as having outsized importance, as reflected in a special 75th Anniversary Tribute issue of *Time* that called D-Day the "24 Hours That Saved the World."[12]

Thus, the invasion on June 6, 1944, is the only item included as a core event by Russians as well as almost every other group in this study.[13] Not a single other item on the Russian list was named by a majority of any other group, and several of the items *never* appeared in others' lists. In decreasing frequency of agreement, the events included by a majority of Russian respondents (indicated by percentage figures) were:

Battle of Stalingrad (93%)
Battle of Kursk (74%)
D-Day (67%)
Battle of Moscow (63%)
Siege of Leningrad (63%)
Nazi invasion of USSR (60%)
Battle of Berlin (59%).

[11] https://www.nytimes.com/2019/06/05/opinion/dday-anniversary.html
[12] *Time. D-Day. 24 Hours that Saved the World*. Introduction by Tom Hanks. 75th Anniversary Tribute. Single issue magazine, January 1, 2019.
[13] In this study, several different ways of referring to the events of June 6, 1944, were included under the general term of "D-Day." Possibilities included opening the second front, Normandy landings, Allied invasion of France, and so forth.

At first glance the absence of, say, the Japanese attack on Pearl Harbor or the American atomic bombings of Hiroshima and Nagasaki on this list might be assumed to indicate what Russians simply do not know because they have not had access to information about it. There is ample evidence, however, that they in fact do know about these events. Indeed, 39% of the Russian respondents listed Pearl Harbor and 44% listed the atomic bombings but in neither case did they rise to the level of 50% agreement of being a crucial event in the war.

The fact that the Russian respondents displayed so much agreement on so many events in comparison to any other group certainly indicates what events were of special interest to them, but leaving it at that says nothing about why this should be so, and it begs the question of why most U.S. respondents, for example, did not include events that are of special interest to *them*. After all, they could have listed items like the Battle of Midway, the Battle of Guadalcanal, Iwo Jima, or the Battle of the Bulge. All of these have been the object of popular movies and novels, but they have not surfaced in strong form in American national memory for World War II, which is consistent with the claim that the war does not serve as a PEN for Americans. In general, then, Russians' unusually high level of agreement on a long list of events in World War II sets them apart from the other 10 national groups.

4.4.3. The Atomic Bombing of Japan in 1945 in American and Russian National Memory

Patterns of selecting most important events is one way of documenting differences between the accounts that Russians and Americans, as well as other groups, provide of World War II. This method does not elicit narrative texts as such, but it does generate data that are suggestive of differences in the narrative templates that guide people's responses. Another way to bring the influence of narrative templates into the open is to focus on the accounts that the two communities provide of a particular event, and for this I turn to the atomic bombing of Hiroshima in August 1945.

I have already touched on this in chapter 1 in my account of the discussion I had with my friend Vitya in 1976 in Moscow. In the survey data just reviewed, I noted that 39% of Russian respondents (as opposed to 78% of Americans) listed the atomic bombings as one of the most important events of World War II. So, Hiroshima and Nagasaki do occupy a significant, though not core, position in Russian national memory, but of more interest for my current purposes are differences between Russians and Americans in the narrative emplotment of the bombings. In American national memory, the atomic bombing of Hiroshima and Nagasaki marked the end of a war that started with the unprovoked attack on the United States at Pearl Harbor on what President Roosevelt declared was a "day that will live in infamy." In this narrative, the bombings were an effort to force the surrender of Japan, and they worked.

Russians, in contrast, tend to emplot World War II in a way that gives Hiroshima and Nagasaki a quite different meaning. The narrative of the Great Patriotic War closes with the Battle of Berlin, so in one sense the war was already over from the Russian perspective. It turns out that it was already over in another sense when it comes to understanding Japan's surrender. In the Russian account Japan was already about to surrender and there was no need for further punishing air raids from the Allies. From this perspective, the use of atomic weapons was wholly unnecessary. Instead, their narrative attributes Truman's decision to use atomic weapons to a desire to intimidate Stalin.

This might appear to be just another case of national narcissism on Russia's part, but it turns out that it is not only in Russian memory that this version of the motive behind Truman's decision can be found; it has also been a topic of study by historians in the West. In his 1965 volume *Atomic Diplomacy*, for example, historian Gar Alperovitz provided a lengthy analysis of Truman's decision and raises the possibility that Truman was motivated, at least in part, by a desire to warn Stalin against postwar expansion in Europe or Asia. Alperovitz's claims have been vigorously disputed,[14] but they do represent a strand of scholarly inquiry that brings into question the standard American account of this episode and are part of a larger discussion that began almost immediately after 1945. In 1950, for instance, Fleet Admiral William D. Leahy, the most senior U.S. military officer who had been on active duty during World War II and a leading adviser of President Truman, stated:

> It is my opinion that the use of this barbarous weapon at Hiroshima and Nagasaki was of no material assistance in our war against Japan. The Japanese were already defeated and ready to surrender . . . My own feeling was that in being the first to use it, we had adopted an ethical standard common to the barbarians of the Dark Ages. I was not taught to make war in that fashion, and wars cannot be won by destroying women and children. (1950, p.441)

The questions raised by Alperovitz, Leahy, and others have been debated for decades. In 2013, for example, Ward Wilson of the British-American Security Information Council revisited the issue in an article in *Foreign Policy* titled "The Bomb Didn't Beat Japan . . . Stalin Did." There he posed the provocative question, "Have 70 years of nuclear policy been based on a lie?" and went on to provide a detailed account of the timing of events in August 1945 that makes it more difficult to attribute the Japanese surrender to the American use of atomic bombs. For example, he reports that Tokyo did not know about the Hiroshima bombing until a day *after* the Japanese leadership had already decided to surrender.

---

[14] http://time.com/4346336/atomic-bombs-1945-history/

The bottom line is that the standard American memory of events of August 1945 continues to have staying power despite the challenges it has faced. In contrast, Russian national memory rejects out of hand the idea that the intent in using atomic weapons was to force a quick surrender of Japan. Just as there has been a high level of certainty in American memory that this was Truman's basic motive, there is great confidence among Russians that the real story was about intimidating Stalin. And historical scholarship also challenges the assertions of American national memory by insisting that facts that bring an existing interpretation into question be taken into consideration. In contrast to collective memory, with its impatience with ambiguity, this scholarship has produced an account in which the motives of historical actors involve multiple, complex forces.

The staying power of American national memory in this case points to some underlying mental habits, namely in the form of a narrative that brings with it a strong assumption that America would never sacrifice hundreds of thousands of Japanese citizens in order to make a point that was not really about them. Such an interpretation conflicts with a story in which Truman used atomic bombs simply to intimidate Russia, and it encourages a kind of what can be called "didn't/couldn't logic" according to which things didn't happen in a certain way because they couldn't have.

Before leaving this issue, it worth noting that anecdotal and other evidence suggests that this national memory may be starting to change among younger generations in America. Zaromb and colleagues (2014), for example, report that college-aged students in the early 21st century do not share the same positive evaluation toward the use of the atomic weapons that older Americans do. This may not amount to a change in the specific narrative of Hiroshima and Nagasaki, let alone a transformation of a narrative template, but it does indicate that the certainty with which older adults accepted Truman's decision to use atomic weapons might be subject to change in the future.

4.5. Summing Up

The selective nature of national memory derives from the combined forces of identifying actors and events for mnemonic focusing and the power of narrative emplotment. Once selectivity is set in motion in national memory, a great deal of work is already done in shaping our understanding of the past, making the understanding of how it works a crucial task. The forms of selectivity outlined in this chapter cannot be reduced to mental processes, to be sure, but the overall effect on social and political processes in a national community is similar to what Kahneman (2011) described as "WYSIATI" (what you see is all there is), as discussed in chapter 3.

In some cases, selectivity in national memory is fairly easy to detect. The intervention of state authorities as they decide what is—and what is not—part of the official past sometimes comes clearly into view with a bit of archival research. The case of the airbrushed Soviet photograph of Yezhov was a case in point. Other efforts to select what should be included in and excluded from national memory have been documented by Loewen (2018) in his discussion of how high school history textbooks shape education in America. These sorts of top-down efforts to control national memory are important, but it would be a mistake to focus on them alone, as if they operate in isolation and can impose any decisions they want. To do so is to overlook the power of narrative tools in shaping national memory. These tools take the form of specific narratives and narrative templates, as well the form of privileged event narratives (PENs) that draw on the strengths of both.

Much of my discussion has focused on underlying codes in the form of national narrative templates. The power exerted by this type of equipment for living and how it shapes the ways we size up situations is easy to overlook. Indeed, part of the power of narrative templates stems from the fact that they operate largely in unnoticed and unconscious ways, leading us to mistakenly assume that we have direct access to what really happened rather than that we are looking through a narrative lens. I have sought to illustrate these claims by examining Russian and Chinese cases of PENs. This led to the claim that World War II occupies a special place in the Russian mnemonic community, setting this community apart from many other national groups. All of which is not to say that other national communities don't have their own PENs. The evidence I reviewed suggests that the Century of Humiliation plays this role for China, and national memory in other societies can be expected to be grounded in narrative templates and PENs. The work involved in identifying what these are is made all the more important by the fact that the key to understanding national identity and clashes between national communities lies, at least in part, in appreciating the equipment for living that it relies on to size up the world around them.

5

Narrative Dialogism
in National Memory

5.1. Introduction

In previous chapters I have focused on how narrative tools shape
national memory. This has included a review of the "strange logic"
of their inner workings, their impact on cognition and memory,
their selectivity, and their function as narrative templates and privileged event narratives. Throughout, I have focused on one or another narrative considered in isolation. But speaking and thinking
about national memory typically involves narratives interacting
with one another and competing to be heard. This suggests the
need to consider national memory as a *"process"* and not just a
"body of knowledge" (Dudai, 2002, p.51). To be sure, understanding
memory as a body of knowledge can provide useful insight. The
survey findings reported in the previous chapter, for instance, reveal important differences between the national groups in their
views of the past. But the larger story needs to attend to memory as
process as well.

   In what follows, my goal is not to present a general review
of memory as process, an effort that would involve all the issues
outlined by Brubaker et al. under the heading of circumstantialism
plus other issues at a societal level. Instead, I approach memory
as process from the more narrowly focused perspective of "dialogism" as outlined by M.M. Bakhtin (1981, 1986b; Holquist, 2002).
This amounts to an elaboration of Cronon's point that "We tell
stories *with* each other and *against* each other in order to speak

How Nations Remember. James V. Wertsch, Oxford University Press (2021). © Oxford University Press.
DOI: 10.1093/oso/9780197551462.003.0005

to each other" (1992, pp.1373–1374). More generally, it builds on MacIntyre's claim that "the narrative of any one life is part of an interlocking set of narratives" (1984, p.217). He asserted that because our life narrative is so thoroughly tied up with other stories already on the scene, "we are never more (and sometimes less) than the co-authors of our own narrative" (p.213). Thus, rather than being independent, unencumbered tellers of our story, we are inherently positioned as responding to, and borrowing from, others. The upshot for MacIntyre is that "Only in fantasy do we live what story we please" (p.213).

MacIntyre develops his line of reasoning as part of an account of the identity and self of individuals, but the patterns of narrative interanimation and habits that he outlines also shape the way we think and act as members of national communities. As is the case for individuals, national groups can be said to "enter upon a stage which we did not design [where] we can find ourselves part of an action that was not of our own making" (1984, p.213). Instead of formulating our national narrative de novo, as a sort of "linguistic Adam" in the words of Bakhtin, we do not have the first word, and it turns out that our national narrative invariably plays "subordinate parts in the dramas of others" (p.213). Bakhtin's contribution to this line of inquiry concerns the many complex ways that narrative voices come into contact and interanimate one another, an effort that takes us far beyond standard notions of dialogue. In particular, it goes beyond dialogue as routine, give-and-take discussion that leads to a meeting of minds. If anything, Bakhtin was more concerned with how voices struggle against one another and in some cases create even *less* agreement than existed before a dialogue commenced.

Introducing dialogism into the study of national memory builds on the claims about narrative mediation outlined earlier but extends them into new conceptual territory. The general concern remains one of how nations remember and how this can be approached in terms of individuals as members of national communities. These individuals continue to be viewed as agents using the narrative tools provided by their community, with all their affordances for grasping events together in the selective ways these tools entail. In addition, however, my analytic focus now expands to how these narrative tools take on new dimensions of meaning as they are embedded in dialogue, sometimes with surprising consequences. For instance, the unique properties of emplotment built into narrative tools (as opposed to other forms of representation such as annals or syllogisms) can act to drive accounts of the past further apart rather than find common ground in dialogue. Taken together, these points provide a foundation for an account of national memory as process, namely process grounded in "narrative dialogism."

5.2. Narrative Dialogism

Bakhtin did not explicitly focus on narratives in his studies of dialogism,[1] but the implications of his approach are obvious. Namely, it encourages us to look at how using narrative tools involves more than describing the past as if this occurs without regard to those around us. Instead, using narratives also involves "addressivity" (Bakhtin, 1986a)—what Cronon calls speaking *to* each other, a process that shapes the content and form of narratives themselves. Accounts of national memory are invariably responses to what other individuals and groups say—sometimes in some very highly charged ways.

A starting point for a Bakhtinian approach to narrative dialogism is the notion of "text," which is defined in terms of two poles. The first is a "language system," or what is "repeated and reproduced" (Bakhtin, 1986b, p.105) across the instances in which a text such as a narrative is used, and the second is the particular use of the

---

[1] I use the term "dialogism" throughout, but in some cases the original English translation of Bakhtin's texts uses "dialogicality," which I use when quoting these texts.

text, which is "individual, unique, and unrepeatable" (p.105). This means that the use of any narrative tool (the "language system" in this case) includes elements shared with other uses of that narrative tool but at the same time involves aspects that are unique to the particular temporal, spatial, and communicative context, especially the context composed of other texts.

Bakhtin's approach to these issues differs from that of formal linguistics as it was being mapped out by the Swiss linguist Ferdinand de Saussure and the Russian Formalists of his time. Their goal was to create a science of language starting with linguistic forms removed from their context, including dialogic context. In this view language was approached as abstract, decontextualized form, a conceptual move that made possible important breakthroughs in the study of areas such as phonology and morphology, but it also precluded the systematic study of utterances. In contrast, Bakhtin began with the observation that "speech is always cast in the form of an utterance belonging to a particular speaking subject" (1986a, p.71), and the implication was that the starting point in his analysis was the contextualized speech act.

Bakhtin's account of text comes with its own notion of a language system, one that differs from what is presupposed in formal linguistics. Specifically, it concerns generic patterns of utterances used repeatedly by a social group. Whereas formal linguistics is concerned with issues such as subject–verb agreement in a sentence, an issue that can be examined independently of any speech context, Bakhtin's focus was on categories of utterances, namely categories or "genres" of utterances indicating membership in a social group. The "social languages" and "speech genres" he envisioned (Bakhtin, 1986a) are characteristic of members of generations, professions, or other groups in which words come to have meanings that reflect the history of a group's usage.

Being part of a social language means that words and meanings have a particular heritage. In contrast to studies of formal linguistics, there are no "neutral" words in this approach. Instead of words belonging to "no one" (Bakhtin, 1981, p.293), the focus is on their history of use in a speech community. Any word we use is part of a social language and for that reason is "half someone else's . . . (it is not, after all, out of a dictionary that the speaker gets his words!)" (pp.293–294). In Bakhtin's account, words acquire the "taste" (p.293) of where they have been. Consider, for example, a social language that emerged around the 2016 presidential election in the United States. After endless repetition of "Make America Great Again" by Donald Trump and his followers, this expression had a history of use tied to a particular group in the larger American speech community. Regardless of political persuasion, Americans could no longer use these words in a neutral way, as if they belonged to no one. Instead, the expression had become "half someone else's" and became so "populated—overpopulated—with the intentions" (p.294) of others that it could no longer be used as if it just comes out of a dictionary. The same could be said of other words such as "Lock her up!" or "American carnage." Taken together, these are part of a pattern of utterances that form the social language of a group in which the heritage of the words gives them a "socially charged life" (p.293).

Bakhtin did not provide a systematic definition of social language in his writings. Instead, he relied on illustrations involving groups who speak one or another social language, groups such as professions, political parties, generations, and government authorities. These descriptions were often ad hoc, with little in the way of specifics about what characterized a social language. In the case of national groups, it is possible to provide a more organized account, however, based on the equipment for living the members of the group share. This equipment includes the specific narratives, narrative templates, and privileged event narratives used by the national community. These support forms of memory as knowledge, but Bakhtin's insights suggest they also need to be considered in the context of dialogic processes involved in memory as process. In order to do this, I outline a few basic categories of narrative

dialogism: "hidden dialogism," "authoritative and internally persuasive discourse," "bivocalism," and "national narrative projects."

5.2.1. Hidden Dialogism Between Narratives

At first glance, the idea of narrative dialogism might seem to suggest two narratives facing off against one another in an explicit
conversation, something that does in fact sometimes occur in
discussions of national memory. Indeed, this was the case in my
conversation about Hiroshima with Vitya outlined in chapter 1.
Another, more extended illustration of this can be found in a
history workbook created by Sami Adwan, Dan Bar-On, Adnan
Musallam, and Eyal Naveh (2003). Collaborating over a period of
years, these authors produced a volume in Arabic and Hebrew for
Palestinian and Israeli high school students who were studying
historical events such as the 1948 war that gave rise to the Israel
state. In the workbook they came up with, each page of "Learning
Each Other's Historical Narrative" was formatted in three
columns: one for the Palestinian narrative, one for the Israeli narrative, and a lined space in the middle for pupils to write their
comments. Two competing narratives were developed by authors
and teachers from the two sides of an ongoing mnemonic conflict,
and the students were charged with considering each before they
wrote down their own account or commentary. This process of
juxtaposing two competing narratives might be called "overt narrative dialogism."

Efforts of the sort pursued by Adwan et al. are inspired, but they
are also rare, which is perhaps to be expected given the massive in-
vestment of time, funding, and good will required to pull them off.
But the infrequent appearance of such projects hardly means that
narrative dialogism is absent from national memory in general.
In fact, it permeates discussions of the past. However, it does so in
ways that are veiled and hence require special effort to be brought

into the open. Such veiled narrative dialogism frequently occurs in the form of what Bakhtin (1984) called "hidden dialogicality."

> Imagine a dialogue of two persons in which the statements of the second speaker are omitted, but in such a way that the general sense is not at all violated. The second speaker is present invisibly, his words are not there, but deep traces left by these words have a determining influence on all the present and visible words of the first speaker. We sense that this is a conversation, although only one person is speaking, and it is a conversation of the most intense kind, for each present, uttered word responds and reacts with its every fiber to the invisible speaker, points to something outside of itself, beyond its own limits, to the unspoken words of another person. (p.197)

This illustration concerns an individual speaker and listener, but Bakhtin's broader interest was with how people speak as members of groups, and in the case of national memory, this involves using the narrative tools provided by a community. Consider, for example, a case introduced in chapter 1: the dialogue between Vladimir Putin and Western journalists at a 2008 press conference about the war between Russia and Georgia that had occurred a few weeks earlier. Again, Putin opened the session by saying:

> Of course, one of the most difficult problems today is the current situation in the Caucasus: South Ossetia, Abkhazia and every-thing related to the recent tragic events caused by the aggression of the Georgian leadership against these two states. I call them "states," because, as you know, Russia has made a decision to recognise [sic] their sovereignty.

In this statement, Putin did not lay out a full narrative of the war, but he clearly sized it up as "aggression of the Georgian leadership," which was perpetrated "against these two states." This formulation skirts the fact that South Ossetia and Abkhazia had been not sovereign states but rather autonomous regions *within* Georgia and became breakaway regions only as a result of the war fought by Russia and Georgia. Putin touched on this in passing by saying, "I call them [South Ossetia and Abkhazia] 'states,' because, as you know, Russia has made a decision to recognise their sovereignty."[2] This amounts to a kind of rhetorical preemptive strike using hidden dialogism. Namely, it involves addressivity in that it anticipates questions and objections that were expected from the reporters, which had a "determining influence on all the present and visible words" of Putin.

Hidden dialogism emerged several times but in more forceful ways at later points in this press conference as well. The journalists' questions began with a statement by Jonathan Steele from *The Guardian*:

> I understand that you have been extremely angered, as indeed most Russian officials have been, by the western reaction and by the western media reaction. But there were elements of western media which did try and report fairly at the beginning, which did say that the Georgians escalated this war and provoked it, which did go to Vladikavkaz and interview refugees from Ossetia who told stories of Georgian atrocities. But then over the next few days the situation changed and you regained control on behalf of the South Ossetians of the territory. Then Russian forces moved forward. And whereas at the beginning you had the moral high ground, if I may say so, the story changed. And the Russian planes were bombing Gori, suddenly there were more Georgian refugees than Ossetian ones and the operation began to look more like something that was almost about revenge rather than defending South Ossetia.

---

[2] The dim view the world took of this decision is reflected by the fact that Russia has been joined in this decision to this day only by Syria, Nicaragua, Venezuela, and Nauru.

Steele's comment about how "the story changed" into one about a massive invasion by Russian forces and about revenge that resulted in Russia's losing the "moral high ground" elicited a strong response from Putin, who viewed Steele's alternative account as not only different but offensive. It challenged the Expulsion of Alien Enemies narrative template, which underlay Putin's statements and positions Russia as a victim and instead casts Russia as an aggressive, expansionist power, which made it no surprise that Putin rejected Steele's formulation out of hand.

When embedded in a dialogic confrontation such as this, the use of narrative, which often operates without being made explicit, can exacerbate existing differences. This stems from the way narrative tools make sense of information. Namely, the "strange logic" of emplotment makes a narrative a kind of self-enclosed whole (Lotman, 1976) that resists the inclusion of contradictory information. When coming into contact with an opposing emplotment, one alternative would be to consider whether another narrative tool should be considered and even might be preferable for understanding the past. But in many cases, the opposite tendency prevails, namely to hunker down and operate with the affordances provided by a familiar narrative tool. The effect is to create a kind of protective shield or "sealed narrative" (de Waal, 2003) that does not allow contradictory information into the account of events, and the result can be to heighten the conflict between one narrative and another. Rather than the sort of "narrative reconciliation" envisioned by Rauf Garagozov (2019), the outcome all too readily can be one such as Putin's outburst that "This is just amazing. This is unbelievable. This is totally incredible."

As another, more nuanced illustration of hidden dialogism, consider the Russian reaction to a 2008 decision by the European Parliament to name August 23 a "Europe-wide Day of Remembrance for the victims of all totalitarian and authoritarian regimes, to be commemorated with dignity and impartiality."[3] One

---

[3] https://en.wikipedia.org/wiki/European_Day_of_Remembrance_for_Victims_of_Stalinism_and_Nazism

might ask, Why August 23? It turns out that it is the date in 1939 when the Molotov-Ribbentrop Pact was signed, the pact that included secret protocols dividing territories between Germany and the USSR (chapter 3), including territories forcibly annexed by the USSR. As outlined in chapter 4, Soviet authorities denied the very existence of these protocols until 1989. After that, the protocols became an embarrassing episode in the official history of the USSR and have remained so for decades in Russia, making it no surprise that Russian authorities objected to the date's being labeled a day of remembrance in 2008.

From a Russian perspective, the European Parliament's decision constituted an element of hidden dialogism. It was a provocation rather than a simple act of remembrance. In this view, the larger picture of World War II was one in which Soviet forces liberated Europe and saved the world from Fascism, and focusing on a relatively unimportant treaty was a way of failing to play proper respect to the victors in the bigger scheme of things. For people in places such as Georgia and Estonia, however, an essential fact about World War II remains that it led to occupation rather than liberation.

At least for a few years after the declaration in 2008 of the Europe-wide Day of Remembrance, the commemorative status of August 23 was observed in several European countries. In Georgia it came to be labeled the Day of Remembrance for Victims of Totalitarian Regimes. In Russia, not surprisingly, it was largely ignored. However, a close reading of Russian media reveals that this hidden dialogue continued in another form. On August 23, 2017, for example, the Russian news agency TASS noted in its "This Day in History" feature that Soviet forces defeated Nazis in the largest armor battle in history at Kursk in 1943.[4] This is a true statement, and given the massive size of the Battle of Kursk, it quite deserving

***

[4] https://twitter.com/tassagency_en/status/900304494331822080?ref_src=t wsrc%5Etfw%7Ctwcamp%5Etweetembed&ref_url=https%3A%2F%2Fwww. dw.com%2Fen%2Feu-begs-citizens-to-reject-extreme-nationalism-on-european-day-of-remembrance-for-victims-of-stalinism-and-nazism%2Fa-40206677

of mention. However, for Georgians and Estonians, the TASS story amounts to an attempt to change the subject and ignore what really should be recognized on that date, namely the Molotov-Ribbentrop Pact. As such, the utterances of voices critical of Russia may not have appeared in explicit surface form in the TASS article, but "deep traces left by these words have a determining influence on all the present and visible words" (Bakhtin, 1984, p.197).

These illustrations of dialogue between narratives demonstrate Bakhtin's general claims that "any utterance, in addition to its own theme, always responds . . . in one form or another to others' utterances that precede it [and reveals how] the speaker expects a response from [others], an active responsive understanding. The entire utterance is constructed, as it were, in anticipation of encountering this response" (1986a, p.94) and in that sense serves as a sort of co-author. Furthermore, the fact that competing narratives are involved, each emplotting information in accordance with its own strange logic, in this case served to encourage intransigent standoffs grounded in sealed narratives.

5.2.2. Dialogism Within Narrative Texts: Authoritative and Internally Persuasive Discourse

The cases that I have discussed so far involve encounters between one narrative utterance and another. I now turn to a second form of narrative dialogism that occurs *within*, rather than between, narratives and concerns the dynamics of how a speaker's voice harnesses the equipment for living provided by a community. Speaking with the help of narrative tools is typically an unconscious process, but in some instances, speakers are more strategic. This is likely to surface, for example, when speakers are confronted with narrative tools that clearly contradict theirs. Thus, in Putin's encounter with the journalists, he not only relied on the Expulsion of Alien Enemies narrative template but also made it clear that he rejected out of hand any narrative that suggests Russia was an aggressive expansionist power. This came out into the open when he was confronted with journalist Jonathan Steele's claim that "the story changed" into one that challenged the Russian view of events. In this case, it seems that Putin not only disagreed with other accounts but viewed them as simply untrue.

In most discussions about national memory, however, the tensions involved in using narrative tools are largely veiled, but that does not mean they are absent. For example, this can involve a distinction between what Bakhtin termed "authoritative discourse" [*avtoritenoe slovo*] and "internally persuasive discourse" [*vnutrenne-ubeditel'noe slovo*]. The former involves the realm of the "religious, political, moral; the word of a father, of adults and of teachers, etc." (1981, p.342), and it "demands that we acknowledge it, that we make it our own; it binds us, quite independent of any power it might have to persuade us internally; we encounter it with its authority already fused to it" (p.342). In this account, authoritative discourse "demands our unconditional allegiance ... [and] one must either totally affirm it, or totally reject it ... One cannot divide it up—agree with one part, accept but not completely another part, reject utterly a third part" (p.343). The result is that the symbolic means used in authoritative discourse are assumed to be magisterial and to be kept at a distance, which often leads to their becoming untouchable, static, and calcified. Texts written in sacred languages such as the Arabic in the Koran, for example, point to this tendency.

In contrast, internally persuasive discourse "is more akin to retelling a text in one's own words, with one's own accents, gestures, modifications" (Holquist, 1981, p.424). Instead of using sacred texts that must be kept at a distance, internally persuasive discourse involves engaging with them and being allowed to change them as one sees necessary to make them one's own. In such discourse, we are allowed, indeed invited, to agree or disagree with part or all of a text, and we can divide it up and accept one part while rejecting other parts. This can be seen in reported speech, for instance, where the utterance "I did not say that" can be rendered as "He denied that he said it" or "He refused to admit that he had said it." In such cases, the speaker reporting the original utterance is "retelling a text in one's own words, with one's own accents, gestures, modifications" instead of reporting it in direct discourse form, where quotation marks create a boundary between reporting and reported utterances.

When it comes to national memory, members of mnemonic communities often treat certain texts about the past as authoritative discourse. In contrast, others are taken to be part of internally persuasive discourse. In the United States, for example, Abraham Lincoln's Gettysburg Address, one of the great texts of American presidential rhetoric, is treated as almost sacred. It is a standard part of American history taught in U.S. schools and is often memorized and publicly recited by students. As such, it does not invite these students to recast it in their own words or to divide it up by agreeing with one part and rejecting another. Instead, it is taken to be an authoritative text to be kept at a distance, and learning it by heart discourages any idea of infiltrating or revising it. The form of habit involved in this case is of the sort envisioned by Bergson for verbatim memory (chapter 2).

Even the fixed, repeatable texts that qualify as authoritative discourse in a community's language system, however, must take on actual life as an utterance when used by a particular speaker in a particular speech setting, and this can produce outcomes that purveyors of authoritative texts may not anticipate or appreciate. It is possible, for example, to reproduce a text verbatim, indexing its status as authoritative, but to do so in a way that suggests the speaker does not accept its authority. This does not amount to making the text one's own as envisioned in Bakhtin's account of internally persuasive discourse. Instead, it involves authoritative discourse with its requirement that "one must either totally affirm it, or totally reject it" (Bakhtin, 1981, p.343) but authoritative discourse that is taken as an object of resistance.

Consider, for example, Peeter Tulviste's (1994) description of discourse practices by ethnic Estonian students in Soviet schools during periods of ideological regimentation. One way they were able to question, or even mock, the authoritative word of Soviet authority was to recite the words of an official text flawlessly in the classroom—but with too *much* enthusiasm. This could take the form, for instance, of using excessive fervor in reciting official accounts of how Estonians zealously joined the "happy Soviet family" when they were "invited" by their "big socialist brothers" in 1940 as part of the forcible annexation resulting from the Molotov-Ribbentrop Pact. The official versions of events that occurred when Moscow was annexing Estonia were widely rejected by ethnic Estonians in private, but doing so in public spaces such as the classroom could be much more dangerous. Instead, they could participate in what Michel de Certeau (1984) called a "tactic of consumption" in which they "poached" the words of others rather than confronting them overtly as a way of criticizing and rejecting them. Such cases involved operating as "guerillas" on the symbolic territory of Soviet authorities. In the terminology of James Scott (1985), these students were employing "weapons of the weak." In Bakhtin's terms, the effect is to transform key segments of authoritative discourse into internally persuasive discourse.

Such tactics of consumption in Soviet Estonia involved treading a fine line when it came to how the voice of the speaker co-authored the text, and it could play out in different ways, depending on whether the classroom teacher chose to focus on the text of the language system or on the unique, unrepeatable pole of a student's utterance. Focusing on the former amounted to giving the student an ideological pass and could signal that the teacher recognized the legitimacy of resistance for ethnic Estonians. Focusing on the latter, however, could lead to a severe reprimand about the student's cynicism and lack of patriotism about official Soviet ideology. In the Soviet setting such practices were part of a larger struggle between official and unofficial history (Tulviste & Wertsch, 1992) where virtually every ethnic Estonian knew two different versions of the past.

Such cases illustrate the possibilities of history instruction as a rich context for studying authoritative and internally persuasive discourse in national memory. Soviet authorities were especially heavy-handed in producing authoritative accounts of the past, but countless stories of subtle resistance by Soviet citizens indicate that they found ways to resist them. These citizens also proved to be effective in harnessing internally persuasive discourse as they worked as "memory activists" (Gluck, 2007) by making accounts of the past objects of engagement and questioning rather than veneration and memorization. These are issues that arise in history instruction just about everywhere, and they touch on the distinction between memory and history outlined in chapter 3. Harnessing that distinction, we might say that national memory is a way of relating to the past that tends to rely on authoritative discourse, whereas history is a way of relating to the past that relies on internally persuasive discourse. As such, authoritative discourse is more helpful in preserving an existing narrative, even at the expense of evidence, whereas internally persuasive discourse is helpful in challenging a narrative in light of criticism and evidence such as newly discovered archives.

From this perspective, analytic history is not distinguished by being simply more true or closer to "what really happened" than national memory. Indeed, it is possible, in principle, for national memory to provide a more accurate account of the past than analytic history. Instead, what sets history apart from memory is that it involves institutionally organized processes such as the disciplined review of evidence and the rational consideration of alternative accounts of the past. Historians may never fully live up to this "noble dream" (Novick, 1988), but their efforts nonetheless shape their discussions in ways that distinguish it from national memory.

The difference between authoritative and internally persuasive discourse typically involves tendencies along a continuum rather than an ironclad, mutually exclusive distinction, and this plays out in understanding the difference between memory and history. For example, it provides a reminder that history instruction, especially in primary and secondary school education, is a kind of hybrid construction. It is called upon to meet the demands of *both* national memory and analytic history. In the former capacity, it serves the effort to socialize informed and loyal citizens, but in the latter, it is tasked with developing critical thinking skills in students that will equip them to challenge authoritative texts in ways similar to how academic historians would. As Sam Wineburg (2018) has noted, the result is a kind of vacillation between these two objectives that plays out in endless arguments that have been part of history and historical pedagogy.

These discussions, which can be found everywhere, often touch on the importance of including heroes in accounts of the past. In posing the question of "why we teach about heroism (and villainy) in the first place," for example, Frederick Hess and Brendan Bell (2017) argue, "We do so because it helps us teach students about our common values and forges a sense of shared purpose,"[5] pointing to the identity project that is part of national memory. It was a concern with this goal of history instruction that led Lynne Cheney, a former head of the National Endowment for the Humanities, to level withering criticism at efforts of some scholars to improve history instruction in the United States. In a 1994 op-ed in the *Wall Street Journal* she called the national history standards created by these scholars as encouraging a "grim and gloomy" picture of America's past driven by political correctness. Gary Nash (2004), one of the creators of the standards, criticized Cheney's comments in turn, noting that she "pronounced the standards project a disaster for giving insufficient attention to Robert E. Lee and

[5] http://www.aei.org/publication/teach-heroes-complexities/

the Wright brothers and far too much to obscure figures (such as Harriet Tubman) or patriotically embarrassing episodes (such as the Ku Klux Klan and McCarthyism),"[6] And in *History on Trial*, Nash, Charlotte Crabtree, and Ross Dunn (1997) go into several additional dimensions of this struggle over national memory.

Such disputes are often framed in terms of which narrative tools should be included in history instruction, and this is clearly important. However, they also turn on differences over narrative dialogism in the form of authoritative versus internally persuasive discourse. The former demands that students accept history textbooks and other materials as they are given and do not challenge them or "agree with one part, accept but not completely another part, reject utterly a third part" (Bakhtin, 1981, p.343). To be sure, students in the United States are generally not required to recite verbatim segments of material from textbooks and refrain from any criticism of them as may have been the practice in Soviet schools. Nevertheless, authoritative discourse enters the picture in the form of standards that guide the selection of history textbooks and the standards used in history examinations. The struggles over official history that occur at this level, though indirect, inject authoritative discourse into history instruction.

In contrast to figures such as Cheney, many analysts have focused less on what heroes and episodes should be included in history textbooks and more on critical thinking skills that students should develop. A well-known proponent of this approach is James Loewen (2018), author of the multi-edition bestseller *Lies My Teacher Told Me: Everything Your American History Textbook Got Wrong*. A former high school history teacher himself, Loewen is highly critical of accounts of America's past provided in standard history textbooks. He sees them as biased and often geared toward skirting difficult issues such as the treatment of Native Americans or Reconstruction. In place of "pathetic pedagogy" (p.xii), Loewen

---

[6] https://historynewsnetwork.org/article/8418

calls for a concerted effort to foster critical thinking in students, a process that "requires assembling data to back up one's opinion" (p.xiii). In the absence of such thinking, students are encouraged to "falsely conclude that all opinions are somehow equal" (p.xiii). Loewen's goal is not to turn every student into a little professional historian but to foster better critical thinking skills in informed American citizens. For him, "When confronting a claim about the distant past or a statement about what happened yesterday, students—indeed, all Americans—need to develop informed skepticism, not nihilistic cynicism" (p.xix).

Loewen's writings are part of a larger discussion that includes research by scholars such as Wineburg (2001, 2018), who has conducted empirical studies of how students and teachers engage with accounts of the past such as those found in history textbooks. Wineburg has expanded this to texts found on the internet in studies of "online civic reasoning." Part of his concern is how "The Internet has obliterated authority" (2018, p.3), making the task of creating shared accounts of the past all the more difficult. If history instruction in the Soviet Union and other authoritarian settings might be viewed as overly restricted in the textual materials that could be used, Wineburg's concern is with having unlimited access to materials about the past. It would appear that we could end up with as many accounts of the past as individuals who have access to the internet, leading to a breakdown of the centripetal forces for binding communities together on the basis of the shared "rich legacies of memory" envisioned by Renan. Such a vision could be part of what Wineburg (2018) calls the "chilling future of learning the past" (p.5). However, data such as those reported in chapter 4 suggest that at least for now, narrative templates and habits seem to be holding mnemonic communities together to a striking degree— sometimes in surprising ways.

In sum, the distinction between authoritative and internally persuasive discourse provides another perspective on how narrative dialogism shapes the use of a narrative. This makes it possible to go a step beyond analyses of narrative dialogism that focus on how one narrative engages with another. Delving into this form of what might be termed "intra-narrative dialogism" is often crucial when trying to understand the dynamics of resistance to official history and the difference between history and memory. It is particularly important when examining processes that are veiled and otherwise likely to be overlooked in discussions of national memory.

5.2.3. "Bivocalism": Dialogism Within Narrative Voices

At many points in his account of dialogism, Bakhtin emphasized that multiple voices can be heard within a single text or even a single word. This suggests that narrative dialogism runs all the way from having two extended explicit narratives laid out side by side to multivoicedness within the confines of a very condensed form. In the previous section I presented authoritative and internally persuasive discourse as an example of the latter. Another condensed form of dialogism occurs when multivoicedness occurs within the speaking voice itself. This is an idea that has been explored by Nutsa Batiashvili (2018) in her account of "bivocal" tendencies in the national memory of the Republic of Georgia.

Elements of bivocalism may be found in nearly all national communities, but Batiashvili has outlined an especially pronounced case in what Bakhtin (1986a) would call a social language that is used in Georgia. This is a social language that has emerged over centuries as Georgians lived through repeated invasions by foreign conquerors but managed to accommodate to their demands while also remaining committed to their own national identity project. In earlier times this involved Persian, Arabic, and Ottoman colonizers, but for the past few centuries this has been largely about maintaining a distinct national identity in the context of being part of imperial Russia.

Batiashvili argues that out of this historical experience "two distinct but mutually constitutive discursive genres" (p.xv) have evolved, "one based in the voice of self-idealization and the other in self-condemnation" (p.xv). The outcome is a "bivocal nation" in which the past "is characterized as series of assaults by powerful enemies and Georgians as heroes who fight for freedom, but also as collaborators who ally themselves with the enemy for their personal gain" (p.xvi). In her extensive analyses, Batiashvili examines the historical origins of Georgian bivocalism and also provides ethnographic accounts of continuing struggles in the present over memory and history.

These two strands of her argument are reflected in a comment by Ketino, a history professor in her fifties who was one of the subjects of Batiashvili's ethnographic study. In an interview, Ketino says, "When I go into a freshmen class, . . . the first thing I tell my students is that Georgia's entire history can be expressed in two proverbs: 'better a glorious death than a life dragged out in shame' and: 'when a bear overpowers you, you should call it papa' " (p.27). Her formulation of dueling proverbs reflects the irreducible tension that Batiashvili sees between two simultaneous proclivities: one toward "self-idealization" and the other toward "self-condemnation" (p.189). This tension is driven by "sub-cultural alterities in which what differentiates 'us' from another version of 'us'—our internal *other*, is a particular reading of the past and hence a particular belief in *who we are*" (p.30). It is a tension that exists "within, as well as between [Georgian] speakers" (p.xvi).

Batiashvili develops several of her ideas by examining the hothouse of national memory debates in post-Soviet Georgia. This was a context involving several camps, each with its own internal tensions. On one side are "two kinds of elitist groups—the 'old intelligentsia' and the 'new NGO[7] intellectuals' (the latter ended up running [President] Saakashvili's pro-Western government)"

---

[7] Non-governmental organization.

(p.xxiii). The other side is made up of conservative nationalist groups committed to Georgian purity based on language and religion. The heated debate between them echoes its "origins in the nineteenth-century rhetorical practices and specifically in the attempts by Georgia's founding fathers to forge a new nation within the margins of the Russian Empire" (p.xix). These origins are reflected in the two proverbs mentioned by Ketino in the previous paragraph. Over the past three centuries a modern Georgian national identity emerged with the help of public intellectuals such as Ilia Chavchavadze (1837–1907), who, significantly, were educated in Russia and took Russia to be a window onto Europe but also brought ideas about nations and nationalism to their project in forming a Georgian nation.

In this setting Georgia did not have the luxury of developing a coherent national identity during a period of peaceful reflection on how members of the nation can be "imagined as a solidarity of like individuals" (p.xviii). Instead, the effort has always involved "fragmentation and a constant tension between different versions of 'us'" (p.xviii). This longstanding struggle has played out in different ways throughout history, and in post-Soviet Georgia Batiashvili focuses on the "rifts between traditionalist and modernist visions of the nation's future" (p.xviii). She argues that these rifts in public debate are reflected within individual Georgians as well, resulting in "not two polarized representations of the national-self, but two voices that stem from a single cultural form, such as a national narrative" (p.xviii).

The illustrations I have used in earlier chapters have emphasized a critical, even anti-Russian stance that is part of Georgian national memory, but that is only part of the story in this bivocal memory project. Georgian history also includes episodes in which Russia came to its aid and served as a protector against invasions of Persian, Ottoman, or Arab enemies. Perhaps not surprisingly, conflicting perspectives are a pervasive part of all these episodes. The best-known such episode is Georgian king Erekle's decision in 1783 to ask for Russian help in defending against an Ottoman invasion, a decision that involved intrigue and double dealing that left Georgia as a colonized entity in the Russian Empire. Reflecting on this, one of Batiashvili's interviewees, an historian named Dodo, pointed to the circumstances that have led Georgia to vacillate between self-idealization and self-condemnation:

> [I]t is often said that small nations should not go to war, because they will be destroyed and it's better for them to be submissive . . . never once did Georgia have an enemy its own size. The Persian Empire was huge, the Ottoman Empire was huge . . . and here we are fighting Russia . . . humans fought and this heroic spirit and this consciousness that a nation must fight for its integrity and for its statehood, this must not be lost, otherwise a nation will become obedient, and nothing, nothing. (p.185)

Dodo's assertive stance would appear to lead straight to the conclusion that Russia is an implacable enemy of Georgia today, but again, bivocality emerges in reflections on the role of Russia as a protector. For example, the Russian Orthodox Church is viewed by many Georgian nationalists as critical for preserving traditional culture in the face of Europeanization. This is part of heated debates between Russophiles and nationalists as political factions, but it is also part of national consciousness at the individual level. Batiashvili reports, for example, a discussion with Dmitri about the "irrational nationalism" of the "pro-Russian 'camp' " in Georgia in which Dmitri reports on a conversation he had had with a Georgian actor Jiani. This actor was from Abkhazia, which had a contentious relationship with Georgia before it became a breakaway region in the 2008 war with Russia, but the sort of ambivalence he shows is not unknown among Georgians more generally. In his interview, Dmitri reflected:

> Considered separately as a person, [Jiani] is a man who loves his country, his homeland, and he is an excellent *tamada*

[toastmaster of the ritualistic Georgian feast]. There's nothing better than sitting with him at the table, he will tell you poems and you will know there is no greater patriot than him. But he is a distinguished Russophile. He despises Europe, he despises the West, hates America. Well, what can one do?! This was caused by our geo-politics—that one part of our society sees salvation there and another one sees it in Europe. (p.182)

As Batiashvili notes, the ambivalence reflected in such reports can be difficult for non-Georgians to understand, but that may have more to do with the ubiquitous and entrenched nature of this ambivalence in Georgia than with a difference in kind. Seeds of ambivalence can probably be found everywhere, though they are often muted or suppressed. Indeed, they are likely to arise in any analysis concerned with narrative dialogism, and figures such as Loewen might celebrate it as the key to developing students' critical capacities.

But Batiashvili's ethnographic and historical study suggests that the Georgian case is unique in certain respects, and perhaps the best way to understand this is in terms of the power of the mental habits involved. Bivocalism seems to be such a fundamental part of national memory in Georgia that it has given rise to mental habits that differ from those of other national communities. It seems difficult in this community to provide accounts of the past that are not grounded in simultaneous self-idealization and self-condemnation of the sort that Batiashvili has outlined and sees as going hand in hand in everyday discourse, official history textbooks, and other aspects of Georgian national life.

5.3. National Narrative Projects

The instances of narrative dialogism I have discussed so far involve specific narratives, narrative templates, and privileged event narratives. In order to fill out the picture of how they contribute to national identity projects, however, at least one additional form of narrative needs to be taken into account—what I term a "national narrative project" (NNP). An NNP is a kind of overall biography or life history of a national community that is directed toward an aspiration or ideal that guides a national community's understanding of itself. It is similar to accounts of events such as World War II in that it has a beginning and a middle, but instead of a "sense of an ending" (Kermode, 1967) of the usual sort, it culminates in an aspiration for the future.

My account of NNPs draws on Alisdair MacIntyre's writings about the narrative organization of individuals' lives and moral choices. In MacIntyre's view, "I can only answer the question 'What am I to do?' if I can answer the prior question 'Of what story or stories do I find myself a part?'" (1984, p.216), a claim that he applied to "enacted narratives" (chapter 4) as well as the stories we tell overtly when reflecting on actions in the past, present, or future. In discussing this issue, MacIntyre took it as a given that the stories involved reflect particular historical and cultural settings. Indeed, "an understanding of any society, including our own [begins with] . . . the stock of stories which constitute its initial dramatic resources" (p.216), with the implication that "the story of my life is always embedded in the story of those communities from which I derive my identity" (p.221). The stock of stories in the European tradition MacIntyre explored, for example, includes accounts of "wicked stepmothers, lost children, good but misguided kings, wolves that suckle young boys, youngest sons who receive no inheritance but must make their own way in the world and oldest sons who waste their inheritance on riotous living and go into exile to live with the swine" (p.216).

Building on these ideas, MacIntyre went on to explore a claim about a larger narrative framework that shapes relationships among the items in a stock of stories. Far from being a random list, this stock comprises an organized meaning system that underpins views about virtue, the good, and a life that is worth living. Not surprisingly, MacIntyre turned once again to narrative to formulate this meaning system, asserting that "personal identity is just that identity presupposed by the unity of the character which the unity of a narrative requires" (p.218). It is an overall life narrative that provides the answer to the question: "In what does the unity of an individual life consist?" (p.218), something that requires "the unity of a narrative embodied in a single life" (p.218), a unity that allows us to interpret the significance of particular stories and acts in our life in light of the larger project. Part of the impetus for these ideas was MacIntyre's objection to movements in analytic philosophy and sociology that question the notion of a coherent, integrated self. He decried, for example, efforts by the sociologist Erving Goffman (1959), who "liquidated the self into its role-playing, arguing that the self is no more than a 'peg' on which the clothes of the role are hung" (MacIntyre, 1984, p.32).

Central to MacIntyre's understanding of the unity of character is the notion of "narrative quest" (p.219). Such quests "sometimes fail, are frustrated, abandoned, or dissipated into distractions, and human lives in all these ways also may fail" (p.219), but it remains the case that the "criteria for success or failure in a human life are the criteria for success or failure in a narrated or to-be-narrated quest" (p.219). Just as the "initial dramatic resources" involved in an identity project differ between communities, narrative quests also vary, and in this connection, MacIntyre mentioned cases ranging from Aristotle's Athenian gentleman to Jane Austen's 18th-century Christian notion of constancy to Benjamin Franklin's ideals of cleanliness, silence, industry, and the drive to acquire wealth. These visions of virtue and the good life differ, but they have in common some narrative quest that shapes the meanings of the specific narratives and narrative templates that individuals use to make sense of their lives.

A narrative quest unfolds as it is being lived, with the result that "at any given point in an enacted dramatic narrative we do not know what will happen next" (p.215). The unpredictability, however, "coexists with a second crucial characteristic of all lived narratives, a certain teleological character" (p.215). The dialectic between lived events and one's sense of where the lifetime is headed means that "There is no present which is not informed by some image of the future and an image of the future which always presents itself in the form of a *telos*—or a variety of ends or goals—toward which we are either moving or failing to move in the present. Unpredictability and teleology therefore coexist as part of our lives" (pp.215–216).

As noted in chapter 2, confusion can sometimes arise when constructs created for individuals are applied to groups, but by maintaining a focus on individuals *as members of a group* (chapter 1), it is possible to trace out some implications of MacIntyre's ideas on narrative quests and how they shape the mental habits of a community used to understand their group and stories they are part of. To be sure, this may involve misguided ideas on the part of the group members themselves about "analytical groupism" (Brubaker et al., 2004), but these ideas nonetheless guide everyday thinking and provide the foundation for understanding the role of NNPs in national memory.

These projects reflect the aspirations of a national community, aspirations that are often discussed in terms of a national idea. Such ideas have long been the focus of political rhetoric and scholarly research, but usually their implications for mental and discursive processes remain unexamined. What follows is not a general review of NNPs that can provide insight into the mental habits of all national communities but instead a set of illustrations geared toward introducing the notion of NNPs. Specifically, it is a discussion of how narrative quests and NNPs play out in the United States, Russia, and China.

A couple of preliminary assumptions are worth noting. First, even though state authorities and other elites routinely try to forge unanimity around a single national narrative among members of their community, competing visions are invariably in play. Hence my comments about America, Russia, and China amount to an effort to identify a leading NNP but leave open the possibility that others are at work as well. The second is an assumption about method and evidence. Perhaps the most obvious place to look for evidence about an NNP is in the political rhetoric used by national leaders, especially when appealing to a national audience in times of crisis. In what follows, I take such rhetorical performances as a key source of evidence for claims about NNPs.

5.3.1. America's Quest for a More Perfect Democratic Union

A good candidate for an NNP for America is the notion of a more perfect union grounded in democracy. Since its founding, the country has struggled with how to form a national community on the basis of a guiding idea rather than ethnic ties or territorial boundaries, and this has involved ongoing tensions among diverse groups and interests that found themselves living together. The nation's founders were deeply concerned with this and sometimes despaired of ever forming a single polity. This was signaled in the first sentence of the preamble of the U.S. Constitution with its mention of the need "to form a more perfect Union." Of course, the founders were not interested in any union forged by any means. A union based on hereditary royalty was what they were seeking to escape, and a union based on authoritarian or totalitarian principles ran counter to the constitution they were writing. Instead, they assumed this union would build on a constitutional democracy, which served to make their task only more challenging.

The product of their efforts was far from perfect, and a century after they created the Constitution, the ongoing struggle, exacerbated by divisions over slavery, resulted in the American

Civil War. Even that traumatic event, however, did not settle how Americans should pursue a more perfect union and live up to the aspiration of the national motto "*E pluribus unum*." Leaping ahead to the 20th century, civil rights leaders such as Martin Luther King were still talking about a dream of a future in which racial divisions would no longer threaten the unity of the nation. And in the 21st century Barack Obama invoked the quest for "a more perfect union" in another memorable speech in 2008 about the continuing racial divides that afflict America.

The very expression "more perfect union" is revealing when trying to understand the ongoing narrative quest of the American national community. The mention of union—including the Union at issue in the America Civil War—reflects both an aspiration and an underlying fear. The centripetal forces drawing Americans together always seem at risk of succumbing to centrifugal forces that could tear society apart, and hence the ideal end point of the national narrative remains a quest, not an accomplishment, an endless process suggested by the "more perfect" part of the expression. But it is a process with a telos of more than simply avoiding disintegration; it is a quest to create a society based on constitutional democracy that could serve as an aspiration for America but also as a model for humankind.

This combined aspiration is reflected in remarks Abraham Lincoln made to Congress on December 1, 1862, during some of the darkest days of the Civil War, when he wrote:

> We *say* we are for the Union. The world will not forget that we say this. We know how to save the Union. The world knows we do know how to save it. We—even *we here*—hold the power, and bear the responsibility. In *giving* freedom to the *slave*, we *assure* freedom to the *free*—honorable alike in what we give, and what we preserve. We shall nobly save, or meanly lose, the last best hope of earth. Other means may succeed; this could not fail. The way is plain, peaceful, generous, just—a way which, if

followed, the world will forever applaud, and God must forever bless.[8]

Lincoln's remarks point to the fact that the more perfect democratic union he envisioned was not only part of a narrative quest for America but also represented "the last best hope" for all of humankind. This assumption that America's aspirations were actually universal is reflected in another expression often associated with the national self-image—a "city on a hill." This is an expression that traces its origins to a sermon by Puritan John Winthrop in 1630, but as Abram van Engen (2020) shows, it actually did not play an important role in American political rhetoric until much later. It is an image based on ideals of freedom and democracy for America that I shall examine in more detail in chapter 6, but for now it is worth noting its limitations as an NNP because it is often taken to suggest accomplishment rather than quest. For this reason, it sometimes has been the focus of stark, seemingly nonnegotiable opposition between those who celebrate America as a beacon to others (e.g., Gingrich and Gingrich, 2011; Reagan, 1989) and those who reject the notion of it as a beacon, sometimes even calling the notion a "sentimental fantasy" (Nguyen, 2016, p.3).

David Blight (2001, 2019) has written extensively about the complex history of America's aspiration to be a more perfect democratic union, including the "tormented relationship between healing and justice" (2001, p.57) it involved. This is a relationship that played out in the decades following the Civil War and gave rise to a misleading semblance of union that managed temporarily to cover over deep divisions about racial justice. The "reconciliationist" vision (2001, p.2) that eventually prevailed provided deeply unsatisfactory accounts of national memory for many people in America and failed to acknowledge that the country remains a deeply "composite nation" (2019). At the same time, however, Blight points to

---

[8] http://www.abrahamlincolnonline.org/lincoln/speeches/congress.htm

an unending quest in that "many Americans still want to believe in a narrative of American history bound up in this perception of the possibilities of multi-ethnic and cultural harmony" (2001, p.4).

This suggests that the aspiration for a more perfect union based on democratic principles is far from dead and the search goes on for "a cohesive narrative of progress and greatness, the story of a special problem-solving nation providing beacons of light and cities on hills for all the world to model" (p.4). In the end, the challenge remains one of how to "imagine a unified national narrative out of our vast multiplicity, our violence, our embrace of and hostility to immigrants, our racism, our profound tragedies" (p.5), especially in light of the fact that "Such a unified story was all but obliterated in the Civil War" (p.5), leaving the "recurring dilemma with white supremacy and white nationalism" (p.5).

Blight's account is a reminder of the bitter divisions over what "more perfect" should be and attempts to find "pleasing narratives" (2019, p.8) about it that stand up to honest scrutiny. Nonetheless, the quest for a more perfect democratic union serves as an NNP and as such provides an interpretive framework for narratives about events in American memory. This sometimes surfaces in overt form, as in Obama's 2016 speech about the continuing struggle with racism in America, and in others it lies just below the surface as reflected in warnings about "class warfare" that continue to be effective in squelching talk about tax increases on wealthy Americans. In such cases, specific narratives derive part of their meaning from the fact that they are in hidden dialogue with an NNP, a form of narrative dialogism that plays a formative role in national memory.

5.3.2. Russia's Spiritual Mission

Much of my discussion of Russia has focused on the Expulsion of Alien Enemies story narrative template, but precisely because it is a template and hence applies to multiple events, it does not qualify as a national narrative project, which, again, is a single extended story of the entire life course of a nation. Furthermore, each instantiation of the Expulsion of Alien Enemies narrative template has an ending, which also disqualifies it as an NNP, given that the latter is an aspiration or a narrative quest toward a general telos.

Instead, good candidates for a Russian NNP are to be found in the countless discussions of the "Russian idea" that have been part of the nation's life for centuries (Berdyaev, 1992; McDaniel, 1996). These discussions typically focus on Russia's unique spiritual mission, but they have expanded to the point that they have been taken up by secular governments as well. The early years of Boris Yeltsin's post-Soviet government, with all of its plans to join the secular European community, for example, saw the establishment of official commissions to search for the Russian idea that could guide society.

In most instances, however, discussions of the Russian idea have focused on spiritual issues, especially those at the heart of Russian Orthodoxy. These issues often come with patriotic, nationalistic, or even xenophobic overtones such as those found in writings by Dostoevsky in the 19th century and Solzhenitsyn in the 20th. One manifestation of the Russian idea that is familiar to virtually every Russian concerns "Moscow as the Third Rome" (Berdyaev, 1992). This notion originated in a missive by Monk Filofei of Pskov, who wrote in 1510 that "Two Romes have fallen. The third stands. And there will be no fourth. No one shall replace . . . Christian Tsardom." In Filofei's account, the decadence and spiritual decay that led to the demise of Christian Rome as head of the church in 330 C.E. and then to the fall of Constantinople in 1453 meant that it was Moscow's destiny to take up the mantle of true Christianity for all time in the form of Russian Orthodoxy. Seeing Moscow as the third Rome is part of vision of Russia as a bulwark against moral degeneracy and decay in the West, and it provides the basis for a narrative quest in pursuit of a unique spiritual mission. It points to the telos that can be used, for example, to make sense of the suffering Russia has been called on to experience at the hand of alien enemies.

To be sure, this narrative quest has sometimes been frustrated and has "dissipated into distractions," as MacIntyre would have said, but in the end the criteria for success or failure in Russian national life based on its spiritual mission are "the criteria for success or failure" (MacIntyre, 1984). Conservative Russian nationalists warn that their nation loses sight of this narrative quest at its own peril. That is the message Aleksandr Solzhenitsyn brought to his fellow Russians in his bitter criticism of Soviet Marxism, which involved the invasion of socialism and communism in accordance with the Expulsion of Alien Enemies narrative template. The larger interpretive context of his condemnation, however, was the NNP concerned with Russia's spiritual mission. From this perspective, the moral leadership of Moscow as the Third Rome may have been subverted for decades, but with the Expulsion of Alien Enemy ideas of Marxism, Russia was able to return to pursuing its true teleological trajectory. For many Westerners, it is difficult to understand how expelling Marxism-Leninism falls under the same interpretive umbrella as expelling Hitler or Napoleon, but the divine mission of Russia and Moscow entailed in the Russian NNP provides a context for how this fits together. It is the larger narrative quest that exists in dialogue with narrative templates, specific narratives, and privileged event narratives that are key to defining the Russian national community.

5.3.3. China's Narrative Quest as the Central Kingdom

Up to this point in my discussion of China, I have focused on the Century of Humiliation as a privileged event narrative. This story does not qualify as an NNP, however, given that it involves a mere century whereas the nation began functioning as an organized state 2,000 years ago. Instead, a more likely candidate for an NNP would be the idea of China as the Central Kingdom. Ethnocentrism and national narcissism are part of countries' memory everywhere (chapter 4), but they take on a special form in the case of China with its longstanding notion of being the Central Kingdom under the heavens. Indeed, the term in Mandarin for China, "Zhonggou," means Middle Kingdom or Central Kingdom and has been used to refer to the country since the Han Dynasty (206 B.C.E.–220 C.E.).

The Central Kingdom (Fairbank, 1969) and "Sinocentrism" (Tin-bor Hui, 2018) have been a topic of scholarship in the West for decades. Fairbank wrote about the "Chinese doctrine of superiority" and how it came to take the form of deeply held assumptions about a "universal kingship" that extends to all peoples of the world. This view became "thoroughly institutionalized and preserved as the official myth of the state" over many centuries, suggesting the existence of a set of mental habits. Starting out in the form of Chinese emperors' view of the "barbarian" groups on its borders, it evolved into a "political theory of the Son of Heaven's superiority over foreigners" from other parts of the world and "was part and parcel of the power structure of the Chinese state" (Fairbank, 1969, p.459).

This worldview is shaped by Confucian assumptions about the natural hierarchy of authority that governs relationships both within and among states. The upshot is that China has "its own long history of international relations that is quite distinct from that of the West" (Acharya & Buzan, 2010, p.2), making it into "the poster child for non-Western IR" (Hui, 2018). Whereas Eurocentric international relations theory has been built on the assumption that there is no natural hierarchy among states and hence that world politics exists a state of anarchy (Waltz, 1979), a Sinocentric approach assumes that hierarchy naturally exists and must be respected. As Wang (2012) notes, this means that "China was not prepared to join the family of nations as an equal member, even after the West forcefully compelled it to open to the world following the Opium War" (p.73). Instead, "China's special 'Middle Kingdom syndrome'" (Xu, 2001, cited in Wang) made it difficult for it to "adapt psychologically to the new reality of international affairs" (p.73).

For centuries, Chinese emperors were supreme within their own state and never had to deal with equals outside of it, and the habits of thought that grew out of this provided, in turn, the means for reinforcing their efforts to remain supreme within it. Some observers have credited this approach with yielding stability and peaceful relations between China and the world. Xuetong Yan (2001) has gone so far as to claim that the Confucian concept of benevolence "will influence international norms and make international society more civilized" (quoted in Hui, 2018). This benign view, however, is hardly shared by all. Robert Kelly (2011) has noted historical episodes where "non-Confucians could be Confucianized by force for their own good by 'righteous war,'" an approach that sounds more like Western ideas about civilizing missions and clashes of civilizations than a benign Confucian vision. The upshot, however, is that a doctrine of superiority, reinforced by Confucian assumptions about a natural hierarchy of nations with China at the apex, has been an imagined telos that underpins the virtue to which the national community aspires, and this has shaped its relations with other nations.

An event often used to illustrate differences between China and the West on these matters is the 1793 visit by English Lord George Macartney to the court of the Qianlong emperor. Macartney was sent by King George to persuade the Chinese emperor to open up port cities to trade and as sites for repairing British ships. He brought with him 600 packages of stunning gifts, including a clock of very advanced design, that he thought would thoroughly astonish his hosts. But the Chinese understood Macartney's mission to be one of supplication and bringing tribute to the emperor, who refused to listen to the British demands. He also ordered Macartney

to perform the kowtow and responded to King George's communication with his own message:[9]

> You, O King from afar, have yearned after the blessings of our
> civilization, and in your eagerness to come into touch with our
> converting influence have sent an Embassy across the sea bearing
> a memorial. I have already taken note of your respectful spirit of
> submission, have treated your mission with extreme favour and
> loaded it with gifts, besides issuing a mandate to you, O King, and
> honouring you with the bestowal of valuable presents. Thus has
> my indulgence been manifested. Our dynasty's majestic virtue
> has penetrated unto every country under Heaven, and Kings of
> all nations have offered their costly tribute by land and sea. As
> your Ambassador can see for himself, we possess all things. I set
> no value on objects strange or ingenious, and have no use for
> your country's manufactures.

This inauspicious beginning of modern relations between China
and Europe unfolded over the next 150 years in conflict and bit-
terness, leaving behind the Century of Humiliation narrative.
What is perhaps most astonishing to the Western eye is that a
basic confidence in China's position seems to have remained in-
tact throughout this century, as well as the devastation of Chairman
Mao's Great Leap Forward and the Cultural Revolution. All of these
were periods in which intellectuals such as Lu Xun (1918) were
excoriating Chinese culture for its failures, but elements of the
"Chinese doctrine of superiority" (Fairbank, 1969) nevertheless
retained its status as a guiding vision.

In the 21st century traumatic events of the sort seen in the
Century of Humiliation have come to an end and the Central
Kingdom idea has re-emerged, perhaps stronger than ever. Piyush
Singh (2013) notes, for example, that Chinese president Xi Jinping

[9] http://afe.easia.columbia.edu/ps/china/qianlong_edicts.pdf

has tied his China Dream program to "the old Confucian concept of the 'Middle Kingdom' whereby China was at the centre [*sic*] of the world affairs and different countries paid homage to it." In dusting off this national project, Xi asserted that "China no longer needs to 'bide its time and hide its capabilities' as propounded by the great reformer Deng Xiaoping."[10] Similarly, in his account of "Sinocentrism for the information age," Christopher Ford (2013) traces mental habits back to China's long-established national view of itself and challenges its "conceptual imperialism, at least in aspiration, suggesting that it is a Chinese strategic objective to control the world's discourse about China."

In sum, the Central Kingdom NNP is a narrative quest that provides a general framework within which the other narrative tools shared by members of this Chinese mnemonic community are interpreted. For example, the Century of Humiliation privileged event narrative gets much of its emotional power through its hidden dialogism with this NNP. If China is assumed to exist at the apex of a natural hierarchy of nations, then being humiliated at the hands of others who were clearly lower in this hierarchy is especially painful. This applies with particular force in the case of Japan with its ancient positioning as the "little brother" of China.

5.3.4. NNPs as Context

The three illustrations from America, Russia, and China that I have outlined are just that—illustrations intended to round out the notion of an NNP. As such, they hardly do justice to the complexities of any of these cases. They do, however, touch on a basic insight of MacIntyre's about an overarching biographical narrative of a nation with which specific narratives and narrative templates exist

[10] http://logos.nationalinterest.in/2013/12/chinese-dream-return-to-the-concept-of-middle-kingdom/

in dialogue—often hidden dialogue—and derive part of their meaning. In this view, members of national communities size up situations and make decisions "in the light of certain conceptions of a possible shared future, a future in which certain possibilities beckon us forward and others repel us, some seem already foreclosed and others perhaps inevitable" (MacIntyre, 1984, p.215).

The larger view that emerges is one in which individuals as members of national groups use the narrative equipment provided by their community to make sense of events in the past and present. But this equipment for living involves more than specific narratives containing concrete information about times, places, and actors. It also operates in the form of narrative templates and mental habits that come to be shared by members of groups. Because these are schematic and abstract, their impact on our accounts of the past is easy to overlook, making it more difficult to detect and reflect on them than is the case with specific narratives. And operating in the background at an even further remove are NNPs. Rather than being concerned with particular events, these cover the entire bi-ography of national communities, and in contrast to narratives with a clear-cut sense of an ending, they culminate in an aspiration for the nation, an ideal outcome that the community strives to ap-proximate. NNPs are even more abstract and lie deeper as an un-derlying code than narrative templates, but the narrative tools we use to make sense of the past often exist as stories "with a sideward glance" in hidden dialogism with them.

5.4. Summing Up: Dialogism and the Meaning of National Narratives

In previous chapters I outlined claims about how the "strange logic" of narrative emplotment shapes the meanings we assign to events in national memory. This involved focusing on narrative tools taken one at a time, as if their sole function is to serve as equipment for living as we think and speak about events from the past. The resulting picture is one of what can be called the "referential" function of narrative. But narrative tools have a fundamental "dialogic" function as well in the sense that they respond to or reflect other narratives in their context, and this shapes the form that they take and the meaning they have in national memory.

The upshot is that the meaning of national narratives needs to be approached in two different but complementary ways. One set of questions concerns what a narrative means by virtue of how it emplots events, often with help of habits grounded in narrative templates. A different assessment of meaning grows out of how a narrative responds to the narratives around it. In some cases, this can involve how one narrative responds to another in a sort of turn-taking dialogue, and in others, the interanimation of multiple narratives is condensed and plays out within a single utterance. And in addition to these forms of dialogism, a more general background framework is provided by NNPs that cover the entire life of a nation in the form of a narrative quest.

Of course, all these dialogic processes involve individuals as active agents. Narratives do not speak in and of themselves or act in consort with other narratives except through the voices of actual speakers or writers. These voices, however, are co-authored by the narrative tools provided by a community. The two issues of referential and dialogic functions are distinct and require different forms of evidence, adding an essential component to the larger story of how members of communities use national narratives as equipment for living in order to size up events from the past.

6

Managing National Memory

6.1. Introduction

Up to this point, I have focused on how memory divides one national community from another, a tendency that stems from the narratives we employ about the past and the truths we assign to them. As noted in chapter 2, narrative truth is a problematic notion even in analytic history, and it is all the more fraught when it comes to national memory. But debates about the past nonetheless rely heavily on narrative truth claims, and this often gives rise to conflict and mnemonic standoffs. The situation is made even more difficult by the fact that narrative habits operate in a veiled fashion, leading us to underestimate or simply overlook their impact.

Like other cultural tools, narratives come with both affordances and constraints (Wertsch, 1998). On the one hand, they are extremely efficient and powerful cognitive instruments for grasping together information into manageable, meaningful packages. They also provide effective means for creating large imagined communities, especially national ones. On the other hand, however, they are constrained by what Cassirer (1953) called the "curse of mediacy," including the tendency to make overconfident assessments of the truth of our accounts of the past. We can hold this in check to some degree by turning to analytic history, but national memory grounded in underlying codes and mental habits leads in directions that are hard to resist.

All this is further complicated by the protean nature of narrative templates, which gives them the flexibility to assimilate or sidestep

How Nations Remember. James V. Wertsch, Oxford University Press (2021). © Oxford University Press.
DOI: 10.1093/oso/9780197551462.003.0006

inconvenient information. It can be exasperating to provide solid evidence and argument when challenging someone's account of the past only to have the effort ignored or dismissed, but narrative templates provide the means for doing just that. Their generalized form makes them flexible, if not slippery, when it comes to dealing with disconfirming or contradictory evidence. Furthermore, they encourage us to see the past from our own perspective, and the resulting "our-side" bias makes our accounts all the more resistant to change.

Given these forces, it is no surprise that mnemonic standoffs arise between national communities. Avoiding them completely would require overcoming the habits of thought and action that William James called "the enormous fly-wheel of society" (1890, p.121) with all of its powerful resistance to change. It can be particularly difficult to change others' habits of emplotting the past, given that this is often taken as a challenge to their basic beliefs and identity commitments. We are likely to resist such challenges ourselves, and we should expect others to do so as well.

In the real world, however, we are routinely left with the need to respond in civil, productive ways when someone tells us that our account of the past is just not true. Indeed, this is something we *must* do if we are to avoid sinking into hopeless, frozen opposition and conflict with others. In these instances, however, we often cannot expect to transcend or neatly resolve our differences. Instead, the more realistic goal is to *manage*[1] differences, which, while not fully satisfying, remains eminently worthwhile, given the alternatives.

---

[1] I use "manage" to reflect on the work of diplomats and other negotiators dealing with an imperfect world where complete agreement over issues is unlikely to occur. This is not the sense of "manage" involved in social engineering to control the beliefs and worldview of entire societies such as that described in Orwell's *Nineteen Eight-Four* (1949).

6.2. Efforts by Professional Negotiators to Manage Mnemonic Conflict

Beginning with my mnemonic standoff with my Soviet friend Vitya over Hiroshima and extending through other cases involving students, journalists, and political figures, I have outlined a range of efforts to deal with differences over national memory. In most instances, these have involved individuals who have little professional experience in negotiation, making it perhaps unsurprising that such encounters often give rise to conflicts that can surprise everyone involved. But for some individuals, strategies for "getting to yes" (Fisher, Ury, & Patton, 2011) are part of professional training, which means they make special efforts to find ways to deal with differences.

In reviewing the lessons from how professional negotiators deal with national memory, three points come to light. First, they tend to know something about the national memory of those with whom they are interacting. In chapter 3, I outlined a case where American students had no knowledge of the 1999 bombing of the Chinese embassy in Belgrade, and this made their effort to engage the Chinese students doomed from the outset. Not knowing about events in national memory that are important to one's interlocutors can be even more problematic than disagreeing over them; it can be insulting.

Second, professional negotiators try to understand not only the concrete facts and positions held by others but why these facts and positions are so sensitive. Fisher et al. touch on this under the heading of understanding an opponent's "interests," a term that is widely used in discussions of international negotiation. When it comes to national memory, this goes beyond obvious material interests and involves delving into the underlying codes and identity projects behind national memory. This invariably takes us into the realm of mental habits as well as the national narcissism (chapter 4) that lurk in all of us.

And third, professionals recognize that despite their best efforts, they will sometimes end up with deep, seemingly nonnegotiable differences over the past, and when they do, it is often wise to accept this but also to maintain elements of a relationship that may be the key to future discussion. For Fisher et al., this falls under the advice "separate the people from the problem."

The first two of these themes amount to knowing what we are up against in mnemonic disputes. Armed with knowledge about the other's account of the past, professionals are in a position to recognize the commitments that go with this knowledge. In some cases, these commitments are so formidable that negotiators avoid bringing up the past at all. But if they find themselves in a position of needing to do so, they often try to take a step back and remember that we are all creatures of mental habits that support claims about deeply held narrative truths for members of a community. This does not mean that we should ignore or excuse claims of others—or ourselves—that are obviously untrue or deeply unethical, but before we accuse others of ignorance or personal animus, it often pays to consider the underlying codes behind what they say that take the form of narrative templates, privileged event narratives, and national narrative projects.

As just noted, negotiators sometimes opt simply to keep accounts of the past off the table, especially when confronted with the need to address some more pressing issue in the present. This is often viewed as a temporary solution that will eventually need to be revisited in an effort to confront the issues at hand. The long term effort may take the form of the "truth and reconciliation" efforts over apartheid in South Africa and violence in other settings (Gibson, 2006; Gibson, Sonis, & Sokhom, 2010) or social and education programs such as "Facing History and Ourselves."[2] The bottom line is that professional negotiators demonstrate sensitivity about national memory and understand that it is something

---

[2] https://www.facinghistory.org/about-us

to be handled with great care. In what follows, I begin with some illustrations of tactics used to avoid discussion of national memory and then move on to more explicit forms of engagement.

6.2.1. Keeping National Memory Out of the Discussion

When professional negotiators avoid issues of national memory, this hardly means that they don't appreciate their importance. Indeed, it often signals that the issues are simply too hot to handle. Consider a case involving Franklin Delano Roosevelt, one of the 20th century's master politicians, both in the United States and on the international scene. During World War II, Roosevelt constantly found himself needing to manage the fragile relationship among Great Britain, the Soviet Union, and the United States. Despite their differences, these allies had to work together in the struggle against Germany, and this often led Roosevelt to avoid or finesse issues of national memory.

An example of this can be found in his handling of Stalin's repeated efforts to bring up the failure of his Allies to open a second front in France in 1942 and again in 1943. Several proposals for this had been considered by the Allies, and it was recognized as a crucial way to help the Soviet Union, which at the time was bearing the lion's share of the effort and losses in the battle against Germany. In Stalin's view, the postponement of the second front was not only a grave shortcoming but also perhaps a plot to weaken the USSR, and for him, this was part of a litany of anti-Soviet efforts by British and U.S. leaders going back to the Russian Revolution in 1917. Roosevelt and Churchill responded by reminding Stalin of other events in their shared past during World War II. For example, they stressed their invasion of North Africa, Sicily, and Italy and their efforts to supply Lend Lease weapons and supplies to the USSR. And Churchill was also quick to remind Stalin of the struggle of Great Britain as it had fought alone against Hitler between 1939 and 1941, a period during which the Soviet Union had remained on the sidelines thanks to the Molotov-Ribbentrop Pact. All of this, however, did little to assuage Stalin's resentments.

These delicate issues lurked in the background of a crucial summit in Tehran at the end of 1943, where Roosevelt, Stalin, and Churchill met to review the progress of their combined efforts and plans for the next phase of the war. When in a good mood, these leaders expressed admiration for the heroism of the others over the preceding years. For example, Stalin toasted to the heroism of the British during the Battle of Britain, and Churchill was effusive in his praise of the sacrifices and accomplishments of the Soviet Army. But resentment based on conflicting national memories and narratives always seemed ready to surface and threaten the working relationship that was required to continue the all-important war effort.

In this setting, Roosevelt emphasized what bound the Allies together and how their common effort was more important than their resentments over past wrongs. His efforts were on display, for example, in a toast he gave at the end of a long day of meetings on November 30, 1943. As the closing banquet wound down at 2 a.m., Roosevelt asked for the privilege of the last word, at which point he said:

> There has been discussion here tonight . . . of our varying colors of political complexion. I like to think of this in terms of the rainbow. In our country the rainbow is symbol of good fortune and of hope. It has many varying colors, each individualistic, but blending into one glorious whole. Thus with our nations. We have differing customs and philosophies and ways of life. Each of us works out our scheme of things according to the desires and ideas of our own peoples. But we have proved here at Tehran that the varying ideals of our nations can come together in a harmonious

whole, moving unitedly for the common good of ourselves and of the world. (Burns, 1970, p.411)

Reflecting his skills as a master negotiator, Roosevelt crafted this toast in a way that skirted all mention of conflicting national memories. He celebrated the Allies' ability to differ over "customs and philosophies and ways of life" stemming from "the desires and ideas of our peoples," but he said nothing about differences over the Molotov-Ribbentrop Pact in 1939, the failure to open a second front in 1943, or other contentious issues. Roosevelt clearly knew that bringing up such episodes could open a Pandora's box of resentments, and his tactic seems to have worked on that evening. Everyone left the banquet in good spirits, and the Allies went on to continue their combined campaign against Germany.

6.2.2. Bringing National Memory into the Discussion

In contrast to this episode, however, professional politicians and diplomats often do not have the luxury of steering clear of national memory. In some cases, this means that the best alternative may be to bring up difficult issues from the past and then simply declare them off limits. This was a strategy used by the American diplomat Richard Holbrooke (1998), for example, as he negotiated with the Serbian leadership in the 1990s to reach an agreement for peace in Bosnia and Herzegovina. Holbrooke was intensely aware that he was dealing with parties who constantly wanted to bring up historical events that were sources of resentment, and this led him at one point to set out a ground rule that there would be "no historical lectures, no bullshit."

In contrast to the tactics employed by Roosevelt and Holbrooke, however, professional negotiators often recognize that national memory must not only be brought up, but must be incorporated

into the discussion, and this can require patience, objective reflection, and the recognition of conflicting perspectives. These are
properties of Kahneman's slow thinking, which can be called on
to supervise the unconscious mental habits of fast thinking. In the
case of national memory this fast thinking is made all the more difficult to detect and control because of the veiled nature of narrative
templates.

These points are consistent with claims that Fisher et al. (2011)
lay out in their advice on "getting to yes" and "negotiating an
agreement without giving in." Starting with the recommendation
to "reconcile interests, not positions" (p.23), their point is the importance of going beyond a concrete demand to underlying beliefs
and emotions. From this perspective, "the basic problem in negotiation lies not in conflicting positions, but in the conflict between
each side's needs, desires, concerns, and fears" (p.23). In the terms
I am using, the proposal by Fisher et al. amounts to a strategy that
includes taking into consideration the narrative habits shared by
members of a national community. But because the narrative tools
are part of a national identity project and not simply neutral cognitive instruments, challenges to others' account of the past can be
taken as challenges to their group and personal integrity.

Coming to grips with issues at this level is especially challenging.
In some instances, struggles over contradictory truths about the
past don't seem to be amenable to patient reflection and the recognition of conflicting perspectives, and we find ourselves groping
for ways to proceed on the basis of vague notions of "trust." This
turns out to be a crucial component in negotiation, but an approach
based on symbolic mediation suggests that trust is not just a property of the "unencumbered individual" (Sandel, 2009). Instead,
it reflects the broader sociocultural context in which one operates,
namely through the influence of symbolic mediation. Instead of
jumping to the conclusion that interlocutors are not to be trusted
because of personal failings or malicious intent, an account of symbolic mediation calls for consideration of the influence of narrative

tools as co-authors of what they think and say. This does not mean that individuals cannot or should not be held responsible for what they do, on the one hand, and it also does not mean that everyone in a group simply parrots a shared narrative, on the other, something that would suggest that all Americans, Russians, Chinese, or members of other groups think alike. Instead, successful efforts to adjudicate disputes over national memory involve recognizing both the narrative tools that an interlocutor uses and her personal agenda in the moment.

In the next section, I examine these issues by returning to a case I raised in chapter 1: the mnemonic standoff between members of the Chinese and American national communities over the 1999 bombing of the Chinese embassy in Belgrade. I revisit this episode from the perspective of how it has been handled by professional diplomats and scholars of international relations. These diplomats and scholars are typically more informed and reflective than the students whose reaction I outlined in chapter 1, but they still often find their efforts shaped, and sometimes stymied, by unconscious mental habits. Even though diplomats and scholars of international relations may be highly skilled in forms of slow thinking that allow them to maintain a distance from their first inclinations to respond, they still struggle with how to recognize, let alone supervise, mental habits of fast thinking.

6.2.3. Chinese and American Accounts of the Bombing of the Embassy in Belgrade

The Chinese and American national communities have sharply different accounts of what happened on the night of May 7–8, 1999. They agree that NATO planes (U.S. Air Force planes flying from the United States) bombed the Chinese Embassy in Belgrade, Yugoslavia, that night, killing three Chinese journalists and injuring 20 other people in the area. But they disagree on

just about everything else. This disagreement surfaced immediately after the event when the Chinese government labeled
the bombing a "barbaric act and a gross violation of Chinese
sovereignty," seeming to signal to a domestic audience that
expressions of outrage would be deemed acceptable. The ensuing
demonstrations quickly spiraled into massive, emotional
outpourings of rage across the People's Republic of China. Tens
of thousands of demonstrators surrounded consular offices of the
United States and other NATO countries, in some cases trapping
embassy officials inside and in others setting fire to the residence
of consular officials, and this forced the Chinese government to
act to calm things down. The intense response by demonstrators
appears to have been as much a reflection of popular opinion
in China as of any government effort, and it came as a complete
shock to U.S. authorities and the American population at large
(Lieberthal, 2014).

Emotions may have cooled since 1999, but a deep gulf between U.S. and Chinese versions of what happened has remained.
U.S. officials have insisted all along that the bombing was an accident stemming from the CIA's use of out-of-date maps of Belgrade.
In this account, the bombs hit the intended geographical coor-
dinates, but instead of being the Federal Directorate for Supply
and Procurement identified in the databases used by NATO, the
building was the Chinese Embassy. As reported in some detail by
figures such as Strobe Talbott (2013), Ambassador-at-Large and
Special Adviser to the Secretary of State at the time, the Clinton administration was shocked and deeply upset by the mistake, especially as it was trying at the time to build better ties with China,
and it responded as quickly as possible with an apology and offer of
compensation.

The Clinton administration followed up a few weeks later by
sending to Beijing a high-level delegation headed by Thomas
Pickering, who was then the U.S. Under Secretary of State, to
make a formal presentation to the Chinese government. Pickering

began his report "Regarding the Accidental Bombing of the P.R.C. Embassy in Belgrade" with the statement:

> The attack was a mistake. Our examination explains how a series of errors and omissions led to that mistake. Let me emphasize: no one targeted the Chinese Embassy. No one, at any stage in the process, realized that our bombs were aimed at the Chinese Embassy. (Pickering, 2001)

In stark opposition to this account, Chinese authorities have consistently insisted that far from being an accident, the bombing was fully intentional. And Chinese citizens seem to agree. Several months after the bombing, for example, surveys and interviews with university students in Beijing found that over three-quarters of them believed the embassy bombing was premeditated by the United States, whereas less than 4% believed it was a technical error.[3] The reasons cited by Chinese for the American attack vary, but one point on which they agree is that it is naïve to believe it was anything other than an intentional attack. Based on my own small, unsystematic sampling of conversations with Chinese colleagues and students, this opinion seems to hold across generations and political perspectives ranging from nationalist to pro-Western, and it left little room for finding a middle ground that would allow for the possibility of American error.

One discussion I had about this issue was at a professional meeting in Beijing several years after the 1999 Belgrade bombing. Over lunch I spoke with three colleagues from Chinese universities and raised the issue of how the episode is remembered in the United States and China. They were not surprised when I said that the American account was that it was an unfortunate accident, but

---

[3] Study conducted by Dingxin Zhao as reported by Wang (2012, p.175). Wang also reports observations by a faculty member at a U.S. institution that Chinese students who were studying there at the time felt strongly that the act was intentional, revealing that the mnemonic community was not contained within the borders of the PRC.

they didn't buy it for a minute. One colleague replied, "Everyone knows that is not true because the CIA could never make such a stupid mistake." I chuckled politely and listed a few other instances where in fact U.S. intelligence services had got things wrong, but it was obvious that my interlocutors were having none of it. They were respectful and professional, but we were clearly at an impasse. An unbridgeable gulf separated my view of the truth from theirs, and nothing I said changed their mind—just as I was not swayed by what they said.

In the years since this encounter I have had many occasions to revisit the topic of the 1999 bombings with Chinese colleagues and friends, and the only thing that changed is that my Chinese colleagues and friends have added to the list of hypotheses about what happened. They often begin with assertions that the bombing was motivated by a desire to intimidate or humiliate China by reminding it of who is boss. They sometimes add to this by saying, for example, that some rogue actor in the Pentagon or CIA may have targeted the Chinese Embassy without the knowledge of President Clinton and his top advisors. Other accounts I have heard from Chinese colleagues and students posit that the CIA mistakenly thought Slobodan Milošević was hiding in the embassy and wanted to "get" him and in the process embarrass China for harboring him. Regardless of the specifics, people in China continue to claim hostile intent was involved while virtually all Americans who are familiar with the episode see it as an unfortunate mistake.

Why do members of the two communities seem so resistant to change in the face of argument and counter-evidence? Once again, the answer appears to be tied to the narrative templates and habits that shape the two communities, especially the "Century of Humiliation" narrative for China. After outlining these in the next section, I examine how they shape arguments put forth by professional diplomats and scholars of international relations about the 1999 bombing and other incidents. Unlike the students' accounts noted in chapter 1, the gulf that separates the versions of events in this case cannot be chalked up to lack of knowledge or information. Instead, it points to the power of narrative habits in separating one national mnemonic community from another even in cases of actors who are experienced diplomats.

6.3. Competing Narrative Templates

In chapter 5 I mentioned the city on a hill story, and in Wertsch (2019) I have outlined it as a narrative template that shapes the habits of American political discourse. As such, it is often invoked to make sense of past and present events in America. The title of this storyline comes from a 1630 sermon by John Winthrop to the Puritans, but as Abram Van Engen (2020) argues, it is not so much knowledge of that particular event but of a more generic sort that is at issue. This involves a storyline about escape from oppression and a quest for freedom, and it takes itself as reflecting a universal aspiration for humankind, which makes America a beacon for others to follow. In its "exemplarist" reading, the moral is that America should focus on serving as a beacon for others to emulate without trying to impose its vision; in its "enforcer" reading, the implication is that America sometimes must help, or even force, other people to escape from oppression and pursue their quest for freedom.

A recent, rather muscular version of the enforcer variant emerged with the collapse of the Soviet Union in 1990, a development that made containment obsolete as a guiding doctrine for the United States. In its place, public intellectuals began to discuss America's role as a "reluctant sheriff" (Haass, 1998). As outlined by Robert Kagan (2012), the history of this storyline goes back at least to the 19th century:

> Americans do not go "abroad in search of monsters to destroy" is the oft-quoted phrase of John Quincy Adams. If someone points out to them that they have, indeed, often done just that, then

they portray themselves as the "reluctant sheriff," their boots on the desk reading the newspaper until some unsavory gang rides into town and forces them to pull their rifle off the rack, whether Japanese imperialists, Nazis, Soviet communists, or Islamic jihadists. "The United States of America never goes to war because we want to," said one prominent politician a few years ago. "We only go to war because we have to."[4] But this self-perception, while sincere, bears no relation to reality. (p.10)

As formulated by Kagan, the reluctant sheriff story bears all the marks of a narrative template. It is a vernacular version of the enforcer version of the city on a hill story and serves as a schematic plot that can be used to size up events, past or present. The fact that it has been invoked to size up multiple events points to its status as a template or schematic code. And the fact that it is invoked by politicians as they seek to appeal to a general political audience indexes that it is part of the habit memory of the American mnemonic community.

The exemplarist variant of the city on a hill narrative template is perhaps a more standard part of the equipment for living in America.[5] In his 1989 farewell address to the nation,[6] for example, Ronald Reagan knew that the narrative of the "shining city upon a hill" would appeal to all Americans and suggested it had universal appeal for others in the world as well. This narrative template was so central to the speech that it could almost be called Reagan's co-author, and in this regard, he was following a practice frequently employed by others. Figures ranging from John Kennedy to George W. Bush, Newt Gingrich, and Barack Obama have all sought to resonate with American audiences by invoking the city on a hill story and use it to draw their audiences into a discussion about

[4] From John Kerry's acceptance speech at the 2004 Democratic National Convention.
[5] Abram van Engen has shown how this story did not actually enter American political discourse until the 19th century, well after Winthrop gave his sermon.
[6] https://www.youtube.com/watch?v=UKVsq2daR8Q

America and its place in the world. It is one of the most popular manifestations of the American national narrative project involving the quest for a more perfect democratic union that I outlined in chapter 5.

Being socialized into the American national community involves mastering the city on a hill narrative, including its variants, through countless encounters with specific stories in school, the media, political speeches, and everyday conversation. The resulting set of narrative habits provides a powerful lens through which contemporary events such as the 1999 Belgrade bombing are viewed, making it nearly inconceivable that America could have been pursuing a nefarious project of bombing an embassy just to demonstrate who is boss.

The Chinese interpretations of the 1999 bombing in Belgrade, of course, involve a quite different perspective, namely one based on a narrative template concerned with the Century of Humiliation. As noted in chapter 4, this is a storyline about foreign invasion and domination over China from the mid-19th century until 1949 with the creation of the People's Republic of China and Mao Zedong's announcement that the Chinese people had stood up. And as outlined in chapter 5 this extended episode of humiliation was made all the more painful due to the national narrative project based on assumptions about China's role as a central kingdom and a "Chinese doctrine of superiority" (Fairbank, 1969).

In the formulation of Zheng Wang (2012), the Century of Humiliation narrative is part of the "deep culture" of China that must be taken into consideration to understand its worldview and approach to international relations. This has especially been the case after the transition that has seen nationalism replace Marxism as the main source of legitimacy in modern China. As outlined by Wang, the key to this new nationalism is the underlying narrative of the Century of Humiliation, whose staying power is striking. All this points to narrative habits that are resistant to change and operate as what James called the "enormous fly-wheel of society." As in the case of Russia, these are narrative habits that have proven to be a resilient resource for mobilizing a population even after decades of top-down efforts by the state to impose a Marxist worldview based on class struggle that specifically eschewed national identity.

6.4. Strategic Trust and Distrust

National narratives and memory are part of a discussion of "strategic distrust" as outlined by Jisi Wang and Kenneth Lieberthal (2012). These two respected scholars collaborated on a report that involved Wang's writing about the Chinese perspective and Lieberthal's writing about the U.S. side and then coming together to collaborate on a final text. One segment of the text about the Chinese perspective is particularly revealing in its view of the American national narrative:

> According to typical Chinese understanding of world history, American politicians are true believers of "the law of the jungle," and their promotion of democracy and human rights are [sic] in reality policy tools to achieve goals of power politics. This cynicism is so widespread that no one would openly affirm that the Americans truly believe in what they say about human rights concerns. The rise of China, with its sheer size and very different political system, value system, culture, and race, must be regarded in the United States as the major challenge to its superpower status. America's international behavior is increasingly understood against this broad backdrop. (p.11)

This passage suggests that Chinese observers of the United States are familiar with some version of the city on a hill narrative template and a national narrative project about a more perfect union based on democracy and human rights. Indeed, it is likely that a Chinese scholar such as Wang knows more about the particulars of these narrative tools than most Americans. The point, however, is that members of the Chinese mnemonic community find it hard to believe that Americans "truly believe in what they say." Instead, they view American assertions largely as a cynical ploy to mask the underlying reality that "American politicians are true believers of 'the law of the jungle.'"[7]

Motivated by suspicions that grow out of viewing the world through the lens of a Century of Humiliation narrative, this can produce interpretations of U.S. intentions and actions that surprise most Americans. In the most benign reading of these claims, Chinese scholars and leaders believe that a strong version of the enforcer reading of the city on a hill national narrative is at work, one that encourages the United States to use force if needed to get other societies to accept its form of governance. This reading contrasts with the more benign exemplarist view often assumed by the American mnemonic community in which the goal is simply to provide a model or beacon for others to follow if they so desire. But if a full-fledged "law of the jungle" interpretation is taken at face value, the disparity between the two communities is even more pronounced.

Analysts sometimes try to make sense of such disagreements in terms of the distinction between "idealist" and "realist" forms of thinking in international relations. Whereas idealists operate in accordance with an ideology based on universal values and strive to find ways to act as part of global institutions, realists assume that actors in international relations recognize that they are in an anarchic state system and pursue their interests without regard to any ideological commitments or hopes for international governance.

---

[7] Before dismissing this outright as simply a Chinese perspective, it is worth noting that scholars of international relations in the "realist" camp sometimes make a similar point. Stephen Walt (1998), for example, has written, "Although U.S. leaders are adept at cloaking their actions in the lofty rhetoric of 'world order,' naked self-interest lies behind most of them" (p.43).

Lieberthal and J. Wang, however, see differences between Chinese and American leaders as reflecting something more, namely differences in "deep thinking," a notion that resonates with Z. Wang's (2012) ideas about deep culture or my claims about narrative templates and national narrative projects. Specifically, Lieberthal and J. Wang are concerned with how leaders on either side understand the deep thinking of leaders of the other and how this understanding is involved in managing strategic distrust. The gulf that separates the two perspectives seems to be so great in this case, however, that it can foster more frustration than mutual understanding. When confronted with Chinese views about American cynicism about the city on a hill story, the result is that Americans might be tempted to agree with Reinhold Niebuhr that "only malice could prompt [such] criticism of any of our actions" (1984, pp.24–25). But Niebuhr took us one step deeper into the dynamics involved by examining irony.

6.5. The Role of Irony

The account Niebuhr provides in his slim volume *The Irony of American History* (1984) makes it possible to avoid overly simple, stark choices between opposing interpretations of our own and others' actions. Instead of assuming that Americans either simply and totally believe the city on a hill story or have no commitment to it whatsoever and only use it cynically, Niebuhr suggests another possible interpretation based on a form of narrative dialogism involving irony.

Irony is generally characterized by the substitution of a statement for its opposite in which what is said in some way contradicts what is meant. In some cases, a speaker is in control of this contradiction in that she intends a meaning at odds with what she says. Consider the utterance of a mother who comes into her teenaged son's messy room and says, "You are going to win an award for neatness one of these days." As any mother knows, what is said is the opposite of what is meant in this case. Burke (1969) views irony as a dialectic struggle between conflicting points of view that leads to an insight beyond the limits of either position, and this is at the heart of Niebuhr's account. For example, it is a type of irony that provides a way to preserve a commitment to one's own national narrative while simultaneously giving rise to unanticipated and unintended interpretations by others. The effects can be difficult to detect due to the fact that it "cannot be directly experienced" by the speaker (Niebuhr, 1984, p.153). Instead, it is a matter of interpretation in which "the knowledge of irony is usually reserved for observers rather than participants" (p.153).

Niebuhr's account of irony involves "an observer who is not so hostile to the victim of irony as to deny the element of virtue which must constitute a part of the ironic situation; nor yet so sympathetic as to discount the weakness, the vanity and pretension which constitute another element" (p.153). For the American "victims" in this case who are committed to the city on a hill national narrative, it is all too easy to see the "element of virtue" but overlook "the vanity and pretension" that they bring to the table. For observers from other national perspectives, such as one fueled by suspicions stemming from the Century of Humiliation narrative, just the opposite may be the case, making it easy to "deny the virtue" of the believer in the city on a hill narrative. Niebuhr's point is that *both* elements must be held in mind at the same time to appreciate the ironic situation and harness this appreciation to overcome misunderstanding and recrimination as members of different national communities. Among other things, this adds a new level of nuance and complexity to the claims about national narcissism outlined in chapter 4.

In American political discourse the exemplarist reading of the city on a hill narrative template, along with the quest for a more perfect democratic union, has long been a cornerstone of political rhetoric. As noted earlier, politicians routinely use these narrative tools not only because they accept the narrative truths they contain but also because they know they are part of the underlying code they have in common with the American mnemonic community. So how do we square this with the fact that others insist, "no one would openly affirm that the Americans truly believe in what they say about human rights" (Lieberthal & Wang, 2012, p.11)? Could it be that Americans truly are indeed completely cynical and don't believe this storyline? Or is an extreme enforcer version the only one at issue? Both of these interpretations would be viewed by Americans as a fundamental misreading of their political culture. But does that then leave us with the conclusion that observers in China and elsewhere are completely misguided in their reading of American culture?

Again, instead of choosing between these stark alternatives, Niebuhr's analysis of irony encourages us to consider how the two interpretations exist in complex, mutually reinforcing patterns of interpretation—and misinterpretation. It is only by simultaneously keeping in mind the interpretations of two informed and intelligent observers such as Lieberthal and J. Wang, interpretations that appear to be polar opposites, that a coherent picture emerges. It is a picture in which members of the American mnemonic community tend to view events through the lens of the exemplarist interpretation of the city on a hill narrative template while observers from countries see only the enforcer reading at work—or perhaps simply take Americans to be pure cynics.

But what if an "element of virtue" is precisely what produces "the weakness, the vanity and pretension" on the part of the American community that give rise to what they see as a fundamental misreading of their motives, a misreading by others that they see as puzzling, indeed offensive? George Packer seems to have this sort of dynamic of irony in mind in his 2019 book *Our Man: Richard Holbrooke and the End of the American Century*, where he examines the efforts of a leading American diplomat whose views were formed during the American war in Vietnam. Packer examines the confusion and frustration of an entire generation of diplomatic and military leaders to which Holbrooke belonged, frustration that is encapsulated in the bitter humor of the chapter title: "Vietnam: How Can We Lose When We're So Sincere?"

Returning to the mnemonic standoff between America and China over the 1999 bombing of the Chinese Embassy in Belgrade, the gulf between the two sides has remained firmly in place. In 2011, for example, I had a conversation with a retired PLA[8] general in China about the bombing, and he related that his hypothesis, undoubtedly based on information from Chinese security services, was that U.S. military leaders thought that Milošević was hiding in the Chinese Embassy in 1999 and wanted to bomb it in order to embarrass the Chinese leadership. He offered that we may never know for certain what occurred, but he expressed the hope that when more archives are eventually opened, we will know the truth.

It is of course possible that this will happen, but most Americans are likely to find this far-fetched and will ask why our Chinese colleagues can't accept the more straightforward conclusion that a terrible mistake was made. And indeed, even if archives do reveal the sort of new information and propositional truths envisioned by the general, deeply embedded American and Chinese mental habits are likely to preserve different accounts of what really happened, even if that involves re-emplotting or otherwise overlooking evidence.

Thus members of the American mnemonic community are likely to continue to reject the idea that the United States had any intention of bombing the Chinese Embassy. As already noted, Ambassador Thomas Pickering (2001) officially stated in 1999, "The attack was a mistake" and "no one targeted the Chinese Embassy." He emphasized that multiple operational procedures had failed in "this tragic set of errors" and provided a detailed account of mistakes having to do with locating and verifying targets

---

[8] People's Liberation Army, the regular armed forces of the People's Republic of China.

for the bombing campaign and with the failure of a procedure for detecting either of these first two blunders. Most of his report was a compilation of claims about propositional truths that were put forth to warrant claims about the U.S. narrative of the event.

The report by Pickering (2001) also implicitly recognized the need to go beyond this and address the issue of motives, which lie at the core of narrative truth. He did this near the end of the presentation under the heading of "U.S. Intentions," where he stated, "Clearly the United States had absolutely no reason to want to attack your protected embassy facility." In laying out this line of argument Pickering noted that bombing the Chinese Embassy would have (a) "been contrary to U.S. doctrine and practice and against international standards of behavior and established international accords," (b) "been completely antithetical to President Clinton's strong personal commitment to strengthening the relationship between the United States and China," and (c) "made absolutely no sense in terms of our policy objectives in Kosovo." Years after writing the report, Pickering (2013) continued to hold to this line of reasoning, as did Strobe Talbott (2013), who was Deputy Secretary of State in 1999. In short, the mnemonic standoff over what happened in Belgrade remained well ensconced more than a decade after the event, even among some of the most distinguished diplomats and scholars of international relations in the United States.

In the end, the continuing mnemonic standoff between the United States and China over this incident may best be understood in terms of the dynamics of irony as outlined by Niebuhr. No matter how sincere Pickering was in explicating the details of what led up to the bombing, the "element of virtue" that underlay his effort apparently could be interpreted by others to reflect "the vanity and pretension which constitute another element" (p.153). Indeed, it appears to almost invite such an interpretation.

Few people who know Pickering would chalk this up to some sort of limitation on his part as an individual. He had long been recognized as one of America's most astute, accomplished, open-minded, and balanced diplomats. But for many of his counterparts in places like China, it was not only Thomas Pickering the individual speaking during his trip to Beijing in 1999; it was Thomas Pickering the individual using American narrative equipment for living. The power of narrative templates, then, can be seen as shaping not only what we say and mean but also how others interpret us in ways we sometimes cannot control, especially once our communication becomes enmeshed in the narrative dialogism of irony. In such cases, our communities' narrative templates seem to have a powerful hold over the narrative truths we will entertain, making negotiation particularly frustrating.

6.6. Managing Mnemonic Standoffs

By way of conclusion, I turn to some concrete ways to manage conflicting national memories. My comments grow out of claims about how narrative tools serve as equipment for living and the recognition that their power to size up a situation can be so pronounced that it is sometimes appropriate to think of them as co-authors of our thinking and speaking. Again, this does not let individuals off the hook when it comes to responsibility for what we say, but it does alert us to the forces—often veiled—that shape our own and others' thinking.

As noted earlier, the goal is not to neatly transcend or resolve conflicting accounts of the past. Given that real people from real national communities are involved, and given that they come equipped with narrative habits and associated identity projects, one can expect limits to shared understanding, especially when the irony noted by Niebuhr is involved. Instead, the goal is to develop effective means for supervising our habits and reining in some of our more dangerous proclivities, and in this spirit I provide a preliminary list of five strategies.

6.6.1. Recognize What We Are Up Against

First, it's essential simply to recognize what we are up against when it comes to mental habits that shape national memory. This may seem to be unnecessary as a warning except for the fact that disputes over national memory often suggest we are prone to remain oblivious to it. Instead of recognizing the power of narrative templates to constrain narrative truth, we routinely focus narrowly on a particular fact or specific propositional truth when responding to others, as if this could settle matters. And when others ignore or brush aside our comment, we often react with frustration and incredulity. This was certainly the case in the first public reaction to the 1999 bombing of the Chinese Embassy in Belgrade, and though less emotional in their response, experienced diplomats from China and the United States were still apparently unconvinced of the other's account of what had happened.

The resistance to change in light of new evidence is reflected in many encounters over national memory. As noted in chapter 3, when Mikhail Gorbachev acknowledged in 1988 that the secret protocols of the Molotov-Ribbentrop Pact indeed existed, many Estonians held out the hope that Russians would be forced to recognize a proclivity for aggressive expansionism at the expense of smaller neighbors. It soon became clear, however, that such recognition was not forthcoming. Instead, the protean nature of the Expulsion of Alien Enemies narrative template made it possible to reinterpret the annexation of Estonia as an act of self-defense in the campaign to save Europe from Fascism. Similarly, reviewing the archival evidence about Truman's decision to drop atomic bombs on Hiroshima and Nagasaki has yielded what appears to be an unending debate based on objective facts and argumentation, but all this effort has left different mnemonic communities largely locked in place on their account of these events. And the encounter between Putin and journalists in 2008 (chapter 3) over what happened in the war between Russia and Georgia produced little other than incredulity on everyone's part.

In short, we often overlook the power of underlying codes when arguing about the past and jump directly into disputing the truth of propositions. This is not to say such disputes are unimportant. Indeed, we *must* attend to the truth of each statement in a narrative, a process to which I return later in the discussion of analytic history versus national memory. But discussions of national memory are likely to remain frustrating if we do not recognize the role of narrative truth grounded in narrative templates and the mental habits that go with them. The fact that narrative templates are schematic, protean, and veiled makes their influence all the harder to recognize, let alone control. But it is at this level that many issues in national memory disputes are decided. Furthermore, it is at the level of underlying narrative codes that irony as envisioned by Niebuhr unfolds, adding a dialogic element to an already complex process.

In general, by recognizing underlying narrative codes, the implications of Niebuhr's call for cognitive humility begins to come into focus. When encountering an account of the past that differs— sometimes fundamentally—from the one we hold, the point is to consider the possibility that the differences are not only about specific narratives but also about narrative templates and national narrative projects. When trying to understand how Russians can have such a different account of Truman's decision to bomb Hiroshima, for example, the point is not to lose sight of documented evidence but to recognize that fundamentally different narrative habits may be at work.

These comments amount to only a partial list of the challenges that come into view when we consider the power of underlying narrative codes to shape national memory. They suffice, however, to make it clear that the frustration and conflict that can emerge between mnemonic communities stems from much more than disputes over particular propositional truths or even the truth of a specific narrative. Recognizing this means recognizing how naïve our hopes often are that if we could just present the facts to another community, they will see the truth of our account of the past. Instead, addressing mnemonic standoffs requires dealing with something deeper in the form of narrative habits.

6.6.2. Use Analytic History as an Antidote to National Memory

In chapters 2 and 5 I outlined a distinction between analytic history and national memory. Again, in a nutshell, analytic history tends to preserve the evidence at the expense of a narrative, whereas national memory tends to preserve a narrative at the expense of the evidence. This does not mean that historical accounts are simply unbiased and true and memory accounts are biased and undependable. Instead, the difference is one of distinct discursive realms that guide history and memory. Analytic history is an institutionalized practice that aspires to put forth and defend claims on the basis of evidence in accordance with norms accepted by members of a professional community. This does not ensure that historians are without bias and cannot arrive at faulty conclusions, but it does mean that there are established procedures for proposing and defending claims, even if these claims come at the expense of embarrassing a national community or threatening the historian's membership in it. National memory, in contrast, is committed to an identity project of a community, and its claims are as likely to be based on what is required to support that community as on whatever evidence comes into play.

As Ernst Renan wrote in his 1882 essay "What Is a Nation?", forgetting and getting things wrong about our past are crucial in creating a nation, which is why "historical studies often constitutes a danger for [the principle of] nationality" (1990, p.11). In this account, analytic history is not only different from national memory but is also a "danger" to it in that memory often relies on "historical error." Renan went on to observe that analytic history differs from national memory in that "Historical inquiry . . . throws light on the violent acts that have taken place at the origin of every political formation" (p.11). This distinguishes it from national memory, which tends to forget that "Unity is always brutally established" (p.11). Renan's primary focus was on the rise of European nations, noting, for example, "The reunion of northern and southern France was the result of a campaign of terror and extermination that continued for nearly a century" (p.11), but his formulation applies just about everywhere. The "westward expansion" in the United States and the growth of the Russian Empire under Catherine the Great are cases in point.

My point is not to compare the countless instances in which "unity is brutally established" but to say something else about what is possible in analytic history—and unlikely in national memory. I do so by drawing on reflections by Viet Tanh Nguyen (2016) on America's struggle over the past in dealing with the Vietnam War. Nguyen introduces a distinction between studies in the humanities and the "inhumanities" and argues that the "ultimate kind of identity politics" is "identifying with the human and denying one's inhumanity" (p.72). This is a standard part of the humanities, but Nguyen is interested in "Reminding ourselves that being human also means being inhuman is important simply because it is so easy to forget our inhumanity or to displace it onto other humans" (p.72). For him, this calls on us to resist the natural tendencies of national memory, which is likely to resist taking into account brutal acts by one's own group as well as by others.

In short, it is easy to recognize and castigate the inhumanity of others, something America has long demonstrated a capacity for. In the 19th century this was evident as Americans waged brutal warfare on the "hostile savages" who impeded westward expansion, and more recently during World War II when we imprisoned thousands of American citizens of Japanese descent in internment camps. In these and other cases, the American national community at least demonstrated some capacity for reflection and remorse, even if this took decades to surface. But as Serguey Erlich (2019) has noted, Americans remain much less likely to accept the notion that massive bombings of civilians in Germany or Japan in World War II represent unjust or inhuman acts and deserve a place in America's study of the inhumanities. This remains the case even in light of statements such as that of a senior U.S. military official who concluded that the atomic bombings "adopted an ethical standard common to the barbarians of the Dark Ages" (Leahy, 1950, p.441). It is in this regard that analytic history can serve one of its most important roles in managing national memory.

To be sure, the general difference between the conscious, rational, objective reflection of historical analysis, on the one hand, and the unconscious habits and fast thinking of national memory, on the other, means that there is no easy way for the former to filter into the latter. Indeed, there are countless cases in which well-documented historical findings fail to be incorporated into national memory—or are rejected outright. This is often due to history's relative openness to considering the issues Nguyen discusses under the heading of the inhumanities and national memory's refusal to do so, but it also reflects the fundamentally different discursive realms in which history and memory operate. In the end, efforts to incorporate analytic history into national memory will rely heavily on formal education, but as figures such as Sam Wineburg (2001) have shown, we are only at the beginning of our understanding of how this can be done.

6.6.3. Educate Narrative Habits Early and Often

I noted in chapter 2 that William James viewed habit as "the enormous fly-wheel of society." As such, habit imparts inertia to social processes that can keep things in place even in the face of conscious desire for change. Indeed, habit can be society's "most precious conservative agent," something that is echoed in the inherently conservative tendencies of collective memory (Wertsch, 2002), and recognizing this can lead to pessimistic conclusions. But James was not all pessimism on this issue and suggested that things need not be so dire as long as the education of habits of thought begins early and is guided by the right inclinations.

From this perspective, the key to managing national memory is narrative habits. To qualify as a habit in James's account, there must be a motor component that stems from embodiment in repetitive bodily actions. This is consistent with the notion of "habit memory" formulated by Connerton (1989), who focused on ritualistic performance, with its component of embodiment, but it is worth noting that verbal performance, as in telling and hearing stories, is also a form of embodied action. With this in mind, the optimistic side of James's message for narrative habits stems from his observation that we can "*make our nervous system our ally instead of our enemy*" (1890, p.121, italics in the original).

In short, national memory owes much of its hold on members of a community to the narrative habits they develop at a young age. This applies not only to those habits that underlie the fast thinking that can seal us off from other communities but also habits that would encourage us to consider the merits of alternative accounts of the past. These observations have major implications for education, and figures such as Wineburg (2001) have spelled some of these out in recent years, including complications involved in balancing the competing forces brought to bear by national memory and analytic history in formal instruction.

6.6.4. Engage with Accounts of the Past That Conflict with One's Own

It is often difficult to see the power that narrative habits have over us until we encounter profoundly different accounts of the

past—especially accounts that we realize are fervently held by intelligent, well-informed, and well-meaning people. If Bruner (2002)
is right, this may be one of the few ways we come to "suspect we
have the wrong story [and] begin asking how a narrative may structure (or distort) our view of how things really are" (p.9). Elsewhere,
I have argued that the best place to look for a national narrative
might be at points where it comes into conflict with another view
(Wertsch, 2018). This idea has come up at several points in previous
chapters, and the implication is that encounters with conflicting
views might be a valuable entry point for managing mnemonic
conflict. We may not agree with a different view. Indeed, we may
dislike it, as well as the people who espouse it, but it may nonetheless be worthwhile to engage with it. Among other things, this
may be crucial to unearthing the unintended ironies built into the
stances we and others bring to our discussions.

But such engagement must be thoughtfully organized to be
productive. Bringing one specific narrative into contact with another can all too easily serve simply to exacerbate differences between sealed narratives and actually increase tension and conflict.
Instead, the ideal is to get the two sides to consider the power of the
underlying codes that shape their own and the other's accounts of
the past. Rather than objecting to particular aspects of a specific
narrative, the effort is likely to be more productive if we engage at
the level of what Lieberthal and J. Wang (2012) call "deep thinking"
or Z. Wang (2012) calls "deep culture" that are the wellsprings of
trust building. Narrative templates are likely to play a crucial role in
this, and one of the best ways to unearth their influence is the sort
of reflection involved in analytic history, as opposed to national
memory, so here again, it is likely be useful to turn to as we enter
into engaging with conflicting accounts of the past.

None of this means that we are obliged to take seriously every version of the past that comes our way. That would require considering
every groundless, conspiracy-based account that we encounter in
modern society. One of the best ways to sidestep such misguided

practices while at the same time engaging with conflicting accounts of the past is to harness the rational discursive practices of historical research. This applies to formal instruction in school as well as to academic research and calls on us to consider how instruction might be changed to help manage mnemonic conflicts of future generations. If we are to make our nervous system our ally instead of our enemy, we need to start the effort early.

6.6.5. Shape Memory Studies to Support Managing Memory

The final point I would make about managing differences over national memory concerns how to organize the study of national memory. As outlined by Astrid Erll (2011), memory studies has gone through various phases in the 20th century. In the afterword of *Memory in Culture* she notes that the first phase started in the 1920s and 1930s when figures such as Maurice Halbwachs, Aby Warburg, and Frederic Bartlett opened up "pioneering research that extended across a broad spectrum of academic disciplines" (p.172). Erll dates the second phase as starting in the 1980s with the writings of Pierre Nora (1989) on *lieux de mémoire*. Like the earlier phase, this touched on several general issues, but it was "more thematically focused on national remembrance and traumatic events" (p.172). For instance, it involved "more than two decades' intensive work done on the Holocaust and the unearthing of historical injustices all across the globe—from the Aboriginals' 'stolen generation' to apartheid" (p.172).

Erll uses these observations as background for discussing where memory studies might be expected to move in the future. Some researchers are not optimistic that such a future even exists. Gavriel Rosenfeld (2009), for example, argues that the field has already peaked and is now in decline. For him, in a world after 9/11, "the study of memory . . . may increasingly appear to be a luxury that a new era of crisis can ill afford" (p.147). I agree with Erll, however, when she writes, "I would rather claim the opposite" (p.172). Indeed, the analyses I have undertaken in this book start with a concern over today's alarming trends of the new nationalism. As for Erll, this is a context where "we cannot afford the luxury of *not* studying memory" (p.172). Indeed, like Erll, I believe that "If we want to understand '9/11', the actions of Islamic terrorists, or the reactions of the West, we must naturally look at certain mental, discursive, and habitual paradigms that were formed in long historical processes" (pp.172–173).

Erll argues that this requires moving beyond "methodological nationalism" (p.173), which involves giving the nation a privileged status as a unit of analysis and starting point in the study of memory. This sort of privileging often comes with the sort of "analytical groupism" or "tendency to treat ethnic groups as substantial entities to which interests and agency can be attributed" that Brubaker, Loveman, and Stamatov (2004) warn against. In chapter 2, however, I noted the paradox that while analytical groupism is not viable as a construct in social science, we are left with the need "to explain the tenacious hold of groupism in practice" (Brubaker et al., 2004, p.31).

It is precisely this paradox that can be addressed by an approach based on symbolic mediation that provides insight into how narratives function as equipment for living. In such an approach, nations are "perspectives on the world rather than entities in the world" (Brubaker et al., 2004, p.31). These are perspectives that have concrete consequences for how national mnemonic communities engage with one another, but they are not perspectives that belong to the unencumbered individual or to a group essence. Instead, they reflect the co-authorship of cultural tools and active agents, and the cultural tools give rise to habit and underlying codes that often escape our attention. Again, this does not let individuals off the hook when it comes to responsibility. If anything, it gives them more responsibilities in the form of needing to understand the narrative tools that shape their thinking as a member of a community.

In short, it is possible to address issues of national memory without falling prey to methodological nationalism by taking into consideration the power of narrative tools and habits. Building an improved version of memory studies of the sort that Erll envisions will require addressing many other issues as well, but this would appear to be one part of the puzzle. All of which is not to say that if we could only understand and appreciate the habits that underlie our own or others' national memory, we could neatly resolve all our disputes about the past. Niebuhr noted the limits of reflection and discussion and the inevitable role of power in resolving some disputes, and this will continue to play a role in conflicts grounded in national memory. But we can enter into these conflicts with better tools at our disposal for managing them, and in the end, that is the hope of this analysis.

Acknowledgments

Many authors begin their acknowledgments by saying their book took longer to complete than they had anticipated. That's true in my case, to be sure, but I can happily report that I have no reason to lament this. Indeed, I spent the years that this book was "delayed" doing something that was both gratifying and instructive—and ended up making the finished product stronger than it otherwise would have been. Namely, I spent 13 years directing a program at Washington University in St. Louis for future global leaders. The McDonnell International Scholars Academy was created in 2005 to recruit and mentor master's and doctoral students from around the world to develop the relationships and trust they will need to thrive as such leaders. For me, it had the added benefit of bringing together a set of brilliant informants to help me work through the themes of this book.

In the process of directing the McDonnell Academy, I met some of the most impressive and inspiring students to be found anywhere in the world. It was a pleasure to watch them participate in seminars on leadership and global issues and hone their skills in discussing crucial issues of the day, including issues over which people from different societies differ strongly. I also watched them emerge as articulate global citizens as they engaged with figures such as United Nations leaders in New York and political leaders in Washington, D.C. And my wife Mary and I loved having these young folks in our home for dinners and receptions, events that often educated us more than them.

All of this was part of a continuing education program for me, and I owe a debt of gratitude to Washington University's Chancellor

Emeritus Mark Wrighton and to the founding benefactor of the Academy, John McDonnell, for the opportunity. The McDonnell Academy Scholars were endlessly patient and generous with their time in trying to explain why ideas and memories from their societies could be so important, inspiring, and sometimes dangerous. Their energy and optimism also provided inspiration and hope for the future in a troubled world. Without this special experience, I would have been unable to take up many of the points I explore in the chapters in this book.

Listing all who have contributed over the decades of my life to the ideas in this volume could go on forever, so I will do so in an abbreviated form and apologize up front for those I can't mention. I start with my parents, who not only had my back but encouraged me to explore the Soviet Union during the depths of the Cold War. They did this in the context of small-town Midwestern life at a time when many Americans everywhere were suspicious of anyone with an interest in, let alone any admiration for, Russia. My parents may have heard pointed comments from others, but they were completely supportive, even when it came to my decision at the age of 10 to subscribe to *Soviet Life*, which I later discovered was more of a propaganda organ than a source of serious insight.

Jumping ahead a few decades, a whole new round of mentors and colleagues inspired me as I lived and worked in Moscow. Foremost among these was Alexander Romanovich Luria, whose impact is obvious in chapter 2, but his was much more than an intellectual mentorship. As a Communist Party member but also as a cosmopolitan citizen of the world, he led a complex and sometimes anxiety-ridden life. But Alexander Romanovich was above all a human being, and that came through in all his dealings with the people around him. At the time I knew him, he was a senior scholar of international repute, but he remained open to ideas from young, naïve visitors, and he provided a model of how a curious mind can continue to grow.

Many roads led to and from Alexander Romanovich in my case. Mike Cole, who had worked with him in Moscow years before I visited, provide the trusted introduction that helped my conversations along the way, and he became a lifelong colleague and friend in the years since. I also had the great fortune of meeting one of Alexander Romanovich's most important students, Peeter Tulviste, whose intellectual and personal companionship I enjoyed for decades after Alexander Romanovich's death in 1977. Another of Alexander Romanovich's students, Vitya Golod, is featured in chapter 1 and was a brilliant guide for me when it came to cultural and political life in Moscow.

So many people from my various visits to Moscow have been so important for me that I hesitate to start listing them, but over the decades, my conversations with a few of them continue to stand out. Early on, Tanya Akhutina was a wonderful and patient guide to understanding not only Soviet life but also the complexities of neuropsychology. Volodya Zinchenko was a steadfast companion as I sought to understand everything about Soviet life as well as the brilliant insights of Russian philosophy, psychology, religion, and literature. Vasya Davydov was not only a dynamic mind but also a larger-than-life character who taught and showed me much about navigating Soviet life. And a student of them all, Sasha Asmolov, has been not only an intellectual fellow traveler but also an example of how to speak up in a system that did not always appreciate what he had to say.

Moscow served as my home base for most of my visits, but it was also a springboard for meeting future colleagues from other regions of the former Soviet Union such as Georgia, Estonia, Azerbaijan, and Ukraine. Peeter Tulviste served as my guide to the intellectual life and history of Estonia. Getting to know him and other colleagues such as Yuri Mikhailovich Lotman opened up new intellectual vistas. Peeter also served as one of the most inspiring models I have encountered of a courageous leader in a difficult time for a society in transition. And even when he took on the daunting and sometimes dangerous task of becoming the first post-Soviet rector of Tartu University, he never lost his vaunted sense of humor.

In the case of Georgia, I was fortunate to meet Tedo Japaridze, a fellow resident in "Zona V" of the giant dormitory of Moscow State University in 1975. He provided a brilliant running commentary on Soviet life and organized my early visits to Tbilisi. After observing some of Tedo's conversations with Americans such as me, the KGB rewarded him with a career setback that kept him at his research institute in Moscow rather than going to the Soviet embassy in Washington, D.C. Fortunately, he weathered these difficult years well and surfaced once again as the first post-Soviet Georgian ambassador to the United States some two decades later, where we were able to resume our collaboration.

It was through Tedo that I met Zurab Karumidze, George Nizharadze, and other leading figures of the new generation of post-Soviet Georgian intellectuals. This was also the conduit for meeting Nutsa Batiashvili and being able to recruit her to the Ph.D. program in anthropology at Washington University, where she wrote a dissertation and book that have tutored me on the complexities of Georgian "bivocalism" that I examine in chapter 5, and through her I met other impressive scholars such as Nikoloz Aleksidze. Today Tedo, Zurab, George, Nutsa, and Nikoloz are all in Georgia contributing to the ongoing, often difficult effort to keep their country on the road to being the most successful laboratory for democracy in the region.

Shifting to other regions of the former Soviet Union, Lena Ivanova of Kharkiv University has been a steady source of insight into Ukraine and its complex relationship with Russia and a helpful colleague in conducting empirical studies about national memory of World War II. And in Azerbaijan, I have benefited from the insights of Rauf Garagazov in Baku. His writings have touched on his country's relationship with Russia, but especially important for me and many others is his work concerned with the complexities of the violent conflict between Azerbaijan and Armenia over the disputed territory of Nagorny Karabakh. He brings a clear-eyed perspective to this while also being one of the very few Azerbaijanis to maintain a working relationship with Armenian colleagues in the search for "narrative reconciliation."

At the same time that colleagues from the Baltics, Ukraine, and the Caucasus have provided insights into national memories that conflict with Russian accounts of the past, it has been a testimony to the intelligence and courage of Russian colleagues that they have remain engaged in international discussions of these issues. This has been true even during tense times in the relationships with other countries, including the United States. People like Tania Venediktova, Olga Malinova, Serguey Erlich, and Sasha Asmolov in Moscow have always been ready to discuss and explain what I would never otherwise understand. They have been steadfast in providing an objective perspective on events that in the end is both cosmopolitan and in the best tradition of Russian critical patriotism.

Many colleagues elsewhere in the world have also been crucial to developing the ideas in the following chapters. The late Mike Holquist of Yale University was a colleague and friend who played an especially important role in guiding me through the ideas of M.M. Bakhtin and other historical figures in the humanities. David Blight at Yale has been a great source of ideas and inspiration about memory and history, and Strobe Talbott of the Brookings Institution has similarly been someone whose scholarship and wisdom I have depended on when trying out new ideas about international relations and diplomacy.

As my efforts to understand national memory have extended beyond Russia, Europe, and the United States, colleagues in China such as Shen Dingli, Chen Li, and Pan Tianshu at Fudan University and Zhang Xiaojun at Tsinghua University have supplied honest, smart insights that helped make sense of things for an American trying to understand their complex society. They have also sent a steady stream of wonderful visiting students to Washington

University, as well as Jing Xu, who received her Ph.D. in anthropology with us and has been an especially good tutor for me of things Chinese as she pursues her career in the United States.

Among the global community of scholars in memory studies, I have benefited greatly from the ideas of Carol Gluck at Columbia University, Yadin Dudai at the Weizmann Institute of Science and New York University, Suparna Rajaram of Stony Brook University, Madgalena Abel of Regensburg University, Sharda Umanath of Claremont McKenna College, Jeff Olick at the University of Virginia, Bill Hirst at the New School for Social Research, Astrid Erll at the Goethe-University Frankfurt, Ann Rigney at Utrecht University, Elizabeth Marsh at Duke, Jeremy Yamashiro at the University of California, Santa Cruz, and James Liu at Massey University.

At my home institution of Washington University in St. Louis, I have been fortunate to have colleagues such as Pascal Boyer, whose writings in psychological and evolutionary psychology have pushed many of us to explore new issues. Over the years, Wayne Fields has provided guidance on issues of political rhetoric, and Jack Knight, now at Duke, has taught me much on issues of trust. I have also benefited immensely from countless conversations with Gerald Early, John Bowen, Abram van Engen, Zhao Ma, Jim Gibson, Andrew Butler, Jeff Zacks, David Cunningham, Rebecca Lester, Brett Gustafson, Kosi Onyenehu, Doc Billingsley, Jennifer Wistrand, and Ruthie Shaffer.

Among colleagues at Washington University, Roddy Roediger has played an especially important role in helping me understand human memory in its various dimensions. He brought an expertise and visibility in experimental psychology that has complemented my interests in collective and national memory, and together we launched several collaborative efforts in team teaching, writing proposals for funding, and organizing meetings such as the one sponsored by the American Academy of Arts and Sciences in 2019 on "National Memory in a Time of Populism."

In the most local of my environments, my wife Mary, our sons Tyler and Nicholas, our daughter-in-law Jess, and now granddaughter Zadie provide the setting for everything else I do. They have been loving family members, traveling companions, and sources of humor, and our children and grandchild inspire me daily in trying to make the world just a bit better. Mary remains especially important in all this. As my life companion, she is a daily source of support and insight about the world. She has mentored not only our immediate family but also many students from around the world. Her acts of generosity to students in need of help in getting through some of life's tough spots, or sometimes just of simple hospitality, are legendary in the McDonnell Academy. An accomplished writer in her own right, she is also the most insightful and honest editor I could wish for. This book would not have been possible without her.

References

Abel, M., Umanath, S., Fairfield, B., Takahashi, M., Roediger III, H.L., & Wertsch, J.V. (2019). Collective memories across 11 nations for World War II: Similarities and differences regarding the most important events. *Journal of Applied Research in Memory and Cognition, 8,* 78–188.

Acharya, A., & Buzan, B. (2010). *Non-Western international ' relations theory: Perspectives on and beyond Asia.* New York: Routledge.

Adwan, S., Bar-On, D., Musallam, A., & Naveh, E. (2003). *Learning from each other's historical narrative: Palestinians and Israelis.* http://vispo.com/PRIME/leohn1.pdf

Alperovitz, G. (1965). *Atomic diplomacy: Hiroshima and Potsdam.* New York: Simon and Schuster.

Alperovitz, G. (1995). *The decision to use the atomic bomb.* New York: Vintage Books.

Anderson, B. (1991). *Imagined communities: Reflections on the origin and spread of nationalism.* London: Verso.

Assmann, A. (2008). Transformations between history and memory. *Social Research, 75*(1) (Special issue, Collective Memory and Collective Identity), 49–72.

Assmann, A. (2011). *Cultural memory and Western civilization.* New York: Cambridge University Press.

Assmann, J. (1997). *Moses the Egyptian: The memory of Egypt in Western monotheism.* Cambridge, MA: Harvard University Press.

Assmann, J., & Czaplicka, J. (1995). Collective memory and cultural identity. *New German Critique, 65,* 125–133.

Bailyn, B. (2001). Considering the slave trade: History and memory. *William and Mary Quarterly, 58*(1), 245–252.

Bakhtin, M.M. (1981). *The dialogic imagination: Four essays* (M. Holquist, ed.). Austin: University of Texas Press.

Bakhtin, M.M. (1984). *Problems of Dostoyevsky's poetics* (C. Emerson, ed. & trans.). Minneapolis: University of Minnesota Press.

Bakhtin, M.M. (1986a). The problem of speech genres. In M.M. Bakhtin, *Speech genres and other late essays* (V.W. McGee, trans.; C. Emerson & M. Holquist, eds.). Austin: University of Texas Press, 60–102.

Bakhtin, M.M. (1986b). The problem of the text in linguistics, philology, and the human sciences: An experiment in philosophical analysis. In M.M.

Bakhtin, *Speech genres and other late essays* (V.W. McGee, trans.; C. Emerson & M. Holquist, eds.). Austin: University of Texas Press, 103–131.

Bamberg, M. (2012). Why narrative? *Narrative Inquiry*, *22*(1), 202–210.

Bartlett, F.C. (1932). *Remembering: A study in experimental and social psychology*. Cambridge, UK: Cambridge University Press.

Batiashvili, N. (2018). *The bivocal nation: Memory and identity on the edge of empire*. London: Palgrave Macmillan.

Beevor, A. (2012). *The Second World War*. New York: Bay Back Books.

Berdyaev, N. (1992). *The Russian idea* (R.M. French, trans.). Hudson, NY: Lindisfarne Press.

Bergson, H. (2014). *Matter and memory*. Tunbridge Wells, UK: Solis Press. [First published as *Matiere et memoire*, 1896.]

Berlin, I. (1991). The bent twig: On the rise of nationalism. In I. Berlin, *Against the current: Essays in the history of ideas* (H. Hardy, ed.). Oxford: Oxford University Press, 238–261.

Berntsen, D. (2009). Flashbulb memories and social identity. In O. Luminet & A. Curci, eds., *Flashbulb memories: New issues and new perspectives*. New York: Psychology Press, 197–206.

Billig, M. (1995). *Banal nationalism*. London: Sage.

Blight, D.W. (2001). *Race and reunion: The Civil War in American memory*. Cambridge, MA: Harvard University Press.

Blight, D.W. (2009). The memory boom: Why and why now? In P. Boyer & J.V. Wertsch, eds., *Memory in mind and culture*. New York: Cambridge University Press, 238–251.

Blight, D.W. (2019). Composite nation. In J.A. Claybourn, ed., *Our American story: The search for a shared national narrative*. Potomac Books: Lincoln, NE.

Boas, F. (1917). Introductory. *International Journal of American Linguistics*, *1*, 1–8.

Bodnar, J. (1992). *Remaking America: Public memory, commemoration, and patriotism in the twentieth century*. Princeton: Princeton University Press.

Bourdieu, P. (1977). *Outline of a theory of practice*. Cambridge, UK: Cambridge University Press.

Bourdieu, P. (1992). *Language and symbolic power*. Cambridge, UK: Polity.

Boyer, P. (2018). *Minds make societies: How cognition explains the world human create*. New Haven: Yale University Press.

Brokaw, T. (1998). *The greatest generation*. New York: Random House.

Brooks, P. (1984). *Reading for the plot: Design and intention in narrative*. Cambridge, MA: Harvard University Press.

Brown, R., & Kulik, J. (1977). Flashbulb memories. *Cognition*, *5*(1), 73–99.

Brubaker, R., Loveman, M., & Stamatov, P. (2004). Ethnicity as cognition. *Theory and Society*, *33*, 31–64.

Bruner, J.S. (1986). *Actual minds, possible worlds.* Cambridge, MA: Harvard University Press.

Bruner, J.S. (1990). *Acts of meaning.* Cambridge, MA: Harvard University Press.

Bruner, J.S. (2002). *Making stories: Law, literature, life.* New York: Farrar, Straus and Giroux.

Burke, K. (1969). *A grammar of motives.* Berkeley: University of California Press.

Burke, K. (1998 [1938]). Literature as equipment for living. In D.H. Richter, ed., *The critical tradition: Classic texts and contemporary trends.* Boston: Bedford Books, 593–598.

Burns, J.M. (1970). *Roosevelt: The soldier of freedom (1940–1945).* New York: Harcourt Brace Jovanovich.

Carr, D. (1986). *Time, narrative, and history.* Bloomington: Indiana University Press.

Carr, D. (1991). *Time, narrative and history (Studies in phenomenology and existential philosophy).* Bloomington: Indiana University Press.

Cassirer, E. (1953). *Language and myth.* New York: Dover Publications.

Cassirer, E. (1968). *The philosophy of symbolic forms.* New Haven: Yale University Press.

Cheney, L.V. (1994, October 20). The end of history. *Wall Street Journal,* A26 (W), A22 (E).

Clark, L. (2011). *The battle of the tanks: Kursk, 1943.* New York: Atlantic Monthly Press.

Cohen, P.A. (1997). *History in three keys: The Boxers as event, experience, and myth.* New York: Columbia University Press.

Cohen, P.A. (2002). Remembering and forgetting national humiliation in twentieth-century China. *Twentieth-Century China, 27*(2), 1–39.

Connerton, P. (1989). *How societies remember.* Cambridge, UK: Cambridge University Press.

Corning, A., & Schuman, H. (2015). *Generations of collective memory.* Chicago: University of Chicago Press.

Cronon, W. (1992). A place for stories: Nature, history, and narrative. *Journal of American History, 78*(4), 1347–1376.

Curci, A., Luminet, O., Finkenauer, C., & Gisle, L. (2001). Flashbulb memories in social groups: A comparative test-retest study of the memory of French President Mitterand's death in a French and a Belgian group. *Memory, 9,* 81–101.

D'Andrade, R. (1995). *The development of cognitive anthropology.* Cambridge, UK: Cambridge University Press.

de Certeau, M. (1984). *The practice of everyday life.* (S.L. Rendall, trans.). Berkeley: University of California Press.

de Cesari, C., & Rigney, A., eds. (2016). *Transnational memory: Circulation, articulation, scales.* Berlin: Walter de Gruyter.

de Waal, T. (2003). *Black garden: Armenia and Azerbaijan through peace and war.* New York: New York University Press.

de Zavala, A.G., Cichocka, A., Eidelson, R., & Jayawickreme, N. (2009). Collective narcissism and its social consequences. *Journal of Personality and Social Psychology, 97,* 1074–1096.

Donald, M. (1991). *Origins of the modern mind: Three stages in the evolution of culture and cognition.* Cambridge, MA: Harvard University Press.

Dostoevsky, F.M. (1994). *Demons: A novel in three parts* (R. Pevear & L. Volokhonsky, trans. & annot.). New York: Vintage Books.

Duara, P. (2000). Response to Philip Huang's "Biculturality in Modem China and in Chinese Studies." *Modern China, 26*(1), 32–37.

Dudai, Y. (2002). *Memory from A to Z: Keywords, concepts and beyond.* Oxford: Oxford University Press.

Duncker, K. (1945). On problem-solving. *Psychological Monographs, 58*(2720), i–113.

Durkheim, E. (1947). *The elementary forms of religious life.* New York: Free Press. [First published as *Les formes élémentaires de la vie religieuse,* 1912.]

Epps, P.L., Webster, A.K., & Woodbury, A.C. (2017). A holistic humanities of speaking: Franz Boas and the continuing centrality of texts. *International Journal of American Linguistics, 83*(1), 41–78.

Erlich, S. (2019). From national pride to global compassion and admiration: Memory and post-memory of the Second World War during transition from modern nation-state to global information civilization. Presentation at the Memory Studies Association Conference, Madrid, June 2019.

Erll, A. (2011). *Memory in culture.* New York: Palgrave McMillan.

Facing History and Ourselves. https://www.facinghistory.org/about-us

Fairbank, J.K. (1969). China's foreign policy in historical perspective. *Foreign Affairs, 47*(3), 449–463.

Fisher, R., Ury, W., & Patton, B. (2011). *Getting to yes: Negotiating agreement without giving in.* New York: Penguin Books.

Fiske, S.T., & Taylor, S.E. (1991). *Social cognition.* New York: McGraw-Hill.

Fivush, R., & Nelson, K. (2004). The emergence of autobiographical memory: A social cultural developmental theory. *Psychological Review, 111*(2), 486–511.

Ford, C. (2013). Sinocentrism for the information age. Hudson Institute. https://www.hudson.org/research/9468-sinocentrism-for-the-information-age

Friedman, T.L. (2005). *The world is flat: A brief history of the twenty-first century.* New York: Farrar, Straus and Giroux.

Fukuyama, F. (1992). *The end of history and the last man.* New York: Free Press.

Garagozov, R. (2019). Narrative intervention in interethnic conflict. *Political Psychology, 40*(3), 449–465.

Garagozov, R. (2020). *Narrativnoe podtalkivanie k miru v zatyazhnom konflikte* [A narrative push toward peace in a protracted conflict]. Baku, Azerbaijan: Eurasia Partnership Foundation.

Gessen, M. (2017). *The future is history: How totalitarianism reclaimed Russia.* New York: Riverhead Books.

Gibson, J.L. (2006). Overcoming apartheid: Can truth reconcile a divided nation? *Annals of the American Academy of Political and Social Science, 603,* 82–110.

Gibson, J.L., Sonis, J., & Sokhom, H. (2010). Cambodians' support for the rule of law on the eve of the Khmer Rouge trials. *International Journal of Transitional Justice, 4*(3), 377–396. https://doi.org/10.1093/ijtj/ijq013

Gingrich, N., & Gingrich, C. (2011). A city upon a hill. The spirit of American exceptionalism. Hosted by Newt and Callista Gingrich. http://www.cityuponahill.com/

Gladwell, M. (2007). *Blink: The power of thinking without thinking.* New York: Little, Brown & Company.

Gluck, C. (2007). Operations of memory: "Comfort women" and the world. In S. Miyoshi Jager & R. Mitter, eds., *Ruptured histories: War, memory, and the post-Cold War in Asia.* Cambridge, MA: Harvard University Press.

Goffman, E. (1959). *The presentation of self in everyday life.* New York: Doubleday.

Goody, J., & Watt, I. (1968). The consequences of literacy. In J. Goody, ed., *Literacy in traditional societies.* New York: Cambridge University Press.

Greimas, A.J. (1966). *Structural semantics: An attempt at method* (D. McDowell, R. Schleifer, & A. Velie, trans.). Lincoln: University of Nebraska Press.

Grossman, V. (2006 [1960]). *Life and fate.* New York: New York Review Books Classics. [First published in Russian.]

Haass, R.N. (1998). *The reluctant sheriff: The United States after the Cold War.* New York: Council on Foreign Relations Press.

Habermas, J., ed. (1984). *Theory of communicative action, Volume One: Reason and the rationalization of society.* Boston: Beacon Press.

Haidt, J. (2012). *The righteous mind: Why good people are divided by politics and religion.* New York: Pantheon Books.

Halbwachs, M. (1980 [1950]). *The collective memory* (translated by F.J. Ditter, Jr., & V.Y. Ditter). New York: Harper Colophon Books. [First published in French.]

Harari, Y.N. (2011). *Sapiens: A brief history of humankind.* New York: HarperCollins.

Havelock, E.A. (1976). *Origins of Western literacy.* Toronto: Ontario Institute for Studies in Education.

Herder, J.G. (2002). *Philosophical writings* (N.N. Forster, trans.). Cambridge Texts in the History of Philosophy. Cambridge, UK: Cambridge University Press.

Hess, F.M., & Bell, B. (2017). Teach the humanity of our heroes: The key figures in American history aren't cartoon characters. https://www.usnews.com/opinion/knowledge-bank/articles/2017-12-19/teach-the-humanity-of-americas-heroes

Hirst, W., & Phelps, E.A. (2016). Flashbulb memories. *Current Directions in Psychological Science, 25*(1), 36–41.

Hobson, J. (2012). *The Eurocentric conception of world politics: Western international theory, 1760–2010*. New York: Cambridge University Press.

Holbrooke, R. (1998). *To end a war: Sarajevo to Dayton*. New York: Random House.

Holquist, M. (1981). Glossary. In M.M. Bakhtin, *The dialogic imagination: Four essays* (M. Holquist, ed.). Austin: University of Texas Press.

Holquist, M. (2002). *Dialogism*. New York: Taylor & Francis, Ltd.

Hui, V.T. (2018). When anti-Eurocentrism becomes Sinocentrism: The "clash of civilization" narrative in Sinocentric IR. Presentation at the panel "Why Global IR Needs Global History." International Studies Association Annual Convention, San Francisco, April 2018.

Hutchins, E. (1995). *Cognition in the wild*. Cambridge, MA: MIT Press.

Isurin, L. (2017). *Collective remembering: Memory in the world and in the mind*. Cambridge, UK: Cambridge University Press.

Jacoby, L., & Kelley, D.M. (1987). Unconscious influences of memory for a prior event. *Personality and Social Psychology Bulletin, 13*(3), 314–336.

James, W. (1884). What is an emotion? *Mind, 9*(34), 188–205.

James, W. (1890). *The principles of psychology*. New York: Dover Publications, Inc.

Kagan, R. (2012). *The world America made*. New York: Alfred A. Knopf.

Kahneman, D. (2011). *Thinking, fast and slow*. New York: Farrar, Straus and Giroux.

Kaplan, B. (1990). Personal communication with the author.

Kelly, R.E. (2011). A "Confucian long peace" in pre-Western East Asia? *European Journal of International Relations, 18*(3), 407–430.

Kermode, F. (1967). *The sense of an ending: Studies in the theory of fiction*. Oxford: Oxford University Press.

Kihlstrom, J. (2012). Remembering the father of cognitive psychology. *Observer*. Association for Psychological Science. https://www.psychologicalscience. org/observer/remembering-the-father-of-cognitive-psychology

King, C. (2019). *Gods of the upper air: How a circle of renegade anthropologists reinvented race, sex, and gender in the twentieth century*. New York: Doubleday.

King, D. (1997). *The commissar vanishes: The falsification of photographs and art in Stalin's Russia*. New York: Henry Holt and Company.

László, J. (2008). *The science of stories: An introduction to narrative psychology*. London: Routledge.

Leahy, W.D. (1950). *I was there: The personal story of the chief of staff to Presidents Roosevelt and Truman based on his notes and diaries made at the time*. New York: Whittlesey House.

Lepore, J. (2019). A new Americanism: Why a nation needs a national story. *Foreign Affairs* (March/April), 10–19.

Lévi-Strauss, C. (1955). The structural study of myth. *Journal of American Folklore, 68*(270), 428–444. (Special issue: Myth: A symposium).

Levy, D., & Sznaider, N. (2002). Memory unbound: The Holocaust and the formation of cosmopolitan memory. *European Journal of Social Theory, 5*(1), 87–106.

Lewis, S. (1998 [1922]). *Babbitt.* New York: Bantam Dell.

Lieberthal, K. (2014). Personal communication.

Lieberthal, K., & Wang, J. (2012). *Addressing U.S.-China strategic distrust.* John L. Thornton China Center at Brookings. https://www.brookings.edu/wp-content/uploads/2016/06/0330_china_lieberthal.pdf

Lilienfeld, S.O., Ammirati, R., & Landfield, K. (2009). Giving debiasing away: Can psychological research on correcting cognitive errors promote human welfare? *Perspectives on Psychological Science, 4*(4), 390–398.

Lim, L. (2014). *People's republic of amnesia.* Oxford: Oxford University Press.

Liu, J.H., Goldstein-Hawes, R., Hilton, D.J., Huang, L.L., Gastardo-Conaco, C., Dresler-Hawke, E., Pittolo, F., Hong, Y.Y., Ward, C., Abraham, S., Kashima, Y., Kashima, E., Ohashi, M., Yuki, M., & Hidaka, Y. (2005). Social representations of events and people in world history across twelve cultures. *Journal of Cross-Cultural Psychology, 36*(2), 171–191.

Loewen, J.W. (2018). *Lies my teacher told me.* New York: The New Press.

Lotman, Y.M. (1976). *Analysis of the poetic text.* (D. Barton Johnson, trans.). Ann Arbor: Ardis.

Lu, X. (2014). *A madman's diary.* Cambridge, UK: Easy Peasy Publishing (originally published in Chinese in 1918).

Luria, A.R. (1976a). Personal communication.

Luria, A.R. (1976b). *Cognitive development: Its cultural and social foundations.* Cambridge, MA: Harvard University Press.

Luria, A.R. (1981). *Language and cognition.* New York: John Wiley & Sons.

MacIntyre, A. (1984). *After virtue: A study in moral philosophy* (2nd ed.). Notre Dame, IN: University of Notre Dame Press.

Malinova, O. (2015). *Aktual'noe proshloe: Simvolicheskaya politika vlastvuyushchei eliti i dilemmy rossiiskoi identichnosti* [The actual past: The symbolic politics of the powerful elite and the dilemma of Russian identity]. Moscow: ROSSPEN.

Malinova, O. (2018). The embarrassing centenary: Reinterpretation of the 1917 Revolution in the official historical narrative of post-Soviet Russia (1991–2017). *Nationalities Papers, 46*(2), 272–289.

Malinova, O. (2019). Constructing the "usable past": The evolution of the official historical narrative in post-Soviet Russia. https://brill.com/view/book/edcoll/9789004366671/B9789004366671_006.xml?lang=en

Mannheim, K. (1952). The problem of generations. In P. Kecskemeti, ed., *Karl Mannheim essays*. New York: Routledge, 276–322.

McAdams, D.P. (1993). *The stories we live by: Personal myths and the making of the self*. New York: Guilford.

McAdams, D.P. (2013). *The redemptive self: Stories Americans live by* (rev. & exp. ed.). New York: Oxford University Press.

McCarthy, T. (1984). Translator's introduction. In J. Habermas, ed., *Theory of communicative action, Volume one: Reason and the rationalization of society*. Boston: Beacon Press, v–xxxvii.

McDaniel, T. (1996). *The agony of the Russian idea*. Princeton: Princeton University Press.

Mead, G.H. (1934). *Mind, self, and society*. Chicago: University of Chicago Press.

Mercier, H., & Sperber, D. (2017). *Enigma of reason: A new theory of human understanding*. Cambridge, MA: Harvard University Press.

Middleton, D., & Edwards, D. (1990). Conversational remembering: A social psychological approach. In D. Middleton & D. Edwards, eds., *Collective remembering*. London: Sage Publications, 23–46.

Miller, M. (2018 [1974]). *Plain speaking: An oral biography of Harry Truman*. New York: Rosetta Books.

Mink, L. (1978). Narrative form as cognitive instrument. In R.H. Canary & H. Kozicki, eds., *The writing of history: Literary form and historical understanding*. Madison: University of Wisconsin Press, 182–203.

Mynatt, C.R., Doherty, M.E., & Tweney, R. (1977). Confirmation bias in a simulated research environment: An experimental study of scientific inference. *Quarterly Journal of Experimental Psychology, 29*(1), 85–95.

Nash, G.B. (2004). Lynne Cheney's attack on the history standards, 10 years later. *History News Network*. Columbian College of Arts & Sciences, George Washington University. https://historynewsnetwork.org/article/8418

Nash, G.B., Crabtree, C., & Dunn, R.E. (1997). *History on trial: Culture wars and the teaching of the past*. New York: Alfred A. Knopf.

Neisser, U. (1967). *Cognitive psychology*. Englewood Cliffs, NJ: Prentice-Hall.

Neisser, U. (1976). *Cognition and reality: Principles and implications of cognitive psychology*. New York: Freeman.

Neisser, U. (1982). Snapshots or benchmarks? In U. Neisser, ed., *Memory observed: Remembering in natural contexts*. San Francisco: W.H. Freeman, 43–48.

Nguyen, V.T. (2016). *Nothing ever dies: Vietnam and the memory of war*. Cambridge, MA: Harvard University Press.

Nickerson, R. (1998). Confirmation bias: A ubiquitous phenomenon in many guises. *Review of General Psychology, 2*, 175–220.

Niebuhr, R. (1984). *The irony of American history*. New York: Scribner.

Nora, P. (1989). Between memory and history: *Les lieux de memoire*. *Representations, 26*, 7–24.

Novick, P. (1988). *That noble dream: The "objectivity question" and the American historical profession*. Cambridge, UK: Cambridge University Press.

Novick, P. (1999). *The Holocaust in American life*. Boston: Houghton Mifflin Company.

O'Connor, F. (1993). The comforts of home. In *Flannery O'Connor: The complete stories*. New York: Farrar, Straus & Giroux, 383–404. [First published in 1965 in *Everything That Rises Must Converge*.]

Olick, J.K. (1999). Collective memory: The two cultures. *Sociological Theory, 17*(3), 333–348.

Olick, J.K. (2007). *The politics of regret: On collective memory and historical responsibility*. New York: Routledge.

Olick, J.K., & Robbins, J. (1998). Social memory studies: From "collective memory" to the historical sociology of mnemonic practices. *Annual Review of Sociology, 24*, 105–140.

Ong, W.J. (1982). *Orality and literacy: The technologizing of the word*. London: Routledge.

Orwell, G. (1949). *Nineteen eighty-four*. London: Martin Secker and Warburg Limited.

Packer, G. (2019). *Our man: Richard Holbrooke and the end of the American century*. New York: Alfred A. Knopf.

Paez, D.R., & Liu, J.H. (2011). Collective memory of conflicts. In D. Bar-Tal, ed., *Intergroup conflicts and their resolution: A social psychological perspective*. New York: Psychology Press, 105–124.

Petersen, R.D. (2011). *Western intervention in the Balkans: The strategic use of emotion in conflict*. Cambridge, UK: Cambridge University Press.

Pevear, R. (1994). Foreword. In F.M. Dostoevsky, *Demons: A novel in three parts* (R. Pevear & L. Volokhonsky, trans. & annot.). New York: Vintage Books, xvii.

Piaget, J. (1953). *The origins of intelligence in the child*. London: Routledge.

Pickering, T. (2001). Oral presentation to the Chinese government regarding the accidental bombing of the P.R.C. embassy in Belgrade, June 17, 1999. U.S. Department of State Archive. https://1997-2001.state.gov/policy_remarks/1999/990617_pickering_emb.html

Pickering, T. (2013). Personal communication.

Polegkyi, O. (2016, May 25). Russia's new "religion": The cult of the "Great Victory." *New Eastern Europe*. https://neasterneurope.eu/2016/05/25/russia-s-new-religion-the-cult-of-the-great-victory/

Propp, V. (1968 [1928]). *Morphology of the folktale (second edition)* (revised and edited by L.A. Wagner). Austin: University of Texas Press.

Reagan, R. (1989). Farewell address, January 11, 1989. https://www.youtube.com/watch?v=UKVsq2daR8Q

Renan, E. (1990 [1882]). What is a nation? In H.K. Bhabha, ed., *Nation and narration*. London: Routledge, 8–22.

Resnick, L.B., Levine, J.M., & Behrend, S.D. (1991). *Perspectives on socially shared cognition*. Washington, DC: APA Science Volume Series.

Ricoeur, P. (1984). *Time and narrative*. Chicago: University of Chicago Press.

Ricoeur, P. (1984–86). *Time and narrative*, 2 vols. (K. McLaughlin & D. Pellauer, trans.). Chicago: University of Chicago Press.

Ricoeur, P. (1991). Life in quest of narrative. In D. Wood, ed., *On Paul Ricoeur: Narrative and interpretation*. London: Routledge, 20–33.

Ricoeur, P. (1992). *Oneself as other* (K. Blamey, trans.). Chicago: University of Chicago Press.

Roediger III, H.L. (2000). Sir Frederic Charles Bartlett: Experimental and applied psychologist. In G.A. Kimble & M. Wertheimer, eds., *Portraits of pioneers in psychology, Vol. IV*. Washington, DC: American Psychological Association, 149–161.

Roediger, H.L., Abel, M., Umanath, S., Shaffer, R.A., Fairfield, B., Takahashi, M., & Wertsch, J.V. (2019). Competing national memories of World War II. *Proceedings of the National Academy of Sciences, 116*(34), 16678–16686.

Roediger, H.L., & DeSoto, K.A. (2017, April 20). How Americans remember and forget U.S. presidents. *Atlas of Science*. http://atlasofscience.org/how-americans-remember-and-forget-the-u-s-presidents/

Roediger III, H.L., Marsh, E.J., & Lee, S.C. (2002). Varieties of memory. In H. Pashler (Series Ed.), *Stevens' handbook of experimental psychology: Vol. 2. Memory for cognitive processes* (3rd ed.). New York: John Wiley & Sons, 1–41.

Rose, G. (2019). The new nationalism. *Foreign Affairs* (March/April), 9.

Rosenfeld, G. (2009). A looming crash or a soft landing? Forecasting the future of the memory "industry." *Journal of Modern History* (March), 122–158.

Rowe, S.M., Wertsch, J.V., & Kosyaeva, T.Y. (2002). Linking little narratives to big ones: Narrative and public memory in history museums. *Culture and Psychology, 8*(1), 96–112.

Russell, B. (1971 [1912]). *Problems of philosophy*. Oxford: Oxford University Press.

Ryle, G. (1949). *The concept of mind*. London: Hutchinson.

Sacks, H., Schegloff, E.A., & Jefferson, G. (1974). A simplest systematics for the organization of turn-taking for conversation. *Language, 50*(4), 696–735.

Sandel, M. (2009). *Justice: What's the right thing to do?* New York: Farrar, Straus and Giroux.

Sarbin, T.R. (1986). *Narrative psychology: The storied nature of human conduct*. New York: Praeger.

Schacter, D.L., Gutchess, A.H., & Kensinger, E.A. (2009). Specificity of memory: Implications for individual and collective remembering. In

P. Boyer & J.V. Wertsch, eds., *Memory in mind and culture*. Cambridge, UK: Cambridge University Press, 83–111.

Schwartz, B. (1997). Collective memory and history: How Abraham Lincoln became a symbol of racial equality. *Sociological Quarterly, 38*(3), 469–496. doi:10.1111/j.1533-8525.1997.tb00488.x

Scott, J. (1985). *Weapons of the weak: Everyday forms of peasant resistance*. New Haven: Yale University Press.

Scribner, S. (1977). Modes of thinking and ways of speaking. In P.N. Johnson-Laird & P.C. Wason, eds., *Thinking: Readings in cognitive science*. New York: Cambridge University Press, 483–500.

Scribner, S., & Cole, M. (1981). *The psychology of literacy*. Cambridge, MA: Harvard University Press.

Shiller, R.J. (2017, January). Narrative economics. *NBER Working Paper No. 23075*. https://www.nber.org/papers/w23075

Shiller, R.J. (2019). *Narrative economics: How stories go viral and drive major economic events*. Princeton: Princeton University Press.

Singh, P. (2013). "Chinese dream"—return to the concept of Middle Kingdom? *Logos: The Takshashila Community Blog*. http://logos.nationalinterest.in/2013/12/chinese-dream-return-to-the-concept-of-middle-kingdom/

Smith, R. (2003). *Stories of peoplehood: The politics and morals of political membership*. New York: Cambridge University Press.

Snyder, T. (2010). *Bloodlands: Europe between Hitler and Stalin*. New York: Basic Books.

Solzhenitsyn, A. (1978). The exhausted West. *Harvard Magazine* (July–August), 20–26.

Solzhenitsyn, A.I. (1985). *The Gulag Archipelago, 1918–1956. An experiment in literary investigation* (T.P. Whitney & H. Willets, trans.). New York: Harper Perennial.

Squire, L. (1987). *Memory and brain*. Oxford: Oxford University Press.

Stahel, D. (2009). *Operation Barbarossa and Germany's defeat in the east*. Cambridge, UK: Cambridge University Press.

Stone, C.B., Coman, A., & Brown, A.D. (2012, January 5). Toward a science of silence: The consequences of leaving the memory unsaid. *Perspectives on Psychological Science*. https://doi.org/10.1177/1745691611427303

Stowe, H.B. (1952) . *Uncle Tom's cabin, or, Life among the lowly*. Boston: John P. Jewett & Company (first published in 1852).

Sumner, W.G. (1906). *Folkways*. Boston: Ginn and Company.

Talbott, S. (2013). Personal communication.

Taleb, N.N. (2007). *The black swan: The impact of the highly improbable*. New York: Random House.

Taylor, C. (1985). *Human agency and language. Philosophical papers I*. Cambridge, UK: Cambridge University Press.

Thapar, R. (2018). https://www.bing.com/videos/search?q=youtube+romila+thapar&view=detail&mid=E5AD1683CB9A5BBF3B16E5AD1683CB9A5 BBF3B16&FORM=VIRE

Thapar, R. (2019, May 17). They peddle myths and call it history. *New York Times*. https://www.nytimes.com/2019/05/17/opinion/india-elections-modi-history.html?action=click&module=Opinion&pgtype=Homepage

Tin-bor Hui, V. (2018). When anti-Eurocentrism becomes Sinocentrism: The "Clash of Civilizations" narrative in Sinocentric IR. Paper presented at the panel "Why Global IR Needs Global History." International Studies Association Annual Convention, San Francisco, April 3–8, 2018.

Toulmin, S. (1958). *The uses of argument*. Cambridge, UK: Cambridge University Press.

Tulviste, P. (1994). Personal communication.

Tulviste, P., & Wertsch, J.V. (1992). Official and unofficial histories: The case of Estonia. *Journal of Narrative and Life History, 4*(4), 311–329.

Tversky, A., & D. Kahneman. (1974). Judgment under uncertainty: Heuristics and biases. *Science, 185*(4157), 1124–1131.

Van Engen, A.C. (2020). *City on a hill: A history of American exceptionalism*. New Haven: Yale University Press.

Volkan, V.D. (1998). Transgenerational transmissions and chosen traumas. Opening address, XIII International Congress, International Association of Group Psychotherapy, August, 1998. https://www.academia.edu/25207644/TRANSGENERATIONAL_TRANSMISSIONS_AND_CHOSEN_TRAUMAS?auto=download

von Humboldt, W. (1997). *Essays on language*. (D. Farrelly & T. Harden, eds.). Bern: Peter Lang Publishers.

Vygotsky, L.S. (1981a). The instrumental method in psychology. In J.V. Wertsch, ed., *The concept of activity in Soviet psychology*. Armonk, NY: M.E. Sharpe, 134–147.

Vygotsky, L.S. (1981b). The genesis of higher mental functions. In J.V. Wertsch, ed., *The concept of activity in Soviet psychology*. Armonk, NY: M.E. Sharpe, 144–188.

Vygotsky, L.S. (1982). *Sobranie sochinenii, Tom pervyi: Voprosy teorii i istorii psikhologii* [Collected works, Vol. 1: Problems in the theory and history of psychology]. Moscow: Izdatel'stvo Pedagogika.

Vygotsky, L.S. (1986). *Thought and language* (A. Kozulin, ed.). Cambridge, MA: MIT Press.

Vygotsky, L.S., & Luria, A.R. (1993 [1930]). *Studies in the history of behavior: Ape, primitive, and child*. (V.I. Golod & J.E. Knox, eds.). Mahwah, NJ: Lawrence Erlbaum Associates, Inc.

Wagoner, B. (2017). *The constructive mind: Bartlett's psychology in reconstruction*. Cambridge, UK: Cambridge University Press.

Walt, S.M. (1998). International relations: One world, many theories. *Foreign Policy, 110,* 29–46.

Waltz, K.M. (1979). The anarchic structure of world politics. In K.M. Waltz, ed., *Theory of international politics.* New York: McGraw-Hill, 79–106.

Wang, Z. (2012). *Never forget national humiliation: History and memory in Chinese politics and foreign relations.* New York: Columbia University Press.

Wayman, E. (2012). When did the human mind evolve to what it is today? https://www.smithsonianmag.com/science-nature/when-did-the-human-mind-evolve-to-what-it-is-today-140507905/

Wertsch, J.V. (1985a). The semiotic mediation of mental life: L.S. Vygotsky and M.M. Bakhtin. In E. Mertz & R.J. Parmentier, eds., *Semiotic mediation: Sociocultural and psychological perspectives.* New York: Academic Press, 49–71.

Wertsch, J.V. (1985b). *Vygotsky and the social formation of mind.* Cambridge, MA: Harvard University Press.

Wertsch, J.V. (1991). *Voices of the mind: A sociocultural approach to mediated action.* Cambridge, MA: Harvard University Press.

Wertsch, J.V. (1998). *Mind as action.* New York: Oxford University Press.

Wertsch, J.V. (2002). *Voices of collective remembering.* Cambridge, UK: Cambridge University Press.

Wertsch, J.V. (2008a). Blank spots in collective memory: A case study of Russia. *Annals of the American Academy of Political and Social Science, 617,* 58–71.

Wertsch, J.V. (2008b). A clash of deep memories. *Profession,* 46–53.

Wertsch, J.V. (2018). National memory and where to find it. In B. Wagoner, ed., *Handbook of culture and memory* (Frontiers in Cultural Psychology series). New York: Oxford University Press, 259–282.

Wertsch, J.V. (2019). National narratives as habits of thought. In J.A. Claybourn, ed., *Our American story: The search for a shared national narrative.* Potomac Books: Lincoln, NE, 19–27.

Wertsch, J.V., & Karumidze, Z. (2009). Spinning the past: Russian and Georgian accounts of the war of August 2008. *Memory Studies, 2,* 377–391.

Wertsch, J.V., & Roediger, H.L., III (2008). Collective memory: Conceptual foundations and theoretical approaches. *Memory, 16,* 318–326.

White, H. (1981). The value of narrativity in the presentation of reality. In J.T.W. Mitchell, ed., *On narrative.* University of Chicago Press, 1–23.

Wilson, W. (2013). The bomb didn't beat Japan... Stalin did. Have 70 years of nuclear policy been based on a lie? *Foreign Policy,* May 30, 2013. https://foreignpolicy.com/2013/05/30/the-bomb-didnt-beat-japan-stalin-did/

Wimmer, A. (2019). Why nationalism works. And why it isn't going away. *Foreign Affairs* (March/April), 27–34.

Wineburg, S. (2001). *Historical thinking and other unnatural acts: Charting the future of teaching the past.* Philadelphia: Temple University Press.

Wineburg, S. (2018). *Why learn history (when it's already on your phone)?* Chicago: University of Chicago Press.

Wood, E.A. (2011). Performing memory: Vladimir Putin and the celebration of WWII in Russia. *Soviet and Post-Soviet Review, 38,* 172–200.

Xu, G. (2001). Internationalism, nationalism, national identity: China from 1895–1919. In G. Wei & X. Liu, eds., *Chinese nationalism in perspective.* Santa Barbara, CA: Greenwood Press, 101–120.

Yamashiro, J., Van Engen, A., & Roediger, H.L., III. (2019). American origins: Political and religious divides in U.S. collective memory. *Memory Studies, 15*(1), 1–18.

Yan, X. (2001). The rise of China in Chinese eyes. *Journal of Contemporary China, 10*(26), 37–38.

Zacks, J.M. (2017). Events in mind, media, and memory. In J.M. Zacks & H.A. Taylor, eds., *Representations in mind and world.* New York: Psychology Press, 184–206.

Zaromb, F., Butler, A.C., Agarwal, P.K., & Roediger, H.L. (2014). Collective memories of three wars in United States history in younger and older adults. *Memory & Cognition, 42,* 383–399.

Zaromb, F.M., Liu, J.H., Páez, D., Hanke, K., Putnam, A.L., & Roediger III, H.L. (2018). We made history: Citizens of 35 countries overestimate their nation's role in world history. *Journal of Applied Research in Memory and Cognition, 7,* 521–528.

Zerubavel, E. (2003). *Time maps: Collective memory and the social shape of the past.* Chicago: University of Chicago Press.

Index

For the benefit of digital users, indexed terms that span two pages (e.g., 52–53) may, on occasion, appear on only one of those pages.

Figures are indicated by *f* following the page number

Abel, M., 150–51, 152
Abkhazia, 21–22, 167–68, 182
abstract reasoning, 57, 58–59
Actual Minds, Possible Worlds
    (Bruner), 61–62
Adams, Herbert Baxter, 94
"addressivity," 163, 167–68
Adwan, Sami, 166
Affordable Care Act, 47
African Americans, 119–20
"age of nationalities," 5–6
Alexander Nevsky (film), 111, 139
Alperovitz, Gar, 155–56
ambivalence, 182–83
America. *See* United States
American Civil War, 67–70, 94, 126,
    187–88, 190
American women, 47
analogies, 99
analytic groupism, 35–36, 186, 230
analytic history, 90–97, 109, 132–33,
    175, 224–26
Anderson, Benedict, 6–7
Andropov, Yuri, 118
anecdotes, 118
anthropology, 11–12
anthropomorphism, 36–37
apartheid, 202–3
Aristotle, 8, 28, 61–62, 65
Armenia, 88–89
"articulation," 53

Assmann, Aleida, 31, 77n.4, 121, 137
Assmann, Jan, 92
atheism, 101–2
atomic bombing of Japan, 2–3, 14,
    129–30, 152, 154–57, 225–26
Atomic Diplomacy
    (Alperovitz), 155–56
"authoritative discourse," 171–79
authority, 94–95
    internet, impact of, 178
    of narratives, 115–16
    resistance to, 116–18, 173–75
    sources of, 70–71
    state as, 89–90, 115–17, 120
autobiographical memories,
    43–44, 48
Azerbaijan, 88–89

Babbit (Lewis), 26
Bailyn, Bernard, 93
Bakhtin, Mikhail, 52–53, 54, 161–62,
    163–67, 172
Bamberg, Michael, 12
"banal nationalism," 6–7
Bartlett, Frederic, 38, 40, 41, 42, 44,
    50–52, 76
Batiashvili, Nutsa, 179–82, 183
Belgians, 43–44
Belgrade, Chinese embassy
    bombing, 19–21, 142–43, 207–
    11, 213, 219–20

Bell, Brendan, 176–77
Benjamin, Walter, 10
Bergson, Henri, 39–40, 79–80, 81
Berlin, Battle of, 16, 17, 153, 155
Berlin, Isaiah, 132–33
bias, 106–7, 109, 150, 199–200, 224
Billig, Michael, 6–7
bivocalism, 179–83
Black Americans, 42–43
Black Swan, The (Taleb), 105
"blank spots," 127–29, 130–31
Blight, David, 69, 70, 94, 126, 189–90
Boas, Franz, 11–12, 35–36
Bodnar, John, 123
Bosnia-Herzegovina, 137–38, 205
Bosnian War, 87–88
bottom-up processes, 33–36,
   71–72, 117
Bourdieu, Pierre, 83
Boxer Rebellion, 64, 140, 142
Boyer, Pascal, 36–38
British students, 50–51
Brooks, Peter, 63–64
Brown, Roger, 42–43, 44, 49–50
Brubaker, Rogers, 34, 35–36, 38, 71,
   78–79, 230
Bruner, Jerome, 1, 8, 13–14, 38,
   61–62, 74
Burke, Kenneth, 26, 27, 28,
   65–66, 216–17
Bush, George H.W., 145–46

capitalism, 101
Carr, David, 60, 61, 72
Cassirer, Ernst, 54, 199
Central Asia, modernization
   efforts, 56–59
Central Kingdom, China as, 192–96
Century of Humiliation, 140–45,
   195–96, 213–14, 215
Cesari, Chiara de, 5
Chapaev (film), 111
Chapaev, Vasily, 110–12

Chavchavadze, Ilia, 180–81
Cheney, Lynne, 185
child development, 56, 59–60, 75–76
China
   Boxer Rebellion, 64
   central kingdom, quest as, 192–96
   Century of Humiliation narrative,
      140–45, 195–96, 213–14, 215
   "chosen glory" rhetoric, 140–41
   Day of Humiliation, 143
   embassy bombing, 19–21, 142–43,
      207–11, 213, 219–20
   international relations,
      193–95, 213–14
   nationalism in, 213–14
   perspective of Americans,
      214–15, 217–18
   Spring and Autumn period, 144
   Tiananmen Square massacre, 33,
      142, 144
China Dream program, 195–96
Chinese Communist Party, 144
"chosen glory," 140–41
"chosen trauma," 137, 138
Christianity, 191–92
chronicles, 63, 68
Churchill, Winston, 203–4
"circumstantialist"
   approaches, 34–36
citizen loyalty, 5
City on the Hill narrative, 146,
   189, 211, 212–13, 214–15,
   216, 217–18
"class warfare," 190
Clinton, Bill, 20, 208–9, 210, 220
cognition. *See* Mental functioning
cognitive anthropology, 38–39
cognitive humility, 223
"cognitive instruments," 25
cognitive psychology, 28, 44–45,
   102–3, 104
"Cognitive Revolution," 73
Cohen, Paul, 64, 90–91, 141–42, 144

Cold War, 1–2, 17–18, 117–18
collective experiences, 136–37
collective memory, 4–5,
 10–11, 51–52
 versus collective remembering,
 32, 157
 individuals and, 40–41, 42, 71–72
 "pastness" of events in, 92–93
 as social phenomenon, 39–40, 41
 two cultures of, 41
 for U.S. presidents, 121
collective remembering, 32
collectives. *See* Groups; Mnemonic
 communities
"collectivist understanding," 41
"Comforts of Home, The"
 (O'Connor), 27–28
"commemogram," 123
common sense, 13–14, 74,
 91–92, 115–16
communism, 101, 123–24, 144, 192
conceptual framework, 31
confirmation bias, 106–7
conflict management, 94–95, 221–
 31. *See also* Negotiations
 engagement with opposing
 accounts, 227–29
 history as anecdote, 224–26
 narrative habits and, 226–27
 recognition of challenges,
 202–3, 222–24
 shaping of memory studies
 and, 229–31
Confucian concepts, 193–94, 195–96
Connerton, Paul, 10–11, 83–84, 227
consciousness. *See* Human
 consciousness
"consequentiality," 42–46, 49–50
contradictory evidence, 96, 132–33,
 169, 199–200, 206–7
"conversational
 remembering," 34–35
"cookie cutter" idea, 13–14, 38

"cosmopolitan memory," 5
counterarguments, use of, 13–14
Cronon, William, 94–95, 115–16,
 161–62, 163
cultural anthropology, 11–12, 35–36
cultural differences, 35–36
cultural factors, 33, 34, 41, 230–31
"cultural memory," 40–41, 121, 137
cultural tools, 9, 10, 84–85
"curse of mediacy," 199
cynicism, 174–75, 214

D'Andrade, Roy, 38–39, 51
Day of Accord and
 Reconciliation, 125
Day of Humiliation, 143
Day of the Great October Socialist
 Revolution, 123–25, 126–28
Day of Victory, 126–28
D-Day, 14, 17, 152, 153, 153n.13
Death of Stalin, The
 (Iannucci), 128–29
de Certeau, Michel, 174
decision making, 102–4,
 105, 196–97
declarative memory, 81
"deep culture," 213–14, 216, 228
"deep thinking," 216, 228
Demons (Dostoevsky), 101–2
Deng, Xiaoping, 195–96
DeSoto, K.A., 121
de Waal, Thomas, 88–89
dialogism, 161–83
 hidden between
 narratives, 166–71
 irony in, 216–17
 meaning of national narratives
 and, 198
 within narratives, 171–79
 within narrative voices, 179–83
 national narrative projects and,
 190, 196–97
 overt example of, 166

differences, 2–4. *See also* Mnemonic
    standoffs
    accounting for, 18, 19–20, 21, 29,
        39, 138–39
    commitment to, 4, 38–39
    illustrations of, 13, 17–19, 20–21
    managing (*see* Conflict
        management)
    opposition, degree of, 3, 29, 31
    rejection of opposing
        narratives, 171–72
    truth and, 3–4, 31, 66–67
    understanding of, 18–19
different worlds, 25n.8, 25–26
diplomats, 88, 205, 207,
    218–19, 220–21
disagreements. *See* Differences
discourse analysis, 34–35
"distributed cognition," 54
distrust, 214–16
Donald, Merlin, 72
Dostoevsky, Fyodor, 101–2, 191–92
Duara, Prasenjit, 35
Dudai, Yadin, 32
Duncker, K., 99
Dunning, William A., 94
Durkheim, Emile, 39–40

Eastern Europe, 89, 130–32
economic narratives, 8–9
education. *See* History instruction
Edwards, Derek, 34–35
"egocentric" speech, 53
Eisenstein, Sergei, 111, 139
elephant/rider allegory, 103
emotions
    behaviors and, 103
    group trauma and, 137
    strategic use of, 89–90, 93
emplotment
    engaging through, 63–64
    exacerbation of differences and,
        162–63, 169

memory and, 65
    organizing function, 62–64,
        65–66, 72
    process of, 62–63
    selectivity of, 121–22, 123, 129–33
"enacted narratives," 60–61,
    184, 185–86
Enemy at the Gates, 16
episodic memory, 81
Epps, Patience, 11–12
"equipment for living," 25–29, 65,
    84–85, 138, 165–66, 197, 221
Erlich, Serguey, 225–26
Erll, Astrid, 10, 31, 40–41,
    42, 229–30
Estonia, 102, 117–18, 130–32,
    174–75, 222–23
ethics, 94–95
ethnicity, 35–36, 38–39, 230
ethnocentrism, 150, 192–93
Eurocentric international relations
    theory, 193–94
"Europe-wide Day of
    Remembrance," 169–71
"event models," 72–73
everyday life, 26, 27, 28–29
evidence, 4, 28, 70–71
    contradictory information,
        resistance to, 96, 132–33, 169,
        199–200, 206–7, 222–23
    forms of, 32–35, 67
    preserving, 97, 132–33
    truth, based on, 70–71, 97
evolutionary psychology, 35–36, 72
"Expulsion of Alien Enemies"
    narrative, 98–102, 109–10,
    112, 127, 132–33, 135, 139–40,
    190–91, 222–23

"Facing History and
    Ourselves," 202–3
false narratives, 18, 28, 117–18, 131
fascism, 130–31, 170, 222–23

"fast thinking," 76–77, 102–9,
    112–13, 205–6
Fatherland War, 99
fiction, 91–92
Filofei, Monk of Pskov, 191–92
Fisher, R., 201, 202, 206
"Five Day War," 21–23, 167–68
Fivush, Robyn, 75
flashbulb memories, 42–50
    consequentiality in, 44–46
    event size and, 47–50
"folk sociology," 37–39
folktales, 77–78
Ford, Christopher, 195–96
Foreign Policy, 156
forgetting, 91, 127–29, 224–25
France, 147–49, 224–25
French citizens, 43–44
Friedman, Thomas, 6

Gagarin, Yuri, 49
Garagozov, Rauf, 8, 169
generational experiences, 136–37
genetic studies, 56
geopolitical scene, 5–6
George, King, 194–95
Georgia, Republic of
    bivocalism in, 179–83
    Day of Remembrance, 170–71
    "Five Day War" with Russia, 21–
        24, 135, 167–69
    origins of, 180–81
    social language used in, 179
Germany, 24
    Nazis, 24, 130–31, 153, 170–71
    Poland invasion, 15, 16,
        129–30, 152
    Soviet invasion, 15, 16, 109–10,
        129–30, 149, 153
    Soviet Union, pact with, 130–31
Gessen, Masha, 135
Gettysburg Address, 173
globalization, 6

Gluck, Carol, 7–8, 117–18
Goffman, Erving, 34, 119, 184–85
Gorbachev, Mikhail, 118,
    131–32, 222–23
Grammar of Motives (Burke), 65–66
Great Communist Beyond, 118
"Greatest Generation," 122–23
Great Fatherland War, 99
"Great Patriotic War," 28–29
    beginning of, 16, 126–27, 129–30
    end of, 126–27, 129–30, 155
    narrative template for,
        98–99, 109–10
    versus Patriotic War, 98–99
    as privileged event narrative, 135–
        40, 144, 145, 146–47
    as specific narrative, 134–35
Great Purge, 128
Grossman, Vasili, 28–29
group experiences, 137
group identity, 44
groupism, 35–36, 37–38, 190, 230
group membership, 41, 43–44,
    82–83, 107–8
groups
    as agents, 37
    between-group differences,
        39, 107–8
    habit and, 82–83
    individuals as members, 39–41, 42
    meaning systems of, 50–51
    memory *in,* 41, 42–50
    memory *of,* 41
    schemata used by, 50–51
    self-centeredness of, 150
Gulag Archipelago
    (Solzhenitsyn), 117–18

Habermas, Jurgen, 116–17
habit, 71–72, 79–84
    as "fly-wheel of society," 80, 82–83,
        200, 213–14, 226–27
    memory and, 79–80, 81, 173

habit (*cont.*)
   mnemonic standoffs and, 200,
     226–27, 231
   narrative templates and, 103–4,
     132–33, 210–11
   national memory and, 82,
     83, 141–42
   resistance to change, 80, 82–83,
     200, 213–14
   social dimension of, 82–83
"habit memory," 10–11, 227
"habitus," 83
Haidt, Jonathan, 103
Halbwachs, Maurice, 4–5,
   39–41, 42, 91
Han Dynasty, 192–93
Harari, Yuval Noah, 73–74
Herder, Johann Gottfried, 11–12, 53, 54
heresy, 130–31, 136
heroism, 176–77
hero narratives, 99–100, 111–12,
   117, 176–77
Hess, Frederick, 176–77
"hidden dialogicality," 166–67
hierarchies, 193–94, 196
Hiroshima, 14, 18, 129–30, 154–57
Hirst, William, 43–44, 47–48
historians
   call to action, 7–8
   challenging of existing
     narratives, 96
   "noble dream" of, 175
   objective analysis by, 93–94, 109
historical analysis, 94
historical error, 91, 220–21
historical focusing, 120–22, 145–46
historical scholarship, 7–8, 69,
   157, 228–29
history
   analytic notions of, 90n.2, 90–97,
     99, 109, 132–33, 175, 224
   as anecdote to mnemonic
     standoffs, 224–26
   archival evidence of, 67, 68–69, 97,
     158, 222–23
   "blank spots" in, 128–29, 130–31
   emplotment of, 62–63
   end of, 6
   versus fiction, 91–92
   flashbulb moments in, 42–50
   versus memory, 7–8, 87, 90–97,
     175–76, 224–26
   myth as, 7–8, 64, 92
   nationalism and, 7–8
   official accounts of, 116–18, 120,
     130–31, 174–75
   origins of narrative, 72–76
   "pastness" of events, 92–93
   preservation of, 83
   "redefinition" of, 64
   retrospection, anticipation of, 64
   "three keys" of, 64
   timelines, 63
   unofficial accounts of, 117–18,
     131, 174–75
History Channel, The, 115
history instruction, 18, 115, 173,
   176–78, 228–29
History on Trial (Nash), 176–77
Hitler, Adolf, 17, 98–99, 145–46,
   149, 203–4
Holbrooke, Richard, 205, 218–19
holidays, 122–24
Holocaust, 14, 137, 151–52
Homo sapiens, 73, 74
How Societies Remember
   (Connerton), 10, 83
human action
   agency and, 52
   as enacting narratives, 60–61
   making sense of, 8
   pentad for interpreting, 65–66
human consciousness
   awareness and, 103–4
   intuitive inference systems
     and, 36

transformation with
literacy, 56–57
versus unconscious processes,
102–4, 105
human development, 56,
59–60, 75–76
human evolution, 73–74, 75–76
humanities, studies in, 225
humankind, 188, 189, 211
Humboldt, Alexander von, 11–12, 53, 54
Hussein, Sadam, 145–46
Husserl, Edmund, 54

Iannucci, Armando, 128–29
idealists, 215
identity, 92–93
enacted narratives and, 60–61, 184
of individuals, 48, 162, 184–85
narrative unity and, 184–85
national notions of, 35–36, 179,
180–81, 213–14
identity politics, 225
ideological extremism, 107
ideological regimentation, 174
ideologies, 66–67, 101, 112, 215
"imagined communities," 6–7
impasses, 3
imperialist aggression, 1–2
implicit memory, 103
Independence Day, 123
"independent recollections," 79
India, history of, 7–8
individualism, 71–72
individuals
collective memory and, 40–41,
42, 71–72
cultural assumptions about, 54
as group members, 39–41, 42, 51–
52, 54, 107–8, 186
identity of, 48, 162, 184–85
mental functioning of, 51–52, 54
personal narratives, 46, 48, 49
private views of, 116–17, 174

"industry of memory," 149–50
information
contradictory, 169
"silencing," 128
suppression, 19–20, 91,
117–18, 132
inhumanity, 225–26
"inner" speech, 53
institutional processes, 33, 34, 71,
84–85, 115–16
"internally persuasive
discourse," 171–79
international relations theory,
193–94, 215
internet, authority and, 178
interpretation, 218
"intra-narrative dialogism," 178–79
intuition, 103, 105
"intuitive inference systems," 36
"intuitive psychology," 36–37
irony, role of, 216–21
Irony of American History, The
(Niebuhr), 216
"irreducible tension," 52, 180
"isms," 101–2
Israel, 166
Isurin, Ludmila, 49

James, William, 80–81, 92–93, 103,
200, 226–27
Japan
atomic bombing of, 2–3, 14, 129–
30, 152, 154–57, 225–26
China, relation to, 196
national narrative of, 117
surrender in WWII, 2, 3, 156
Jews, 89, 137, 149

Kagan, Robert, 211–12
Kahneman, D., 104–6
Kant, Immanuel, 38
Kaplan, Bernard, 127–28
Kelly, John, 194

Kennedy, John F., 42, 45–46
Kihlstrom, John, 44–45
King, Martin Luther, Jr., 42–43, 48–
    49, 122, 187–88
knowledge
    creation, 34
    of events in WWII, 150–54
    "knowing how" *versus* "knowing
        that," 81
    lack of, 19–20, 201, 210–11
    memory as, 32, 161
    sources of, 25–26
Koran, 172
Kosovo, Battle of, 88, 137–38
Kukryniksy group, poster by,
    109–13, 110*f*
Kulik, James, 42–43, 44, 49–50
Kursk, Battle of, 16, 17–18,
    153, 170–71

language
    mental functioning and, 54, 56, 59
    role of, 52–53, 73
    science of, 164
    "semiotic potential" of, 59–60
    systems of, 163–64
    transparency in, 13–14
László, János, 12
"law of the jungle" narrative, 214–15
Leahy, William D., 155–56
Leningrad, siege of, 153
Leninism, 1–2, 99–100, 192
Lenin Vladimir, 127–28
Lepore, Jill, 5–6, 7
Levy, Daniel, 5
Lewis, Sinclair, 26
Lieberthal, Kenneth, 214, 216, 228
Lies My Teacher Told Me (Loewen),
    115, 177–78
Life and Fate (Grossman), 28–29
Lim, Louisa, 33
Lincoln, Abraham, 69–70, 121,
    173, 188–89

linguistic anthropologists, 11–12
linguistics, 164
literacy, symbolic mediation
    and, 55–60
literature, as "equipment for
    living," 26–29
Liu, James, 145–46
living memories, 121, 136
Loewen, James, 115, 158, 177–78
logic, of narratives, 12, 61–66, 75,
    157, 169
"logico-scientific" thinking, 61–62
Lu, Xun, 141, 195
Luria, Alexander, 13–14, 52–53, 54,
    55*f*, 56–59

Macartney, George, 194–95
MacIntyre, Alisdair, 48, 60–61,
    161–62, 184–85
Madman's Diary, A (Lu), 141
"Make America Great
    Again," 164–65
Malcolm X, 42–43
Malinova, Olga, 124
Marxism, 1–2, 54, 99–100, 112, 120,
    192, 213–14
materialism, 101–2
McAdams, Dan, 8, 12
Mead, George Herbert, 34
meaning-making, 75
media, 1–2, 6–7, 10, 115, 116–17
mediation. *See* Symbolic mediation
memorization, 79–80, 81, 173, 175
memory. *See also* Collective memory
    emotional appeal, 93
    fading of, 121, 123
    in groups, 41, 42–51
    of groups, 41
    habit and, 79–80, 81
    versus history, 7–8, 87, 90–97,
        175–76, 224–26
    "industry of," 149–50
    national memory as, 39–42, 51–52

as process *versus* knowledge, 32–
33, 161–62, 165–66
selectivity and, 115
social framework of, 41
standard tests of, 81–82
types of, 40–41, 81–82
"memory activists," 7–8, 117–18,
124, 131, 175
Memory in Culture (Erll), 229
memory politics, 124
mental functioning, 102–3, 104. *See
also* Human consciousness
fast and slow thinking, 102–9
of individuals, 51–52, 54
language and, 54, 56, 59
mediation of, 12, 55–56, 59, 61
perspective on national
memory, 11, 12
practical *versus* theoretical
thinking, 57
pre-narrative forms of, 59–60,
72–73, 75
two modes of, 61–62
mental habits. *See* Habit
Mercier, Hugo, 107
"methodological nationalism," 5, 230
methods, of inquiry, 32–35
Middleton, David, 34–35
Miloševic, Slobodan, 87–88,
89–90, 137–38
Mink, Louis, 61, 62–63, 67–68, 70,
91–92, 94–95
mnemonic communities
belonging in multiple, 119–20
negotiations between authorities
and, 116–17
norms of, 120–21
mnemonic focusing, 122–28
mnemonic standoffs, 13–25, 108–9
counterarguments in, 4, 13–14,
199–200, 210–11
fast thinking responses to, 108–9
illustrations of, 2–3, 13, 14–25

intractability of, 4, 18–19, 29,
199–200
managing (*see* Conflict
management)
truth and, 66–67, 199
Molotov, Vyacheslav, 128, 129*f*
Molotov-Ribbentrop Pact, 130–33,
169–70, 203–4, 222–23
monuments, 92, 102, 115, 127–28
moral authority, 25
moral superiority, 141
Morphology of the Folktale
(Propp), 77–78
Moscow, 1, 191–92
Moscow, Battle of, 15, 16, 153
Moses the Egyptian (Assmann), 92
"motor mechanisms," 79, 80
myths, 7–8, 64, 74, 90–91, 92

Nagasaki, 14, 129–30, 154–57
Nagorny Karabakh, dispute over,
8, 88–89
Napoleon, 98–99
narcissism, 146–47, 150, 192–93
"narrative anthropology," 12
narrative approach
to consequentiality in
FBMs, 44–46
differences in national memory
and, 18–19
rationale for, 8–11
"narrative conventions," 45–46
narrative dialogism. *See* Dialogism
"narrative economics," 8
"narrative fallacies," 105, 106
narrative psychology, 12
narrative quests, 185–86. *See also*
National narrative projects
"narrative reconciliation," 8, 169
narrative resources, 116, 120–33
narratives. *See also* National
narratives
abbreviated mentions of, 24–25

narratives (*cont.*)
  actor intentions in, 21
  "addressivity" of, 163, 167–68
  affordances of, 28–29, 52, 59–60,
    162–63, 169, 199
  analysis, two levels of, 76–79
  big and little, 47–50
  constraints of, 28–29, 52, 199
  as cultural tools, 9, 10
  emplotment of (*see* emplotment)
  enacting, 60–61
  as "equipment for living," 25–29
  general forms, 76
  as interpretive lens, 24–25, 135–36,
    141–42, 145–46, 213, 215
  lining up of personal and national,
    46, 48, 49
  logic of, 12, 61–66, 157
  mediation by, 12
  "moralizing impulse" of, 109
  origins in human history, 72–76
  "pentad" organization, 65–66
  preserving, 97
  "referential" function of, 197–98
  rules for construction of, 68, 70
  scene in, 65–66
  social consequences of, 74
  specific, type of (*see* Specific
    narratives)
  structure of, 60–61
  as symbolic mediation, 59–61, 90
  templates for (*see* Narrative
    templates)
  versus theories, 68
  unity of, 67–68, 184–85
  visual arts and, 65
narrative templates, 12–13, 24–25
  access to, 133–34
  agent use of *versus* engagement
    with, 108
  competing, 211–14
  habit and, 103–4, 132–33, 210–11
  illustrations of, 98–102, 109–10,
    112, 142–43, 144

  power of, 98, 100–1, 158–59
  protean nature of, 132–33,
    199–200, 222–23
  relation to specific narratives, 76–
    77, 78–79, 98–102, 133, 134
  schemata and, 76–77, 78–79
  as underlying codes, 78–79, 84, 85,
    132–33, 223
  unifying function of, 112
  of world wars, 146
"narrative" thinking, 61–62
"narrative truth," 18–19, 66–72, 97,
    199. *See also* Truth
narrative voices, 162, 179–83
Nash, Gary, 176–77
national histories, 7–8
national holidays, 122–24
national identity, 35–36, 179,
    180–81, 213–14
nationalism, 5, 137–38
  as bent twig, 132–33
  dangers of, 5, 7, 89
  emergence of, 5–6
  globalization and, 6
  igniting of, 35
  types of, 5–7, 230
  understanding of, 6–8
nationalities, age of, 5–6
national memory, 4–8
  accuracy of, 18–19
  analytic history and, 87, 90–97
  authority over, 115–17
  avoiding issues of, 202–5
  blank spots in, 127–29
  Chinese embassy bombing, 19–21
  conceptual framework for
    studying, 31
  conscious reflection on, 108–9
  dark pasts in, 124–26
  disciplinary collaboration in study
    of, 11–13
  emotion and, 93
  evidence for, 32–35
  forgetting in, 127–29

habit and, 82, 83
versus history, 7–8, 87, 90–97
incendiary effects of, 88, 89–90
incorporation into
    negotiations, 205–7
as interpretive lens, 21–25,
    141–42, 145–46
legacy of, 6, 7
memory types involved in, 81–82
mental functioning
    perspective, 11, 12
methods of studying, 32–35
as mobilizing force, 112
narrative approach to, 8–11
narrative templates, shaping by,
    98, 100–1
national narratives role in, 90, 121
power of, 87
as process *versus* body of
    knowledge, 161
as real memory, 39–42, 51–52
selectivity (*see* Selectivity)
staying power of, 157
studies of, shaping, 229–31
"symbolic mediation" for, 11, 12
top-down *versus* bottom-up
    processes, 33–34, 115–17
truth of, 3–4, 18–19
vision of, 32, 39
of WWII, American *versus*
    Russian, 14–19, 154–57
national narcissism, 146–47,
    150, 192–93
national narrative projects, 183–97
    China as central kingdom
        narrative, 192–96
    competing visions of, 186–87
    as context, 196–97
    evidence about, 186–87
    Russia's spiritual mission, 190–92
    U.S. quest for democratic
        union, 187–90
national narratives, 49
    abbreviated expressions of, 24–25

alignment with personal
    narratives, 48
challenging of, 96, 97
contradictory evidence on, 96, 97
emotions, strategic use of,
    89–90, 93
falsehoods in, 130–32
flashbulb memories and, 48–49
implicit *versus* explicit, 77n.4
meaning of, approaches to, 198
national memory, role in, 90
"strange logic" of, 64, 66, 75,
    84, 169
uncertainty about, 49
of United States, 48–49
national pride, 1–2, 49
nation-states
    citizen loyalty to, 5
    definition of, 6
    emergence of, 5–6
    globalization effects on, 6
    hierarchies of, 193–94
    historical writings of, 7
    origin stories, 66, 123
    as social constructs, 35–36
    spirit of, 6–7
    top-down *versus* bottom-up
        processes, 33–34
    traumatic or criminal pasts
        of, 124–26
Native Americans, 50–51
NATO, 20, 22
natural language, 52–53
Nazis, 24, 130–31, 153, 170–71
"neglection," 127–28
negotiations, 88, 116–17. *See also*
    Conflict management
    between Allies in WWII, 203–5
    avoiding issues of national
        memory, 202–5
    conflicting "interests" *versus*
        positions, 201, 206
    efforts by professional negotiators,
        88, 201–11, 220–21, 222

negotiations (*cont.*)
  incorporation of national
    memory, 205–7
  for peace in Bosnia, 88, 205
Neisser, Ulric, 44–46, 47, 48, 50, 79–
    80, 99, 133
Nelson, Catherine, 75
neurophysiology, 42–43, 44
Nevsky, Alexander, 99–100, 110–12
"new nationalism," 5–6, 229–30
"new unconscious," 102–3
Nguyen, Viet Tanh, 39, 136, 146,
    149–50, 218–19, 225
Nickerson, Raymond, 107
Niebuhr, Reinhold, 216–17
nihilism, 101
9/11 terrorist attack, 136,
    137, 145–46
Nineteen Eighty-Four (Orwell), 26,
    28–29, 116–17
Nora, Pierre, 91, 229
norms, 120–21, 145–46
North Atlantic Treaty Organization
    (NATO), 20, 22
Novick, Peter, 92–94

Obama, Barack, 187–88, 190
O'Connor, Flannery, 27, 28
O'Connor, Sandra Day, 47
"off-the-shelf technology," 25–26,
    93, 106
Olick, Jeffrey, 31, 33, 41, 42, 71–72
ontogenesis, 75
Operation Barbarossa, 97
*Operation Barbarossa and
    Germany's Defeat in the East*
    (Stahel), 96–97
opinions, 3–4, 18–19,
    66–67, 177–78
Opium Wars, 140
Orwell, George, 26, 28–29, 116–17
Ottoman Empire, 88, 181–82
Our Man (Packer), 218–19

Packer, George, 218–19
Palestinian narrative, 166
"paradigmatic" thinking, 61–62
"Patriotic War," 98
patriotism, 49, 174–75
Pearl Harbor, 14, 17–18, 129–30,
    145–46, 152, 154, 155
People's Republic of Amnesia
    (Lim), 33
perception, 102–3
personal narratives, 48
Petersen, Roger, 89
Pevear, Richard, 101–2
Phelps, Elizabeth, 43–44, 47–48
photography, 10, 128–29
"phronesis," 61–62
Piaget, Jean, 38, 75
Pickering, Thomas, 208–9, 219–21
Plato, 103
Poetics (Aristotle), 28
Polegkyi, Oleksii, 126–27
political correctness, 176–77
political discourse, 87
political forces, 66, 70, 71, 115–16.
    See also State authorities
political rhetoric, 186–87, 217–18
popular culture, 149–50
pre-narrative understanding, 59–60,
    61, 72–73, 75
primordialism, 35–39
"privileged event narratives," 24–25,
    133–45, 158–59
  Chinese Century of Humiliation
    as, 140–45
  "Great Patriotic War" as, 135–40,
    144, 145, 146–47
  as lens, 135–36, 141–42,
    144, 145–46
  living memories and, 136
  World War II as, 145–46
procedural memory, 81–82
professional negotiators, 201–7
propaganda, 2, 23, 109–10, 110*f*, 112

Propp, Vladimir, 77–78
proverbs, 26
psychological anthropology,
    12–13, 51
psychological factors, 33, 34
"psychological tools," 56n.2
public discourse, 1–2, 33
Putin, Vladimir, 21–24, 25, 124–26,
    167, 169

race, 35–36
Race and Reunion (Blight), 126
racial divisions, 187–88, 189–90
racism, 149, 190
rational argumentation, 71, 97
Reagan, Ronald, 212–13
realists, 215
reality, 13–14, 55–56, 89, 115–16
recall, 42–43
reconciliation, 8, 169,
    189–90, 202–3
remembering
    collectively, 32
    conversational type of, 34–35
    covertly, 128
    as group members, 42–43
    by individuals, 40–41
    as mental process, 42, 55–56
    pre-narrative forms of, 59–60
    procedural component of, 82
    in social context, 40–41
    of Soviet Union, 123–24
Remembering (Bartlett), 40
Renan, Ernst, 6–7, 76, 91, 224–25
resistance
    to change, 80, 82–83, 116–17, 200,
        213–14, 222–23
    to contradictory evidence,
        96, 132–33, 169, 199–200,
        206–7, 222–23
    against official accounts,
        116–17, 173–75
retrospection, anticipation of, 64, 65

rhetorical efforts, 23–24, 134–35,
    167–68, 186–87
Ricoeur, Paul, 61–63
Rigney, Ann, 5
Robbins, Joyce, 31
Roediger, Henry, 81–82, 121, 150
Roosevelt, Franklin D., 155, 203–5
Rosenfeld, Gavriel, 229–30
Russia, 1. *See also* Soviet Union
    Civil War, 111
    Estonian conflict, 102, 130–32
    "Expulsion of Alien Enemies"
        narrative, 98–102, 109–10,
        112, 127, 132–33, 135, 139–40,
        190–91, 222–23
    "Five Day War" with Georgia, 21–
        23, 102, 135, 167–68
    Georgian national identity
        and, 181–82
    "Great Patriotic War" (*see* "Great
        Patriotic War")
    national heroes, 99–100, 110–11
    national holidays, 125, 126–27
    national memory as interpretive
        lens, 21–25, 135, 145
    national pride, 1–2
    "Patriotic War," 98–99
    spiritual mission project, 190–92
    World War II, contribution
        to, 147–49
    World War II, national memory
        of, 2–3, 14–19, 145–46, 153–57
Russian Formalists, 164
"Russian idea," 191–92
Russian Orthodoxy, 182, 191–92
Russian Revolution, 123–26, 124n.4
Russo-Georgian War, 21–23, 102,
    135, 145
Russo-Japanese War, 141
Ryle, Gilbert, 81

Sacks, Harvey, 34
Sarbin, Theodore, 12

Saussure, Ferdinand de, 164
schemata
    definition, 51
    formation of, 79–80
    group-specific content of, 51
    in infants, 38
    memory, shaping of, 45–46
    narrative-based, 38–39
    narrative templates, parallels with,
        76–77, 78–79
    role in groups, 50–51
    sharing of, 51
school textbooks, 115, 128–29, 158,
    166, 177–78
Schwartz, Barry, 69–70
Scott, James, 174
"sealed narratives," 169
selective memory, 145–57
selectivity, 115, 120, 158–59
    of events and actors, 121–27
    example of, 128–29
    forgetting and, 127–29
    of narrative emplotment, 121–22,
        123, 129–33
    resources for, 120–33
self-condemnation, 180, 181–82, 183
self-idealization, 180, 181–82, 183
semantic memory, 81
Serbia, 87–88, 137–38, 205
shared understandings, 29
Shiller, Robert, 8–9
Shpet, Gustav, 54
silencing of information, 117, 128
Singh, Piyush, 195–96
"Sinocentrism," 193–94, 195–96
situations, "sizing up," 26–27, 65,
    158–59, 196–97, 212
slavery, 68–69, 126, 187–89
slow thinking, 102–9, 112–13, 205–6
Smith, Rogers, 96, 125–26
social context, 34, 41, 42
social forces, 42, 44–45, 51
social identity, 44–45

socialism, 101, 192
"social languages," 164–66, 179
"socially shared cognition," 54
social memory, 121, 137
social oblivion, 120–21, 128,
    130, 132–33
social order, 80
"social organization," 41
social revolution, 123–26
social sciences, narrative turn of, 9
Solzhenitsyn, Alexander, 101,
    117–18, 191–92
South Africa, 202–3
South Ossetia, 21–22, 22n.6, 168
Soviet propaganda, 2, 109–10,
    110f, 112
Soviet Union. See also Russia
    America, perspective on, 1–2
    anecdote of mythical
        telephone, 118–19
    censorship by, 1
    collapse of, 88, 123–24, 125–26,
        132, 211
    communism, interpretation
        of, 101
    German invasion of, 15, 16, 109–
        10, 129–30, 149, 153
    Germany, pact with, 130–33
    Great Purge, 128
    liberation of Eastern
        Europe, 130–31
    military leaders, 110–11
    national events in, 49
    national holidays, 123–24
    origin story, 123–24
    public versus private views in,
        117–19, 174
    Red Army, 17, 110–11, 112–13,
        130–31, 149
    revolutionary narrative,
        123–26, 127–28
    World War II, Allied
        support, 203–4

World War II, contribution
to, 147–50
World War II, national memory
of, 2–3, 14–19
specific narratives, 76, 77–78
illustration of, 77
"privileged event narratives"
and, 134–35
relation to narrative templates,
76–77, 78–79, 98–102, 133–34
role in habits, 133
in Russia's past, 98–99,
102, 134–35
speech, 164–65, 171–73
Sperber, Dan, 107
spirit, 6–7
Squire, Larry, 81
Stahel, David, 96–97
Stalin, Joseph, 2, 3, 99–100, 111,
129f, 203–4
Stalingrad, Battle of, 15, 16, 153
state authorities, 89–90, 115–17, 120
statues, 92, 102, 115, 127–28
Steele, Jonathan, 22–23, 168
stereotypes, 37–38
stories. See Narratives
Stowe, Harriet Beecher, 26
strategic distrust, 214
student learning, 128–29
Suvorov (film), 111
Suvorov, Alexander, 110–13
syllogistic reasoning, 58–59, 61, 62, 67
symbolic form, philosophy of, 54
"symbolic interactionism," 34
"symbolic mediation," 37–38,
52–79, 84
cultural memory and, 137
forms of, 52–53, 55–56, 85
literacy as illustration of, 55–59
narratives as, 11, 12,
59–61, 230–31
selectivity and, 138
thinking and, 104

"symbolic politics," 123–24
symbols, 56n.2
Systems 1 and 2 thinking,
104–6, 107–9
Sznaider, Natan, 5

"tactic of consumption," 174
Talbott, Strobe, 208, 220
Taleb, Nassim, 105, 106
Taylor, Charles, 53
technology, equipment for
living, 25–26
teleology, 185–86
telos, 185–86
terrorism, 136
text
internally persuasive, 172–73
notion of, 163–64
rejection of, 172–73
as sacred, 172, 173
verbatim memory of, 173–74, 177
textbooks, 15, 115, 128–29, 132, 158,
166, 177–78
Thapar, Romila, 7–8
theoretical thinking, 57, 58–59, 68
thinking. See Mental functioning
Thinking Fast and Slow
(Kahneman), 104–5
Tiananmen Square massacre,
33, 142
Time, 153
"time maps," 120–21
top-down forces, 33–34, 71–72, 115–
16, 127, 158
totalitarian regimes, 28–29, 117–18,
119–20, 169–71, 187
Toulmin, Stephen, 70–71
transnational memory projects, 5
traumatic events, 43, 47–49, 137,
138, 139–40
Truman, Harry, 2, 3, 70–71, 155–56
Trump, Donald, 164–65
trust, 214–16

truth, 3–4, 18–19, 21, 89
  analytic *versus* synthetic, 67
  authority on, 70–71
  distortion of, 20–21
  evidence for, 67, 70–71
  in managing differences, 202–3,
    206–7, 223–24
  of propositions, 67–69, 222, 223
  rational argument, based
    on, 70–71
Tulviste, Peeter, 117–18, 174, 235–36

Ukraine, 1
Uncle Tom's Cabin (Stowe), 26
unconscious processes, 102–4, 105,
  138–39, 141
underlying codes, 78–79, 84, 85,
  132–33, 223
United Kingdom
  British students in, 50–51
  China, relations with, 194–95
  in World War II, 147–49
United States
  Air Force, 19
  atomic bombing of Japan, 2–3, 14,
    129–30, 152, 154–57, 225–26
  bombing of Chinese embassy,
    19–21, 142–43, 207–11,
    213, 219–20
  Central Intelligence Agency,
    20, 209–10
  Chinese perspective on,
    214–15, 217–18
  City on the Hill narrative, 146,
    189, 211, 212–13, 214–15,
    216, 217–18
  Civil War, 67–70, 94, 126,
    187–88, 190
  democratic union, quest
    for, 187–90
  diplomatic efforts, 88, 205,
    207, 218–21
  founders of, 187

generational experiences, 136
history instruction in, 173, 176–78
history of, 115–16
irony of history in, 216, 217
"law of the jungle" narrative
  about, 214–15
minority group
  perspectives, 119–20
national holidays, 122–23
nationalism, 5–6
national motto, 187–88
national narratives of, 48–49, 146
origin story, 66
political rhetoric, 217–18
presidents, recall of, 121
as "reluctant sheriff," 211–12
slavery in, 68–69, 126, 187–89
Soviet perspective of, 1–2
20th century events, 146
westward expansion, 224–26
World War II, contribution
  to, 147–49
WWII, national memory of, 3–4,
  14–19, 146, 154–57
unity, 224–25
universal values, 215
U.S. Constitution, 187–88
USSR. *See* Soviet Union
utterances, 164–65, 171, 172–73

Van Engen, Abram, 189, 211
"vernacular memory," 117–18
Veterans Day, 122–23
victim narrative, 25
Vietnam War, 39, 136, 146, 149–50,
  218–19, 225
violence, cycles of, 89
virtue, 217
visual arts, 65
Volkan, Vamik, 137–38
Voroshilov, Kliment, 128, 129*f*
Vygotsky, L.S., 52–53, 54, 55–58,
  57*f*, 59

Walt, Stephen, 215n.7
Wang, Jisi, 214, 216, 228
Wang, Zheng, 140–41, 144, 193–94, 213–14, 216, 228
"War of the Ghosts," 50–51
Wayman, Erin, 73
"weapons of the weak," 174
Wertsch, James V., 117–18, 211
Western Enlightenment, 101
Western ideas, 101–2
Western popular culture, 149–50
"What Is a Nation?" (Renan), 6, 91, 224–25
"what you see is all there is" ("WYSIATI"), 106–7, 158
White, Hayden, 61, 63
Wilson, Ward, 156
Wilson, Woodrow, 122–23
Wimmer, Andreas, 5–6
Wineburg, Sam, 176, 178, 227
Winthrop, John, 189, 211
worldviews, 4, 18, 213–14
World War I, 122–23
World War II
    Allied discussions during, 203–5
    American *versus* Russian national memories of, 2–3, 14–19, 32, 129–30
    atomic bombing of Japan during, 2–3, 154–57

emplotment of, 129–30
Japanese narrative of, 117
Jews, killing of, 89
knowledge of events in, 150–54
major events in, 14, 15–17, 24, 151–54
narrative as interpretive lens, 23–25, 145–46
nation narcissism and remembering, 146–47
nations' contributions to, 147–50
as privileged event narrative, 145–46
selective memory of, 145–57
veterans of, 122–23

Xi, Jinping, 195–96
Xiaoping, Deng, 142
Xuetong, Yan, 194

Yamashiro, Jeremy, 66
Yeltsin, Boris, 124–25, 191
Yezhov, Nikolai, 128, 129f
Yugoslavia, 87–88, 89–90, 137–38. *See also* Belgrade, Chinese embassy bombing

Zacks, Jeffrey, 72–73
Zaromb, F., 157
Zerubaval, Eviatar, 120–21, 123